A Still More Excellent Way
Transforming your life

Reflections on the gifts and fruits
of the holy spirit

WILLIAM SYKES

William Sykes

Copyright © William Sykes
A Still More Excellent Way
Transforming your life
William Sykes

2nd Edition Published in 2013

First published in 2012 by
William Sykes
University College
High Street
Oxford
OX1 4BH

All rights reserved. Apart from limited use for private study, teaching, research, criticism or review, no part of this publication may be reproduced, stored or transmitted without prior permission in writing of the copyright owner and publisher of this book. Enquiries for reproduction outside the terms of this statement should be made to the publisher at the address above.

ISBN-13: 978-1484083598

ISBN-10: 1484083598

The view from above the village of Mürren of The Eiger, Mönch and the Jungfrau. I have been going to Mürren for over thirty years to take the Christmas and New Year Services in The English Church and this area has been a great source of inspiration. I think it is one of the most beautiful places in the world.

CONTENTS

1	Inspiration	Pg 12
2	Wisdom	Pg 22
3	Counsel	Pg 33
4	Understanding	Pg 42
5	Knowledge	Pg 51
6	Fear	Pg 62
7	Power	Pg 75
8	The Spirit Of The Lord	Pg 85
9	Love	Pg 101
10	Joy	Pg 118
11	Peace	Pg 130
12	Patience	Pg 141
13	Kindness	Pg 153
14	Goodness	Pg 163
15	Faithfulness	Pg 175
16	Gentleness	Pg 187
17	Self-Control	Pg 198
18	Life	Pg 210
19	Light	Pg 222
20	Truth	Pg 231
21	Hope	Pg 241
22	Grace	Pg 251
23	Glory	Pg 261
24	Beauty	Pg 270
25	Character	Pg 281
26	Courage	Pg 292

William Sykes

Preface

We live in the digital age, the information age, the age of science, the clash of civilization – that the labels for our times jostle in all directions tells us much about them. We are barraged with information, much of it unsought and some of it unsound, some of it technical and some of it farcical – hurled by speakers after our acceptance, or fear, or envy, the better to gain our money, time, or vote. So, as the English author W.H. Auden realized half a century ago, we live in an age of anxiety.

How we deal with that anxiety defines each of us.

Ages ago, that definition was rooted in the spirit – that spark in each person's being that is shared with a deeper aspect of the universe. The spirit is the divine element in each human being. A source of solace despite our tragedies and doubt and a source of care despite our luxury and power, spirit is essential to the human soul as much as to the understanding of God.

Where is spirit? For a smart person in anxious times, what survives the deluge of science, advertisement, cannibalistic politics, religious strife, economic conflict, and reality television? The answer varies for each of us, and perhaps it changes with time, but there is an answer available, which is ... a great deal indeed.

Bill Sykes, the author and steward of this project, is remarkably well prepared to help us seek that answer. Once an officer in a Gurkha regiment of the British army, the Revd. in a challenging and difficult situation as chaplain to the "Godless Student of Gower Street" – ie. University College London – and then chaplain for twenty seven years to skeptical over-achievers of a great university (Oxford) he is now Emeritus Chaplain Fellow of University College, Oxford.

To reach all the misbegottens in his charge, he realized he could use the help of three sources: the teachings of the church fathers, the writings of wise people, and the spirit in the people he was trying to reach. To gather the teachings and writings in a useful way was a monumental task, but to reach that spirit was more daunting still.

To reach the spirit in each of us, he knew, was a task each of us must do for ourselves. And, he has used the writings and teachings to help us along two different roads to reach it.

The first road he developed is conversation. By that, he learned gently to nudge people into groups of two to five or so, people who had some quest to understand better the spirit in themselves, even if that quest seemed to them to be about understanding other people, or money, or bosses, or exams. Each member of the group would encounter the readings and teachings of great minds and spirits on a given topic, and then be inspired by the need to share with the others and to integrate the thoughts of the others in return.

The second road was a reflection of the first, and that is to reflect inwardly rather than outwardly. This approach is really to accept a modern form of the ancient art of meditation, focusing on a single idea that embraces a broader wisdom.

In the collection you hold in your hand (or see on your screen), you have the maps to travel along either, or both, roads in engaging the spirit. The readings are organized intuitively, because it is our intuition that best guides our reason on these journeys. The road is wide enough for a conversation from these writings and compelling enough to carry a lone traveller to a far distance.

The materials make for a great conversation. To use them jointly, gather a group first (two to five or less). Leave time to select a topic that matters at that moment to a person in the group. It will not matter at all if the topic is one already much used: these are deep wells that offer plenty of new refreshment in later visits. It is probably best not to ask too much of why a person selects a topic. Then give time for everyone to read what seems attractive in it and then a period for silent reflection – say five to ten minutes but not more. Then start a conversation, in which the person who selected the topic goes first with whatever seemed interesting, agreeable or disagreeable in the readings and what that seems to mean. Then let the free-for-all commence, though hopefully with good will among all. Someone should keep time, and the conversation cannot go too long, probably to a preset limit but not more than twenty to forty-five minutes. With luck, it will end just as people think it is getting good. My experience has been that these conversations continue for each person long after they have left the group, and the sense of calm and clarity that may arise will last even longer.

The materials are also beautifully arranged for solitude. They are objects for contemplation, not completion. The point is to allow yourself to wander idly among the writings until one seems more important than others and then to let yourself explore it by repetition. Just repeat the phrase, silently or aloud, let it echo in the mind. Three, five, eight, or four times–that is yours to choose. When it is time to move on you will. It really makes for a calming journey.

When I was younger I was quite willing to accept the rewards for such travels like the holiday snaps that might come back from vacation. If I better understood what people mean when they talk of Love, or Fear, I was perfectly content. Over time, though, I've come to see that what I had looked at in each of these was more than a nice view or an interesting building or some other box to tick off on a travelogue; what mattered was the journey itself. Obvious as this might seem to others, I was surprised to see that the joy, the spirit, was in the search for the understanding and in the knowledge there was understanding: the specifics of Love, Fear, and the rest just mattered less than the whole process of them. The spirit was the same in all of them, and in all of us when we explored them.

Whether you choose to travel alone or with friends, these materials are a delightful journey in search of the spirit. As one of the hundreds and hundreds of Bill Sykes's students and friends who have travelled with him, in person or with his books, I hope you enjoy your journeys with him as much as I have.

Bon voyage.
Steve Sheppard
Steve Sheppard teaches and writes about the law in Arkansas.

Introduction

"We have lost our spiritual roots." Such was the conclusion of a shrewd observer of the scene. This is an indisputable sign of our times. How then do we get back to our spiritual roots? I am going to answer this question by telling you a story.

For twenty seven years I was Chaplain Fellow of University College, Oxford. Our College, along with Balliol and New College, has an interest in a Chalet on the slopes of Mont Blanc. For over a hundred years we have been taking small groups of undergraduates and graduate students on Reading Parties during Summer Vacations. In all, I have probably been on about twenty of these Parties.

On one of these Parties a very bright Junior Research Fellow called in for a couple of days en route for Greece. He asked me if I could take him for a walk the next day which would enable him to get the feel of the French Alps. I readily agreed and the two of us set off early next morning.

My plan was to walk up by the side of the Bionnassey Glacier to a point called *Le Nid Aigle* (The Eagle's Nest). It took us an hour to reach the bottom of the Glacier, where we had a rest and admired the view. After a couple of minutes he asked me the dreaded question. "Bill, can you tell me exactly what it is that you believe?" "Oh gosh", I thought. "He's so bright he's never going to believe this."

My starting point was the Genesis story of the creation of "Man." "Man" here means "Man" and "Woman". I regard this story as a mighty parable of the human soul. A reminder – a parable is an earthly story with a heavenly meaning.

In this story God is depicted as fashioning and shaping "Man" in his own image and likeness. The last thing He did was to breath into "Man", and "Man" became a living being. I take this to mean that something of the Divine Nature was breathed into our nature. God also said "Let us make man in our image." To whom is he referring? We believe He was prefiguring the coming of Christ and the Holy Spirit, so the potential of the Divine Life in our inner being is colossal – Father, Son and all the gifts and fruits of the Holy Spirit!

One further point. That which was fashioned and shaped in the image and likeness of God was taken from the dust of the earth. This means that "Man" in addition to having something akin to a divine potential is at one and the same time earthy and creaturely, having all the passions of the animals in the depths of his being. Thinking about this positively, I see a value in the earthy and creaturely, for example - a valuable source of energy, power and dynamism. There is, though, a potential danger here, as we know from our own experience of passion, and observing passion in the animals.

"Are you with me so far?" He nodded affirmatively, so I went on. "If we want to see this fully worked out in a life I would want to go to the Gospels, to the person of Jesus Christ. In His early years He seemed to enjoy a unique relationship with the Father. However we know little of his life between the ages of 12-30, except this, that "He grew in wisdom and in stature, in favour with God and man." Aged thirty, Jesus was baptized in the river Jordan, and the descent of the dove symbolized the coming of the Holy Spirit into His life. From then onwards His life was increasingly transformed. He experienced all the gifts and fruits of the Holy Spirit and in the latter part of the Gospels worked these out in His own life to their fullest and highest extent.

"Let me now outline the gifts and fruits of the Holy Spirit.

First, Gifts. These are Wisdom, Counsel (Guidance), Understanding, Knowledge, Fear (not Fright, but Reverence, Sacred Awe, Holiness and Wonder), Power, and the Spirit of the Lord.

Second, the fruits of the Spirit are: Love, Joy, Peace, Patience, Kindness, Goodness, Faithfulness, Gentleness and Self-Control.

Other gifts and fruits of the spirit are:

Inspiration, Life, Light, Truth, Hope, Grace, Glory, Beauty, Character and Courage."

"I believe Jesus worked out all these gifts and fruits of the Holy Spirit to their highest and fullest extent. In addition He accepted the earthy and creaturely side of His nature, integrating the passionate side of his nature with the gifts and fruits of the Holy Spirit. But this was achieved at an enormous ongoing cost – an early experience of the cross. In "dying to self" every scrap of selfishness and self-centredness had to go, in order to make way for the gifts and fruits of the Holy Spirit. His inner integration was achieved at an enormous cost. So it is with anyone who follows this way of life. Imagine for a moment Jesus holding all these gifts and fruits of the Holy Spirit as One. His charisma would be colossal! In my search for the Divine I cannot think of anything higher. This is the God I can believe in. The disciples reached the same conclusion. Jesus was to them "Very God and Very Man."

"All right so far?" "Yes, I am following you."

"I now want to go to a resurrection appearance in the Upper Room, where the disciples were gathered together. Jesus stood among them and said "Peace be with you" and when He had said this He breathed on them (reminiscent of the Genesis story of the creation of Man) and then said to them: "Receive the Holy Spirit." From that moment onwards the lives of the disciples were changed and transformed. In a little time they became Apostles.

"We now move on to the Epistles. It was St Paul who realized what Christ had experienced we can all in some measure also experience. "It is no longer I who live," he said, "but it is Christ who lives in me," and in addition, "For in him (in Christ) the whole fullness of deity dwells bodily and you have come to fullness of life in him."

"In the Epistle to the Ephesians Paul is even more explicit. In one of the greatest passages in Scripture he wrote: "For this reason I bow my knees before the Father, from whom every family in heaven and earth is named, that according to the riches of his glory he may grant you to be strengthened with might through his Spirit in the inner man, and that Christ may dwell in your hearts through faith; that you being rooted and grounded in love may have power to comprehend with all the saints what is the breadth and length and height and depth, and to know the love of Christ which surpasses knowledge, that you may be filled with all the fullness of God." What I am really on about is that final phrase – "so that you may be filled with all the fullness of God."

There are other passages which speak of something similar are: "In him (in Christ) are hidden all the treasures of wisdom and knowledge," and "But we have this treasure in earthen vessels."

"There was a pause. We gazed into the far distance, to the top of the Bionnassey Glacier, and then we saw an extraordinary sight. We saw the start of an avalanche.

We suddenly became aware of a huge block of snow, ice and rock, suspended in mid-air for what seemed a long time before it came crashing down. We were both excited by this spectacle. Something seemed to click into place with my friend. "Do you know," he said "I've never heard the Christian faith put over in this way before. I could go on that!" And he did "go on that!" A few weeks later, he was baptized and confirmed in Christ Church Cathedral, in Oxford!

That is the end of the story. I must now say a word about "Reflection." In Reflection we bring into play the whole of our inner being. We "ponder" over phrases or expressions in this book. We mull over them. We read, mark, learn, and inwardly digest them. We consider them. We inwardly ruminate on them. Doing this in depth we move into meditation and contemplation. This is how we use the whole of our inner being. Let me spell this out more clearly.

In Reflection, we bring into play the whole of our inner being.

First, there is the mind. We take a phrase or a short sentence from this book, and repeat it to ourselves several times. A good example would be: "In your presence there is fullness of joy." Within a few days, having reflected on this sentence, we might well become conscious of experiencing a little more joy in our lives. In Reflection we think and use our minds as far as they will go.

Second, we also make use of the feeling side of our nature – by this I mean our heart, our instinct, our intuition, our feelings, our emotions, and our gift of discernment.

Third, we use our imagination in Reflection, and is there here a connection between "image of God," "and imagination"?

Fourth, we use our experience of life so far – a valuable resource in the practice of Reflection.

Fifth, in the silence of Reflection we keep ourselves open and receptive to whatever the Spirit might come up with.

Sixth, for many years I have taken a short phrase and armed with writing material, have spent an hour looking at the phrase and writing down whatever came to mind. This has been an invaluable practice for me over the years, and some of you might benefit by adopting this practice.

I have come to believe that the gifts and fruits of the Holy Spirit are our most treasured possession. To this end I have searched two thousand years of Spirituality and have selected an average of a hundred and forty phrases and short sentences for each gift and fruit of the Holy Spirit. Reflection has greatly transformed my life. I hope this will be your experience too, using the book in the way suggested.

One exciting discovery! By Reflecting on the gifts and fruits of the Spirit, I feel I have come to "know" the Spirit of Jesus Christ as never before - an increase of at least a thousand-fold! I hope many others will experience something similar.

I want to end on a challenging note, by quoting some words of the Scottish New Testament Scholar – Professor William Barclay. He wrote in his commentary on *The Gospel of Matthew*: "If we refuse the invitation of Christ, some day our greatest pain will lie, not in the things we suffer, but in the realization of the precious things we have missed, and of which we have cheated ourselves."

To conclude – the "Still More Excellent Way" is about growing to our highest level of development and expression by Reflection on the gifts and fruits of the Holy Spirit. A great adventure can be experienced and as someone said "Adventure is the champagne of life." Go for it!

1 INSPIRATION

Inspiration is extremely important. We recall the Genesis story of the creation of human kind. After God fashioned and shaped "man" in His image and likeness He breathed into "man" and "man" became a living being.

What is depicted in this story is God 'inspiring' man; God 'breathing' His own nature into man. As we have pointed out elsewhere inspiration is multi-faceted and mysterious. It is active in all the gifts and fruits of the Holy Spirit and ultimately is what "A Still More Excellent Way" is all about. Reflection, Meditation and Contemplation are ways and means of being open and receptive to inspiration.

I came across an interesting illustration of inspiration whilst sitting in my rooms in University College. On the same staircase was an American graduate, reading for an honours degree in modern history. His grandfather and great uncle had both been eminent theologians. Unlike his forbears Gustav was not an overtly religious person, but from time to time he came to Evensong and occasionally would drop in to my rooms for a chat and a coffee.

When he returned to the States he became a journalist. After three years, he came back to England on holiday and popped in to see me. After sharing a few pleasantries he said, "You know, Bill, I have come to realize Oxford is a very spiritual place." I was taken aback by this observation and expressed my feeling that Oxford is practically spiritually dead. "No, no," he said, "I do not mean the current generation of undergraduates, graduate students and Fellows. *I think the Spirit is in the walls."*

The penny dropped. I saw exactly what he meant. Oxford is in an inspirational city. *The Spirit is, indeed, in the walls."*

Now go, and I will be with your mouth and teach you what you are to speak –
Exodus 4.12

Inspiration – drawing in of breath, divine influence, sudden happy idea, inspiring principle – *The Concise Oxford Dictionary*

Inspiration will always sing; inspiration will never explain – *Kahlil Gibran*

The soul may be so inspirited by the Divine Spirit as to be certified of its relationship to God – *Henry Ward Beecher*

Find inspiring people. Inspiring people are vitamins for our spirit – *Sark*

An inspiration – a long deep breath of the pure air of thought – could alone give health to the heart – *Richard Jefferies*

The spirit of the Lord speaks through me, his word is upon my tongue –
2 Samuel 23.2

Spirit gives meaning to his (man's) life, and the possibility of the greatest development – *C.G. Jung*

When a man has given up the one fact of the inspiration of the Scriptures, he has given up the whole foundation of revealed religion – *Henry Ward Beecher*

Grace only visits them in moments of inspiration, and then it is of noble character, enhanced as it is by the ever present gift of strength – *S. de Madariaga*

People in whom…God has awakened the enjoyment of music, painting, poetry, drama, should use these tastes deliberately in their fostering of their religious life – *J. Neville Ward*

Christ reformed man by inspiring the love of goodness, as well as by hatred or evil. He controlled the passions by the inspiration of the moral goodness – *Henry Ward Beecher*

But truly it is the spirit in a mortal, the breath of the Almighty, that makes for understanding. It is not the old that are wise, nor the aged that understand what is right. Therefore I say, "Listen to me; let me also declare my opinion" – *Job 32.8-10*

It is the man who puts the vigour and enthusiasm which God inspires into the life that now is who will be fitted for the world that is to come. 'Having done all, stand' – *Henry Ward Beecher*

The greater the spiritual activity within a man, the less he is able to ascribe this activity to himself. And this fact, however paradoxical, is the root of religion – *A.C. Bradley*

That prayer and its time and its reverent and unstinted gestures were the condition of God and of his return to all those who barely expect it, who only kneel down and stand up and are suddenly filled to the brim? – *Rainer Maria Rilke*

Goodness rather than talent had given her a wisdom, and goodness rather than courage a power of using that wisdom, which to these simple folk seemed almost an inspiration – *Charles Kingsley*

Every good deed comes from God. His is the ideal; His the inspiration, and His its fulfilment in time, and therefore no good deed but lives and grows with the everlasting life of God Himself – *Charles Kingsley*

There is in human life very little spiritual inspiration; very little that they can get from each other; very little that they can get from society; very little that they can get from laws and institutions. Its source is above us – *Henry Ward Beecher*

How lovely is your dwelling-place, O Lord of hosts! My soul longs, indeed it faints for the courts of the Lord; my heart and my flesh sing for joy to the living God – *Psalm 84.1-2*

A god has his abode in our breast; when he rouses us, the glow of inspiration warms us; this holy rapture springs from the seeds of the divine mind sown in man – *Ovid*

There is something in our minds like sunshine and the weather, which is not under our control. When I write, the best things come to me I know not where – *G.C. Lichtenberg*

I become a transparent eyeball; I am nothing; I see all; the currents of the Universal Being circulate through me; I am a part of particle of God – *Ralph Waldo Emerson*

And do we not all agree to call rapid thought and noble impulse by the name of inspiration? After our subtlest analysis of the mental process, we will still say…that our highest thoughts and our best deeds are all given to us – *George Eliot*

The authority of the inspired scriptures resides, not in an intrusive control of the writing process, not in an error free presentation, but in a reliable expression of the faith in the unique period of its earliest gestation – *James Tunstead Burtchaell, CSC*

When they bring you before the synagogues, the rulers, and the authorities, do not worry about how to defend yourselves or what you are to say; for the Holy Spirit will teach you at that very hour what you ought to say – *Luke 12.11-12*

Perpetual Inspiration, therefore, is in the Nature of the Thing as necessary to a Life of Goodness, Holiness, and Happiness, as perpetual Respiration of the Air is necessary to animal life – *William Law*

Those divinely possessed and inspired have at least the knowledge that they hold some greater thing within them though they cannot tell what it is, from the movements that stir them and the utterances that come from them they perceive the power, not themselves, that moves them – *Plotinus*

Now this continual knocking of Christ at the door of the heart sets forth the case or nature of a continual, immediate divine inspiration within us; it is always with us, but there must be an opening of the heart to it;

and though it is always there, yet it is only felt and found by those who are attentive to it, depend upon it, and humbly wait for it – *William Law*

God should be in the Christian's soul, in his living consciousness, vital, active, fiery. He should inspire him and fill him with admiration. His God should be one that loves him, inspires him, rebukes him, punishes him, wounds him, heals him, and rejoices him – one whose arms and whose bosom he feels – *Henry Ward Beecher*

When he had said this, he breathed on them and said to them, 'Receive the Holy Spirit.' – *John 20.22*

To dare to listen to that inspiration from within which voices the ultimate reality of one's own being requires an act of faith which is rare indeed. When the conviction is borne in upon one that anything which is put together, or made up, has no ultimate reality and so is certain to disintegrate, one turns to one's own final reality in the faith that it and it alone can have any virtue or any value – *Esther Harding*

Sometimes when I have come to my work empty, I have suddenly become full, ideas being in an invisible manner showered upon me, and implanted in me from on high, so that through the influence of divine inspiration I have become filled with enthusiasm, and have known neither the place in which I was nor those who were present, nor myself, nor what I was saying, nor what I was writing, for then I have been conscious of a richness of interpretation, an enjoyment of light, a most keen-sighted vision, a most distinct view of the objects treated, such as would be given through the eyes from the clearest exhibition – *Philo*

The artist's inspiration may be either a human or a spiritual grace, or a mixture of both. High artistic achievement is impossible without at least those forms of intellectual, emotional and physical mortification appropriate to the kind of art which is being practised. Over and above this course of what may be called professional mortification, some artists have practised the kind of self-naughting which is the indispensable pre-condition of the unitive knowledge of the divine

Ground.
Fra Angelico, for example, prepared himself for his work by means of prayer and meditation – *Aldous Huxley*

Now we have received not the spirit of the world, but the Spirit that is from God, so that we may understand the gifts bestowed on us by God – *1 Corinthians 2.12-13*

The uninitiated imagine one must await inspiration in order to create. That is a mistake. I am far from saying that there is no such thing as inspiration, quite the opposite. It is found as a driving force in every kind of human activity, and is in no wise peculiar to artists. But that force is only brought into action by an effort, and that effort is work. Just as appetite comes by eating, so work brings inspiration, if inspiration is not discernible at the beginning. But it is not simply inspiration that counts; it is the result of inspiration – that is, the composition – *Igor Stravinsky*

It is by long obedience and hard work that the artist comes to unforced spontaneity and consummate mastery. Knowing that he can never create anything on his own account, out of the top layers, so to speak, of his personal consciousness; he submits obediently to the workings of 'inspiration'; and knowing that the medium in which he works has its own self-nature, which must not be ignored or violently overridden, he makes himself its patient servant and, in this way achieves perfect freedom of expression. But life is also an art, and the man who would become a consummate artist in living must follow, on all the levels of his being, the same procedure as that by which the painter or the sculptor or any other craftsman comes to his own more limited perfection – *Aldous Huxley*

But strive for the higher gifts. And I will show you a still more excellent way – *1 Corinthians 12.31*

Consider the people we usually think of as having been inspired – William Shakespeare. What was the source of his inspiration? The composers, Mozart, Beethoven and Bach. What about their inspiration? Where did their melodies come from? Could they have come from within their souls? The artists, Michelangelo and Leonardo da Vinci. Was this divine influence or merely genes? – or possibly a combination of both? The poets, Shelley, Wordsworth and Keats: What was the source of their inspiration? Was it environment and hereditary, or something deeper? The scientist Marie Curie. Where did her inspiration come from? – *Anon*

'In the time of the philosophers,' he (Al-Ghazzali) writes 'as at every period, there existed some of these fervent mystics. God does not deprive this world of them, for they are its sustainers'. It is they who, dying to themselves, become capable of perpetual inspiration and so are made the instruments through which divine grace is mediated to those whose unregenerated nature is impervious to the delicate touches of the Spirit – *Aldous Huxley*

No man was ever great without a touch of divine inspiration – *Cicero*

I press on towards the goal for the prize of the heavenly call of God in Christ Jesus – *Philippians 3.14*

The true genius is a mind of large general powers, accidentally determined to some particular direction – *Samuel Johnson*

Genius is the clearer presence of God Most High in a man. Dim, potential in all men; this man it has become clear, actual – *Samuel Johnson*

Poets do not effect their object by wisdom, but by a certain natural inspiration and under the influence of enthusasm like prophets and seers – *Socrates*

Set your minds on things that are above, not on things that are on earth – *Colossians 3.2*

Poesy was ever thought to have some participation of divineness, because it doth raise and erect the mind by submitting the shews of things to the desires of the mind – *Francis Bacon*

Cleanse the thoughts of our hearts by the inspiration of thy Holy Spirit, that we may perfectly love thee, and worthily magnify thy holy Name

– *Holy Communion, The Collect*

My holy of holies is the human body, health, intelligence, talent, inspiration, love, and the most absolute freedom, imaginable – *Chekhov*

Whatever a poet writes with enthusiasm and a divine inspiration is very fine – *Democritus*

True music…must respect the thought and inspirations of the people and the time – *George Gershwin*

The two qualities which chiefly inspire regard and affection (are) that a thing is your own and that it is your only one – *Aristotle*

What sacred instinct did inspire my soul in childhood with a hope so strong? – *Thomas Traherne*

Thou, my all! My theme! My inspiration! and my crown! – *Edward Young*

The scene changes but the aspirations of good men will persist – *Vannevar Bush*

Love is a spirit all compact of fire, not gross to sink, but light, and will aspire – *William Shakespeare*

Each of us aspires to goodness, each of us desires the good and desires it for himself – *Theodore Agrippa d'Aubigne*

Far away there in the sunshine are my highest aspirations. I may not reach them, but I can look up and see their beauty, believe in them, and try to follow where they lead – *Louisa May Alcott*

Aspiration – draw of breath; desire earnestly – for or after – *The Concise Oxford Dictionary*

Thou who canst *think* as well as *feel*. Mount from the earth. Aspire! Aspire! – *William Wordsworth*

It's not a matter of chasing sensations, but welcoming those which come to us legitimately, and directing them towards the goals we aspire to –

Michel Quoist

By the word soul, or psyche, I mean that inner consciousness which aspires. By prayer I do not mean a request for anything preferred to a deity; I mean soul emotion, intense aspiration – *Richard Jefferies*

But I do hold to a something more, far higher than the actual human, something to which it is human to aspire and to seek to translate into life, individual and communal; this something translates itself to me best as the Holy Spirit – *Stephen MacKenna*

It is true, no doubt…that many persons 'go through life' without being consciously aware of their high endowment, they accumulate 'things', live in their outside world, 'make good'…but…the *push for the beyond,* is always there in us – *Rufus M. Jones*

I have immortal longings in me – *William Shakespeare*

A good man, through obscurest aspiration, has still an instinct of the one true way – *Johann Wolfgang von Goethe*

By aspiring to a similitude of God in goodness or love, neither man nor angel ever transgressed, or shall transgress – *Francis Bacon*

And thou my mind aspire to higher things; grow rich in that which never taketh rust – *Sir Philip Sidney*

Strong souls live like fire hearted suns to spend their strength in farthest striving action – *George Eliot*

Enflam'd with the study of learning, and the admiration of virtue; stirr'd up with high hopes of living to be brave men, and worthy patriots, dear to God and famous to all ages – *John Milton*

Yet some there be that by due steps aspire to lay their just hands on that golden key that opes the palace of eternity – *John Milton*

The sensual man is at home in worldliness because he has no higher aspiration. The spiritual man, however much attracted to worldliness, cannot be at home in the world of sense because he is groping towards the world of spirit – *Hubert van Zeller*

A man who loves Jesus and the truth, who is delivered from undisciplined desires and really lives the inward life, can turn to God with nothing to hold him back. In spirit he can rise beyond himself and rest in peace and joy – *Thomas à Kempis*

The religious spirit is in us. It preceded the religions, and their task as well as that of the prophets, of the initiated, consists in releasing, directing, and developing it.
This mystical aspiration is an essentially human trait. It slumbers at the bottom of our souls awaiting the event, or the man capable, in the manner of an enzyme, of transforming it into true mysticism, into faith – *Lecomte du Noüy*

The inspiration of the Almighty alone gives understanding – *George MacDonald*

2 WISDOM

A reminder of the Introduction. There is the divine inbreathing in the Genesis story of the creation of humankind. To see this fully worked out in a life we go to the Gospels, to the person of Jesus Christ. We move on to a resurrection appearance in the upper room. The disciples were gathered together. Jesus said, "Peace be with you." And when he had said this He breathed on them (reminiscent of Genesis story of the creation of humankind) and said "Receive the Holy Spirit." Lives were transformed. St Paul realized what Christ had experienced we can all in some measure also experience. One main way of bringing this about is Contemplation.

We are now going to concentrate on Wisdom, but don't be surprised if other gifts and fruits of the Holy Spirit make their presence known. Cross-fertilization is extremely valuable! All the gifts and fruits of the Holy Spirit are also linked together as One.

With God are wisdom and strength – *Job 12.13*

The wisest have the most authority – *Plato*

The truly wise are those whose souls are in Christ – *St Ambrose*

The more accurately we search into the human mind, the stronger traces we everywhere find of the wisdom of him who made it – *Edmund Burke*

Knowledge stamped on the heart makes one wise – *Beth Moore*

The price of wisdom is above pearls – *Job 28.18*

Sophia, wisdom - the knowledge of the most precious things - *Aristotle*

Christ teaches by the Spirit of wisdom in the heart, opening the understanding to the Spirit of revelation in the Word – *Matthew Henry*

Great is wisdom; infinite is the value of wisdom. It cannot be exaggerated; it is the highest achievement of man – *Thomas Carlyle*

You have the wisdom of Love…and it was the highest wisdom ever known upon this earth, remember – *Charles Dickens*

A wise man makes his own decisions, an ignorant man follows public opinion – *Chinese proverb*

"Let days speak, and many years teach wisdom." But truly it is the spirit in a mortal, the breath of the Almighty, that makes for understanding – *Job 32.7-8*

Wisdom alone is true Ambition's aim – *William Whitehead*

The most evident sign of wisdom is continual cheerfulness – *Michel de Montaigne*

Wisdom springing up within him from the Life of the Spirit – *Rufus M. Jones*

Wisdom hath four virtues: prudence, temperance, courage, and righteousness – *King Alfred*

The days that make us happy make us wise – *John Masefield*

You desire truth in the inward being; therefore teach me wisdom in my secret heart – *Psalm 51.6*

There can be no wisdom disjoined from goodness – *Richard Trench*

The height of wisdom is to take things as they are, and look upon the rest with confidence – *Michel de Montaigne*

Sophia, knowledge of things both human and divine. *Sophia* was a thing of the searching intellect, of the questing mind, of the reaches of the thoughts of men – *Cicero*

God waits for man to regain his childhood in wisdom – *Rabindranath Tagore*

The fear of the Lord is the beginning of wisdom; all those who practise it have a good understanding – *Psalm 111.10*

Wisdom is not cheaply won. It is achieved through hard sacrifice and discipline, through the endurance of conflict and pain – *Sir Sarvepalli Radhakrishnan*

Nothing is a waste of time if you use the experience wisely – *Rodin*

The Scriptures declare all wisdom to be a divine gift – *St Clement of Rome*

Who is the wise man? He who learns from all men – *William Gladstone*

Wisdom cometh by suffering – *Aeschylus*

Happy are those who find wisdom, and those who get understanding – *Proverbs 3.13*

Accumulated knowledge does not make a man wise. Knowledgeable people are found everywhere, but we are cruelly short of wise people – *Michel Quoist*

Knowledge is the power of the mind, wisdom is the power of the soul – *Julie Shannahan*

Seek the wisdom of the ages – *Ron Wild*

Continual cheerfulness is a sign of wisdom – *Thomas Fuller*

The beginning of wisdom is this: Get wisdom, and whatever else you get, get insight – *Proverbs 4.7*

Wisdom is concerned with how we relate to people, to the world, and to God – *Edmund Clowney*

The wisdom of the wise is an uncommon degree of common sense – *W.R. Inge*

There is a deep wisdom inaccessible to the wise and prudent but disclosed to babes – *Christopher Bryant SSJE*

He who knows others is wise; He who knows himself is enlightened – *Tao Te Ching*

Wisdom makes one's face shine, and the hardness of one's countenance is changed – *Ecclesiastes 8.1*

Perfect wisdom hath four parts, viz., wisdom, the principle of doing things aright; justice, the principle of doing things equally in public and private; fortitude, the principle of not flying danger but meeting it; and temperance, the principle of subduing desires and living moderately – *Plato*

Common sense mellowed and experienced is wisdom; and wisdom in its ripeness is beauty – *A.R. Orage*

You were the signet of perfection, full of wisdom and perfect in beauty – *Ezekiel 28.12*

The true sage is not he who sees, but he who, seeing the furthest, has the deepest love for mankind – *Maurice Maeterlinck*

Pain makes people think. Thought makes a person wise. Wisdom makes life endurable – *John Patrick*

I have heard of you that a spirit of the gods is in you, and that enlightenment, understanding, and excellent wisdom are found in you – *Daniel 5.14*

Wisdom begins with wonder – *Socrates*

Of all things which wisdom provides to make us entirely happy, the greatest is the possession of friendship – *Edmund Burke*

Music is a higher revelation than all wisdom and all philosophy – *Ludwig van Beethoven*

Whoever loves her (wisdom) loves life – *Ecclesiasticus 4.12*

Some hold…that there is a wisdom of the Head, and that there is a wisdom of the Heart – *Charles Dickens*

The child grew and became strong, filled with wisdom; and the favour of God was upon him – *Luke 2.40*

Wisdom cannot be pass'd from one having it to another not having it, Wisdom is of the soul, is not susceptible of proof, is its own proof – *Walt Whitman*

Let us be poised, and wise, and our own today – *Ralph Waldo Emerson*

Wisdom…is a knowledge exercised in finding out the way to perfect happiness, by discerning man's real wants and sovereign desires – *Thomas Traherne*

One can have knowledge without having wisdom, but one cannot have wisdom without having knowledge – *R.C. Sproul*

Where did this man get all this? What is this wisdom that has been given to him? – *Mark 6.2*

In all created things discern the providence and wisdom of God, and in all things give Him thanks – *St Teresa of Avila*

Dare to be wise – *Horace*

Wisdom is ofttimes nearer when we stoop than when we soar – *William Wordsworth*

It is part of the Christian spiritual tradition that God dwells in the centre of every man, an unseen, largely unknown Strength and Wisdom, moving him to be human, to grow and to expand his humanity to the utmost of its capacity – *Christopher Bryant SSJE*

Everyone then who hears these words of mine and acts on them will be like a wise man who built his house on rock. The rain fell, the floods came, and the wind blew and beat on that house, but it did not fall, because it had been founded on rock – *Matthew 7.24-25*

Wisdom lies more in - affection and sincerity - than people are apt to imagine – *George Eliot*

Wisdom is the perfection of human living – *Sir Sarvepalli Radhakrishnan*

Only when we offer our minds to God do we receive the illumination of his wisdom – *Bede Griffiths OSB*

Health is the condition of wisdom and the sign is cheerfulness – an open and noble temper – *Ralph Waldo Emerson*

I am sending you out like sheep into the midst of wolves; so be wise as serpents and innocent as doves – *Matthew 10.16*

Sophia (Wisdom) is the answer to the eternal problems of life and death, and God and man, and time and eternity – *William Barclay*

Wisdom…is an inpouring and a source of all graces and all virtues – *John of Rysbroeck*

What is the price of Experience (wisdom)? It is bought, with the price of all that a man hath, his house, his wife, his children – *William Blake*

He (God) is the source of your life in Christ Jesus, who became for us wisdom from God - *1 Corinthians 1.30*

Celestial wisdom calms the mind – *Samuel Johnson*

Wisdom…is intent living, the most fruitful act of man – *Sir Sarvepalli Radhakrishnan*

Wisdom denotes the pursuing of the best ends by the best means – *Frances Hutcheson*

It is the privilege of wisdom to listen – *Oliver Wendell Holmes*

Christ himself, in whom are hidden all the treasures of wisdom and knowledge – *Colossians 2.3*

The first step in wisdom is to know what is false – *Latin proverb*

Nine-tenths of wisdom consists in being wise in time – *Theodore Roosevelt*

Courage is a virtue only insofar as it is directed by prudence – *Francois Fénelon*

Wisdom is the ability to use knowledge so as to meet successfully the emergencies of life. Men may acquire knowledge, but wisdom is a gift direct from God –
Bob Jones

The cross on Golgatha will never save thy soul. The cross in thine own soul, alone can make thee whole – *Angelus Silesius*

Let the word of Christ dwell in you richly; teach and admonish one another in all wisdom – *Colossians 3.16*

Adversity makes a man wise, not rich – *Romanian proverb*

Tracing our Wisdom, Power and Love, in earth or sky, in streams or grove – *John Keble*

Knowledge dwells in heads replete with thoughts of other men, wisdom in minds attentive to their own – *William Cowper*

To love wisdom as to live according to its dictates, a life of simplicity, independence, magnanimity, and trust – *Henry David Thoreau*

Wisdom is the right use of knowledge – *Charles H. Spurgeon*

Who is wise and understanding among you? Show by your good life that your works are done with gentleness born of wisdom – *James 3.13*

May the outward and inward man be as one – *Socrates*

Common sense in an uncommon degree is what the world calls wisdom – *Samuel Taylor Coleridge*

Theology deserves to be called the highest wisdom for everything is viewed in the light of the first cause – *St Thomas Aquinas*

To neglect the wise sayings of great thinkers is to deny ourselves our truest education – *William James*

Philosophy has shown itself over and over again to be full of arguments but lacking in conclusions – *Hugh Sylvester*

The first thing we can say of God is to be silent concerning him from the wisdom of inner riches – *St Augustine*

A wise man will always be a Christian, because the perfection of wisdom is to know where lies tranquillity, and how to obtain it – *W.S. Landor*

Strengthen them…with the Holy Ghost the Comforter, and daily increase in them thy manifold gifts of grace; the spirit of wisdom… – *Confirmation Service, The Book of Common Prayer*

There is a time when a man distinguishes the idea of felicity from the idea of wealth; it is the beginning of wisdom – *Ralph Waldo Emerson*

Teach a child what is wise, that is morality. Teach him what is wise and beautiful, that is religion – *T.H. Huxley*

Wisdom is not an art that may be learned; wisdom comes from the stars – *Paul Fleming*

To know what lies before us in daily life, is the prime wisdom – *John Milton*

The hours of a wise man are lengthened by his ideas – *Joseph Addison*

There needs but one wise man in a company, and all are wise, so rapid is the contagion – *Ralph Waldo Emerson*

Always wise men go back to leap the furthest – *French proverb*

Wisdom is the knowledge of truth in its inmost reality, expression of truth, arrived at through the rectitudes of our own soul. Wisdom knows God in ourselves, and ourselves in God – *Thomas Merton*

The Wisdom of God is working through all created life, and far and wide is the sustainer and the inspirer of the thought and the endeavour of men – *Michael Ramsey*

Deep and grave enthusiasm for the eternal beauty and the eternal order, reason touched with emotion and a serene tenderness of heart – these surely are the foundations of wisdom – *Henri Frédéric Amiel*

The art of being wise is the art of knowing what to overlook – *William James*

And we shall be truly wise if we be made content; content, too, not only with what we can understand, but content with what we do not understand – the habit of mind which theologians call – and rightly – faith in God – *Charles Kingsley*

Wisdom in its ripeness is beauty – *A.R. Orage*

Abundance of knowledge does not teach a man to be wise – *Heraclitus*

True wisdom is gazing at God. Gazing at God is silence of the thoughts – *Isaac of Nineveh*

The wise man looks inside his heart and finds eternal peace – *Hindu proverb*

Wisdom must be sought…'Tis never sought in vain – *Edward Young*

Honesty is the first chapter in the book of wisdom – *Thomas Jefferson*

Wisdom sends us back to our childhood – *Blaise Pascal*

We profess two wisdoms in Christ, the uncreated wisdom of God, and the created wisdom of men – *St Thomas Aquinas*

Intuition is knowledge which derives not from observation and experience or from conception and reason, but from the mind's reflection on itself – *Bede Griffiths OSB*

The only wisdom we can hope to acquire is the wisdom of humility – *T.S. Eliot*

The first key to wisdom is assiduous and frequent questioning. For by doubting we come to enquiry and by enquiry we arrive at truth – *Peter Abelard*

The Word of Wisdom that opens all things, and come to know the hidden Unity in the eternal being – *Rufus M. Jones*

Wisdom is of the soul – *Walt Whitman*

Prudent in life's difficulties – *Rufus M. Jones*

So does the heart become open to divine wisdom – *Bede Griffiths OSB*

Wisdom's best nurse is contemplation – *John Milton*

Wonder is the beginning of wisdom – *Greek proverb*

3 COUNSEL

At school we were taught to say our prayers. At the end of the day, before going to sleep, we were to start with Thanksgiving – thanking God for all the blessings of that day. We were then to move on to Confession, owning up to where we had gone wrong during the day, "in thought, word, deed and omission." This was followed by accepting God's forgiveness, and moving on to say the Lord's Prayer. After this we were to engage in Intercession, ending up with Petition, requesting that our own needs would be met.

In my late teens, there was a major shift. I came to realize my prayer life was one-sided for I was doing all the talking. A crucial breakthrough came with the discovery of a "listening form of prayer." This was closely connected with starting a spiritual diary (or journal). I would take a verse of Scripture, and spend an hour writing down all that came to mind. For me this was the start of a valuable Counselling form of prayer. This practice is probably the most valuable thing I have done in life.

And Samuel said, "Speak, for your servant is listening" - *1 Samuel 3.10*

The only real valuable thing is intuition – *Albert Einstein*

The counsellor helps the soul to see itself and thorough direction shows the way to fullness and joy – *N.W. Goodacre*

Keeping a spiritual diary (journal) enables a person to be counselled

Listen long enough and the person will generally come up with an adequate solution – *Mary Kay Ash*

They listened to me, and waited, and kept silence for my counsel – *Job 29.21*

A minister is not only for public preaching, but to be a known counsellor for their souls – *Richard Baxter*

We ought… to give more time to listening to God than we do to speaking to Him – *Cyril H. Powell*

Take up the practice of quiet forethought, to avoid anxieties and worries

I bless the Lord who gives me counsel; in the night also my heart instructs me – *Psalm 16.7*

No gift is more precious than good advice – *Desiderius Erasmus*

Write down the advice of the person who loves you, though you like it not at present – *Proverb*

Let no one give advice to others, that they have not first given themselves – *Seneca*

Make me to know your ways, O Lord; teach me your paths. Lead me in your truth, and teach me – *Psalm 25.4-5*

The best and most wonderful thing that can happen to you in this life, is that you should be silent and let God work and speak – *Dag Hammarskjöld*

Silence is a listening to the truth of things – *Heraclitus*

Jesus gives to us the moral standard of life, the ethical ideal – *Bishop Boyd Carpenter*

He leads the humble in what is right, and teaches the humble his way – *Psalm 25.9*

Jesus is only heard well in a peaceful soul surrounded by an atmosphere of silence – *D. Columba Marmion*

The value of prayer; it is precious beyond all price – *Thomas Buxton*

Often you just have to rely on your intuition – *Bill Gates*

Do not open your heart to everyone, but discuss your affairs with one who is wise and who fears God – *Basil Hume OSB*

I will instruct you and teach you the way you should go; I will counsel you with my eye upon you – *Psalm 32.8*

He (God) cannot be seen but he can be listened to – *Martin Buber*

The more faithfully you listen to the voice within you, the better you will hear what is sounding outside – *Dag Hammarskjöld*

Listening is a conscious, willed action, requiring alertness and vigilance, by which our whole attention is focused and controlled – *Mother Mary Clare, SLG*

This is God, our God for ever and ever. He will be our guide for ever – *Psalm 48.14*

For me a crucial breakthrough came with the discovery of a "listening" form of prayer – *Anon*

Meditation is not an end in itself; it is a means to an end; in it we listen to God that we may hear, and obey Him – *Olive Wyon*

Contemplation is to see and to hear from the heart – *Bede Griffiths*

OSB

A discipline of meditation, entering into silence, stilling the activity of the mind, allowing feelings and intuitions to rise from the depths of our being – *George Appleton*

O that my people would listen to me – *Psalm 81.13*

From the day I came into public life, I have been directed by an inner life and an inner voice – *George Lansbury (one time leader of the Labour Party)*

We are not meant to live solely by intellectual convictions, we are meant more and more to open ourselves to the Spirit – *Basil Hume OSB*

But those who listen to me will be secure, and will live at ease, without dread of disaster – *Proverbs 1.33*

Jesus promised that his Spirit would guide his disciples into all truth, both truth of mind and direction of life – *George Appleton*

I was guided by an implicit faith in God's goodness – *Thomas Traherne*

Guidance does not end when calamity begins. In every situation He meets us and out of every situation He can lead us to a greener pasture and a sphere of wider view – *W.E. Sangster*

God shall be my hope, my stay, my guide, and lantern to my feet – *William Shakespeare*

The integrity of the upright guides them – *Proverbs 11.3*

The Holy Spirit is the true counsellor. He shows us what is to come and also gives us the strength to face the difficulties that lie ahead of us – *Martin Israel*

There is a spirit that works within us, and develops a power in us that teaches us how to accomplish what we will, and guides us by its inspiration to successful results – *Henry Ward Beecher*

Where there is no guidance, a nation falls, but in an abundance of counsellors there is safety – *Proverbs 11.14*

The most difficult and decisive part of prayer is acquiring this ability to listen – *Mother Mary Clare, SLG*

The experience of a guiding inward Spirit – *Rufus M. Jones*

In silence he (Jesus) will listen to us, then he will speak to our soul, and there we will hear his voice – *Mother Teresa*

Silence does not reveal its treasures until we are willing to wait in darkness and emptiness – *Olive Wyon*

For a child has been born for us, a son given to us; authority rests upon his shoulders; and he is named Wonderful Counsellor, Mighty God, Everlasting Father, Prince of Peace – *Isaiah 9.6*

The very best and highest attainment in this life is to remain still and let God act and speak in you – *Meister Eckhart*

The gospel was not good advice but good news – *William E. Gladstone*

I will put my law within them, and I will write it on their hearts; and I will be their God, and they shall be my people – *Jeremiah 31.33*

Reference to God of all problems, attitudes, opportunities and decisions of our lives – *George Appleton*

Patient waiting upon God until a persistent feeling of oughtness comes – *George Appleton*

When they bring you before the synagogues, the rulers, and the

authorities, do not worry about how you are to defend yourselves or what you are to say; for the Holy Spirit will teach you at that very hour what you ought to say –
Luke 12.11-12

All spiritual experience must be subject to the moral test, it must further be tested by the light of God in other men and in history, and by the *spirit of Scripture* – *Rufus M. Jones*

The illumination, grace and power of God the Holy Spirit – *Bede Griffiths OSB*

Learn from me – *Matthew 11.29*

Listen to His 'word' within us – *John Main OSB*

All we have to do is listen to our heart to the silence of God – *Sister Jeanne D'Arc OP*

Conscience illuminated by the presence of Jesus Christ in the heart must be the guide of every man – *R.H. Benson*

The only listening that is worth while is the listening which listens and learns. There is no other way to listen to God – *George Appleton*

This is my Son…listen to him – *Matthew 17.5*

Readiness to receive insights from others but not let them decide for us – *George Appleton*

How do we seek the Spirit's guidance? – *George Appleton*

I will ask the Father, and he will give you another Advocate, to be with you for ever. This is the Spirit of truth, whom the world cannot receive, because it neither sees him nor knows him. You know him, because he abides with you, and he will be in you –
John 14.16-17

Listen to what God inspires – *Francois Fénelon*

Wait upon Him for guidance and direction – *David Hoste*

When the Spirit of truth comes, he will guide you into all the truth; for he will not speak on his own, but will speak whatever he hears, and he will declare to you the things that are to come – *John 16.13*

How can you expect God to speak to you in that gentle and quiet voice which melts the soul, when you are making so much noise with your rapid reflections? Be silent, and God will speak again – *Francois Fénelon*

An enemy may chance to give you counsel – *English proverb*

A moment's insight is sometimes worth a life's experience – *Oliver Wendell Holmes*

He that will not be counselled cannot be helped – *French proverb*

May the Lord direct your hearts to the love of God and to the steadfastness of Christ – *2 Thessalonians 3.5*

Conscience is God's presence in men – *Emanuel Swedenborg*

A good conscience is a mine of wealth. And in truth, what greater riches can there be, what thing more sweet than a good conscience? – *St Bernard of Clairvaux*

Listen for the meaning beneath the words

I'm become, re-become…more of a Listener, a deeper sense of the possibilities of something stirring, emerging from There Back-of-things – *Stephen MacKenna*

The most precious messages are those which are whispered – *Mark Rutherford*

Men, as by a natural inspiration, have agreed to speak of conscience as the voice of God, as the Divinity within us – *William E. Channing*

The value of experience is not in seeing much, but in seeing wisely – *Sir William Osler*

If we listened more we would learn more about spirit and truth – *Hubert van Zeller*

There is a great need today for hearts that listen – *Elizabeth Bassett*

Prayer is not so much a matter of talking as listening; contemplation is not watching but being watched – *Carlo Carretto*

Give me, O Lord, a heart that listens – *Sister Jeanne D'Arc OP*

We can look back, and see a guiding and a directing hand in it and through it all – *William Barclay*

Without a guide it is difficult to recognize the fruits of the Presence of God in our lives – *Jean Vanier*

Give us grace to listen well – *John Keble*

We need only listen to what Jesus has told us. It's enough to listen to the Gospel and put into practice what it tells us – *Carlo Carretto*

I cannot hear what you say for listening to what you are – *Robert Louis Stevenson*

How does the heart become open to Divine Wisdom? – *Bede Griffiths OSB*

I don't think some decisions are made by the reasoning faculties, but by some instinct. One *knows* what one can do and what one cannot do, when the time arrives – *A.C. Benson*

A STILL MORE EXCELLENT WAY

And I will place within them as a guide my umpire *Conscience*, whom if they will hear, light after light well us'd they shall attain, and to the end persisting, safe arrive – *John Milton*

For a time will come when your innermost voice will speak to you, saying: "This is *my* path; here I will find peace. I will pursue this path, come what may –
Grace Cooke

We have two ears and one mouth so that we can listen twice as much as we speak –*Epictetus*

God never ceases to speak to us, but the noise of the world without and the tumult of our passions within bewilder us and prevent us from listening to him – *Francois Fénelon*

No true disciple of mine will ever be a Ruskinian; he will follow, not me, but the instincts of his own soul, and the guidance of its Creator – *John Ruskin*

It takes a great man to be a good listener – *Arthur Helps*

4 UNDERSTANDING

Whilst doing National Service with the Gurkhas in the Far East I remember reading a book entitled "Love is a Many-Splendoured Thing" by Han Suyin. One sentence challenged me in particular. "To realize how difficult, agonizing, is the process of understanding and how long it takes." My reaction was – surely the process of understanding is not that difficult or painful? Fifty years on, and I have developed a certain respect for what she wrote. Having been ordained for most of that time I have come to realize how complicated human nature is and how difficult it is to understand. Unlike the author I have enjoyed the challenge and hope that contemplating on the following material will ease the burden for others.

But where shall wisdom be found? And where is the place of understanding? – *Job 28.12*

What one has not experienced, one will never understand in print – *Isadora Duncan*

The highest of all is not to understand the highest but to act upon it – *Søren Kierkegaard*

The real thing is to understand, and love that you may understand – *J.B. Yeats*

But truly it is the spirit in a mortal, the breath of the Almighty, that makes for understanding – *Job 32.8*

The greatest gift that any human being can give to another is the gift of understanding and of peace – *William Barclay*

Such good things as pass man's understanding – *The Book of Common Prayer*

Life can only be understood by living – *W. MacNeile Dixon*

The more you understand, the better you can believe – *Raymond Lull*

I have more understanding than all my teachers, for your decrees are my meditation…for I keep your precepts – *Psalm 119. 99-100*

It is with the soul that we grasp the essence of another human being, not with the mind, not even with the heart – *Henry Miller*

To understand a matter properly, a man must dominate it, instead of allowing it to dominate him – *Ernest Hello*

A person can never fully be *understood*, but can be fully *loved* – *J. Neville Ward*

All the glory of greatness has no lustre for people who are in search of understanding – *Blaise Pascal*

Making your ear attentive to wisdom and inclining your heart to understanding – *Proverbs 2.2*

For the rights of understanding to be valid one must venture out into life – *Søren Kierkegaard*

To realize how difficult, agonizing, is the process of understanding and how long it takes – *Han Suyin*

That which enables us to know and understand aright in the things of God must be a living principle of holiness within us – *John Smith the Platonist*

Nobody sees with his eyes alone; we see with our souls – *Henry Miller*

For the Lord gives wisdom; from his mouth come knowledge and understanding – *Proverbs 2.6*

Spirituality needs theology, spirituality needs understanding, and it is such understanding that theology supplies – *John Macquarrie*

Grant that I may not so much seek to be understood as to understand – *St Francis of Assisi*

I believe in Jesus Christ, in whom I get a picture of God within the limits of my comprehension – *Hugh Redwood*

The Spirit of God has been understood as God in the midst of men – *John Macquarrie*

The fear of the Lord is the beginning of wisdom, and the knowledge of the Holy One is insight – *Proverbs 9.10*

He understood the leprosy of the leper, the darkness of the blind, the fierce misery of those who live for pleasure, the strange poverty of the rich – *Oscar Wilde*

Life must be understood backwards…but it must be lived forwards – *Søren Kierkegaard*

Of course *understanding* of our fellow-beings is important. But this understanding becomes fruitful only when it is sustained by sympathetic feeling in joy and in sorrow – *Albert Einstein*

How much better to get wisdom than gold! To get understanding is to be chosen rather than silver – *Proverbs 16.16*

We should not pretend to understand the world only by the intellect;

we apprehend it just as much by feeling – *C.G. Jung*

Much learning does not teach understanding – *Heraclitus*

Effects of prayer – increased physical buoyancy, greater intellectual vigour, moral stamina, and a deeper understanding of the realities underlying human relationships – *Alexis Carrel*

Had he done as the Master had told him, he would soon have come to understand. Obedience is the opener of eyes – *George MacDonald*

We are to answer for any truth we have understood – *Anthony Bloom*

I have heard of you that a spirit of the gods is in you, and that enlightenment, understanding and excellent wisdom are found in you – *Daniel 5.14*

If one is master of one thing and understands one thing well, one has at the same time insight into and understanding of many things – *Vincent van Gogh*

Love is life. All, everything that I understand, I understand only because I love – *Leo Tolstoy*

The whole of God's being cannot be understood but enough of it can be understood to trust it – *Henry Ward Beecher*

A comprehended god is no god at all – *Gerhard Tersteegen*

Those who trust in him will understand truth – *Wisdom of Solomon 3.9*

My words are spiritual and cannot be comprehended fully by man's intelligence – *St Thomas à Kempis*

This is the true power of God, the power of an infinite understanding – *Stuart Jackman*

It is by loving that you understand – *Carlo Carretto*

He (Jean Vanier) comes over as a man of great compassion and understanding, mingled with kindness and sympathy – *Anon*

I will light in your heart the lamp of understanding, which shall not be put out – *2 Esdras 14.25*

"Thou must thyself be the way." The spiritual understanding, must be born in thee – *Rufus M. Jones*

No man has understanding, if he is not humble, and whoever lacks humility, is devoid of understanding – *Isaac of Nineveh*

Adoration is among the most powerful of the educative forces which purify the understanding, form and develop the spiritual life – *Evelyn Underhill*

But as for what was sown on good soil, this is the one who hears the word and understands it, who indeed bears fruit and yields, in one case a hundredfold, in another sixty, and another thirty – *Matthew 13.23*

Understanding is the reward of faith. Therefore seek not to understand that thou mayest believe, but believe that thou mayest understand – *St Augustine*

To be surprised, to wonder, is to begin to understand – *José Ortega Y Gasset*

To understand any living thing you must, so to say, creep within, and feel the beating of its heart – *W. MacNeile Dixon*

Now we have received not the spirit of the world, but the Spirit that is from God, so that we may understand the gifts bestowed on us by God – *1 Corinthians 2.12*

No human being can really understand another, and no one can arrange another's happiness – *Graham Greene*

The understanding that comes from God is true wisdom, unlike the knowledge that is the fruits of human endeavour … it is broad, expansive, all embracing and of transfiguring intensity – *Martin Israel*

And the peace of God, which surpasses all understanding, will guard your hearts and your minds in Christ Jesus – *Philippians 4.7*

Christ teaches by the Spirit of wisdom in the heart, opening the understanding to the Spirit of revelation in the Word – *Matthew Henry*

Contact with God, faith, is the spirit of understanding and of wisdom – *E.C. Blackman*

God is the most important object of understanding – *E.C. Blackman*

What man does not understand, he does not possess – *Johann Wolfgang von Goethe*

Understanding is the wealth of wealth – *Arab proverb*

Seek first to understand, then to be understood – *Stephen Covey*

I want their hearts to be encouraged and united in love, so that they may have all the riches of assured understanding and have the knowledge of God's mystery, that is, Christ himself, in whom are hidden all the treasures of wisdom and knowledge – *Colossians 2.2-3*

No one can develop freely in this world and find a full life without feeling understood by at least one person – *Paul Tournier*

You never really understand a person until you consider things from his point of view…until you climb into his skin and walk around in it – *Harper Lee*

The way to understand the Scriptures and all theology is to become holy. It is to be under the authority of the Holy Spirit – *Martyn Lloyd-Jones*

A moment's insight is sometimes worth a life's experience – *Oliver Wendell Holmes*

He who would fully and feelingly understand the words of Christ, must study to make his whole life conformable to that of Christ – *St Thomas à Kempis*

Think over what I say, for the Lord will give you understanding in all things – *2 Timothy 2.7*

What is most necessary for understanding divine things is prayer – *Origen*

I want, by understanding myself, to understand others. I want to be all that I am capable of becoming – *Katherine Mansfield*

By faith we know His existence; in glory we shall know His nature – *Blaise Pascal*

I believe in order that I may understand – *St Anselm*

We must learn to *understand* – *William Barclay*

The best-educated human being is the one who understands most about the life in which he is placed – *Helen Keller*

To know someone here or there with whom you feel there is understanding in spite of distances or thoughts unexpressed – that can make of this earth a garden – *Johann Wolfgang von Goethe*

Religion has its origin in the depths of the soul and it can be understood only by those who are prepared to take the plunge – *F.D. Maurice*

To possess Him who cannot be understood is to renounce all that can be understood – *Thomas Merton*

As we acquire more knowledge, things do not become more comprehensible, but more mysterious – *Albert Schweitzer*

Faith is the first step in understanding; understanding is the reward of faith – *St Augustine*

With great doubts come great understanding; with little doubts come little understanding – *Chinese proverb*

Seek not so much to have thy ear tickled as thy understanding enlightened – *Nehemiah Rogers*

It is neither necessary, nor indeed possible, to understand any matter of faith farther than it is revealed – *Benjamin Whichcote*

Each generation of Christians makes its own contribution to the understanding of the riches of Jesus Christ – *C.B. Moss*

Understanding ourselves in the light of God, and the growth in the life of faith and prayer – *Norman Goodacre*

A clear understanding of God makes one want to follow the direction of things, the direction of oneself – *André Gide*

Whoever has helped us to a larger understanding is entitled to our gratitude for all time – *Norman Douglas*

The Holy Spirit raises us far beyond the limitations of our own understanding so that we may drink deeply of the knowledge of God – *Martin Israel*

The understanding that comes from God is true wisdom – *Martin Israel*

The comprehension of life, of its living flow is beyond conceptual thought, which, in the very effort to comprehend, arrests, divides and falsifies it – *W. MacNeile Dixon*

The first condition under which we can know a man at all is, that he be in essentials something like ourselves – *J.A. Froude*

But, in faith, there is one source alone of all knowledge , and that is God Himself – *Martin Israel*

It was the man in the street who understood our Lord, and all the doctor of the law who was perplexed and offended – *R.H. Benson*

Peace cannot be kept by peace. It can only be achieved by understanding – *Albert Einstein*

Faith opens the door to understanding – *St Augustine*

Never try to reason the prejudices out of a man. It was not reasoned into him and cannot be reasoned out – *Sydney Smith*

5 KNOWLEDGE

Harry James Cargas gives us an excellent introduction to "Knowledge." He wrote about there being two types of knowledge – the knowledge of things created and self-knowledge. He suggested that the two should be complementary and held in balance.

As a former pastoral chaplain most of my work was to do with self-knowledge, which at some point involved a knowledge of God. As a modern writer reminds us, to know God is not merely to have an intellectual knowledge of God. It is to have an intimate relationship with God. At the same time I had to remember I was in an academic institution, and so concerned with the pursuit of academic knowledge, or what we have been calling "knowledge of things created."

For the Lord is a God of knowledge – *1 Samuel 2.3*

Knowledge is vain and fruitless which is not reduced to practice – *Matthew Henry*

The best way to know God is to love many things – *Vincent van Gogh*

This is how people get to know God – by doing his will – *Henry Drummond*

But those who know do not theorize, they merely bear witness to what they have seen and experienced – *Kathleen Raine*

Knowledge is the action of the soul – *Ben Jonson*

The fear of the Lord is the beginning of knowledge – *Proverbs 1.7*

An extensive knowledge is needful to thinking people – *John Keats*

What is the best thing in life? – to know God – *J.I. Packer*

As knowledge increases, wonder deepens – *Charles Morgan*

If you indeed cry out for insight, and raise your voice for understanding; if you seek it like silver, and search for it as for hidden treasures - then you will understand the fear of the Lord and find the knowledge of God. For the Lord gives wisdom; from his mouth come knowledge and understanding – *Proverbs 2.3-6*

The aim of meditation… is to come to know him through the realization that our very being is penetrated with his knowledge and love for us – *Thomas Merton*

The people who know God best are those who least presume to speak of him – *Angela of Foligno*

True knowledge lies in knowing how to live – *Baltasar Gracian*

For the earth will be full of the knowledge of the Lord as the waters cover the sea – *Isaiah 11.9*

Not I, the I that I am, know these things, but God knows them in me – *Jacob Boehme*

To know Him therefore as He is, is to frame the most beautiful idea in all Worlds – *Thomas Traherne*

To know yourself is to realise that you're at once unique and multiple – *Michel Quoist*

The knowledge of the secret godliness that each one of us bears within him – *Herman Hesse*

No one knows the Son except the Father; and no one knows the Father except the Son and anyone to whom the Son chooses to reveal him – *Matthew 11.27*

Two types of knowledge – the knowledge of things created and self-knowledge – *Harry James Cargas*

The tragedy of much modern life is that the abandonment of the knowledge of God means that futility has taken over – *Leon Morris*

The knowledge of God is very far from the love of him – *Blaise Pascal*

One must spend time in gathering knowledge to give it out richly – *Edward C. Steadman*

I am the good shepherd. I know my own and my own know me, just as the Father knows me and I know the Father – *John 10.14-15*

Only a rare person now and then is curious enough to want to know God – *A.W. Tozer*

Knowledge is not the most important thing in the world. Love is essential – *Francois Fénelon*

The aim of education is the knowledge not of facts but of values – *W.R. Inge*

Knowledge without integrity is dangerous and dreadful – *Samuel Johnson*

And this is eternal life, that they may know you, the only true God, and Jesus Christ whom you have sent – *John 17.3*

Seek to grow in knowledge… for the benefit of your souls – *Jonathan Edwards*

Self-knowledge comes to us only in the dark times, when we are stripped of illusion and naked to truth – *Mary Craig*

To know, to get into the truth of anything, is ever a mystic act, – of which the best Logics can but babble on the surface – *Thomas Carlyle*

The best treasure that a man can attain unto in this world is true knowledge; even the knowledge of himself – *Jacob Boehme*

O the depth of the riches and wisdom and knowledge of God! How unsearchable are his judgements and how inscrutable his ways! – *Romans 11.33*

Knowledge of God is not merely intellectual knowledge of God; it is a personal relationship with God – *William Barclay*

Knowledge is not something to be packed away in some corner of our brain, but what enters into our being, colours our emotion, haunts our soul, and is as close to us as life itself – *Sir Sarvepalli Radhakrishnan*

Knowledge which is acquired under compulsion has no hold on the mind – *Plato*

Knowledge is happiness, because to have knowledge – broad, deep knowledge – is to know true ends from false, and lofty things from low – *Helen Keller*

But anyone who loves God is known by him – *1 Corinthians 8.3*

Truth is the foundation of all knowledge and the cement of all societies – *John Dryden*

What we feel matters much more than what we know – *George Moore*

But only to our intellect is he incomprehensible; not to our love – *The*

Cloud of Unknowing

To know is not to prove, nor to explain. It is to accede to vision – *Antoine de Saint-Exupéry*

Accumulated knowledge does not make a man wise. Knowledgeable people are found everywhere, but we are cruelly short of wise people – *Michel Quoist*

And to know the love of Christ that surpasses knowledge, so that you may be filled with all the fullness of God – *Ephesians 3.19*

Nothing is more excellent than knowledge – *St John of Damascus*

The knowledge of love – *Bede Griffiths OSB*

I often wonder if my knowledge about God has not become my greatest stumbling block to my knowledge of God – *Henri J.M. Nouwen*

He who would know God must first know himself – *Meister Eckhart*

I want to know Christ and the power of his resurrection – *Philippians 3.10*

Human things must be known to be loved; but Divine things must be loved to be known – *Blaise Pascal*

A man may be theologically knowing and spiritually ignorant – *Stephen Charnock*

Wonder (which is the seed of knowledge) – *Francis Bacon*

Knowledge is love and light and vision – *Helen Keller*

We know, and it is our pride to know, that man is by his constitution a religious animal – *Edmund Burke*

For this reason, since the day we heard it, we have not ceased praying for you and asking that you may be filled with the knowledge of God's will in all spiritual wisdom and understanding – *Colossians 1.9*

For the attainment of divine knowledge, we are directed to combine a dependence on God's Spirit with our own researches – *Charles Simeon*

There is but one thing in the world worth knowing – the knowledge of God – *R.H. Benson*

He who suffers much will know much – *Greek proverb*

It is eternal life, God's life, to know what God is like – *William Barclay*

I want their hearts to be encouraged and united in love, so that they may have all the riches of assured understanding and have the knowledge of God's mystery, that is, Christ himself, in whom are hidden all the treasures of wisdom and knowledge – *Colossians 2.2-3*

If you have knowledge, let others light their candles at it – *Margaret Fuller*

To know God is therefore not merely to have an intellectual knowledge of God; it is to have an intimate relationship with God – *William Barclay*

Our knowledge of God must lead to a more intimate relationship with Him or we run the risk of becoming pharisees – *Douglas Rumford*

Progress in the Christian life is exactly equal to the growing knowledge we gain of the Triune God in personal experience – *A.W. Tozer*

The most basic requirement for an authentically integrated self is knowledge of one's own inherent value – *Katherine Zappone*

The highest and most profitable reading is the true knowledge and consideration of ourselves – *St Thomas à Kempis*

A scrap of knowledge about sublime things is worth more than any amount of trivialities – *St Thomas Aquinas*

Knowledge unused for the good of others is more vain than unused gold – *John Ruskin*

Knowledge is proud that she knows so much; Wisdom is humble that she knows no more – *William Cowper*

To know God is to know Goodness. It is to see the beauty of infinite Love – *Thomas Traherne*

There is no knowledge at all unless it is also and equally action – *R.H.J. Steuart SJ*

It is deep within ourselves that the meaning of the universe is to be found –
Harry James Cargas

Lord, teach me to know Thee, and to know myself – *St Augustine*

Wonder, rather than doubt, is the root of knowledge – *Abraham Heschel*

An ounce of love is worth a pound of knowledge – *John Wesley*

If a man believes and knows God, he can no longer ask, 'What is the meaning of my life'? But by believing he actually lives the meaning of his life – *Karl Barth*

Philosophical knowledge is a spiritual act, where not only the intellect is active, but the whole of man's spiritual power, his emotions and his will – *Nicolas Berdyaev*

Oh, the fullness, pleasure, sheer excitement of knowing God on Earth

– *Jim Elliot*

We can no more find a method of knowing God than for making God, because the knowledge of God is God himself dwelling in the soul. The most we can do is to prepare for his entry, to get out of his way, to remove the barriers, for until God acts in us there is nothing positive that we can do in that direction – *Alan W. Watts*

All knowledge is sterile which does not lead to action and end in charity – *Joseph Mercier*

Knowledge, love, power – there is the complete life – *Henri Frédéric Amiel*

What we want is to see the child in pursuit of knowledge, not knowledge in pursuit of the child – *George Bernard Shaw*

My words are spiritual and cannot be comprehended fully by man's intelligence – *St Thomas à Kempis*

Make it thy business to know thyself, which is the most difficult lesson in the world – *Miguel de Cervantes*

The message the mystics have for us is that while there is indeed a very real world "out there", there is a more real world within each of us – *Harry James Cargas*

In faith, there is one source alone of all knowledge, and that is God Himself – *Martin Israel*

There is a great deal of unmapped country within us – *George Eliot*

Men are born equal but they are also born different – *Erich Fromm*

To know what God is like does make the most tremendous difference to life...
We enter into a new life, we share something of the life of God Himself, when, through the work of Jesus, we discover what God

is like – *William Barclay*

Divine knowledge flows to the receptive human soul in the practice of contemplative prayer – *Martin Israel*

The humble knowledge of yourself is a surer way to God than the deepest search after science – *St Thomas à Kempis*

In proportion as we have the Spirit of Jesus we have the true knowledge of Jesus – *Albert Schweitzer*

The knowledge of one human being, such as love alone can give…is worth more than all the book learning in the world – *Charles Kingsley*

The highest stage man can reach is to be conscious of his own thoughts and sentiments, to know himself – *Johann Wolfgang von Goethe*

Nature has concealed at the bottom of our minds talents and abilities of which we are not aware – *Francois, Duc de La Rochefoucald*

To know God and to live are one and the same thing – *Leo Tolstoy*

Know all and you will pardon all – *St Thomas à Kempis*

Knowledge and human power are synonymous – *Francis Bacon*

To know how to use knowledge is to have wisdom – *Charles H. Spurgeon*

The great end of life is not knowledge but action – *T. H. Huxley*

Knowledge comes, but wisdom lingers – *Alfred, Lord Tennyson*

Knowing all things, therefore, and providing for what is profitable for each one, he revealed that which it was our profit to know, but what we were unable to bear, he kept secret – *St John of Damascus*

People who lean on logic and philosophy and rational exposition end by starving the best part of the mind – *J.B. Yeats*

Of all kinds of knowledge that we can ever obtain, the knowledge of God and the knowledge of ourselves are the most important – *Jonathan Edwards*

He who knows his own self knows God – *Mahammed Hadith*

Believers who have most knowledge, are not therefore necessarily the most spiritual – *John Newton*

Cease from an excessive desire of knowing, for you will find much distraction and delusion in it – *St Thomas à Kempis*

Doubt is the key to knowledge – *Persian proverb*

To be conscious that you are ignorant is a great step to knowledge – *Benjamin Disraeli*

Seek not to grow in knowledge chiefly for the sake of applause, and to enable you to dispute with others; but seek it for the benefit of your souls – *Jonathan Edwards*

Knowledge of God can be fully given to man only in a Person, never in a doctrine. Faith is not the holding of correct doctrine, but personal fellowship with the living God – *William Temple*

The knowledge of God is naturally implanted in all – *St Thomas Aquinas*

The difference between knowledge of God and love of Him! – *Blaise Pascal*

It is in silence that God is known, and through mysteries that He declares Himself – *R.H. Benson*

Innocence and knowledge make a man blessed – *St Ambrose*

No man was ever great without some degree of inspiration – *Cicero*

The first and most important thing we know about God is that we know nothing about him except what he himself makes known – *Emil Brunner*

The saints of the past have never known God otherwise than by looking to him in his Son, as in a mirror – *John Calvin*

God is continually drawing us to himself in everything we experience – *Gerard Hughes*

In order to come to union with the wisdom of God, the soul has to proceed rather by unknowing than by knowing – *St John of the Cross*

Once you become aware that the main business that you are here for is to know God, most of life's problems fall into place of their own accord – *J.I. Packer*

It is not only impossible but useless to know God without Christ – *Blaise Pascal*

We both exist and know that we exist, and rejoice in this existence and this knowledge – *St Augustine*

Never mistake knowledge for wisdom. One helps you make a living and the other helps you to make a life – *Sandra Carey*

6 FEAR – (SACRED AWE, REVERENCE, HOLINESS, WONDER)

The gift of the spirit of fear does not mean fright. Here fear means sacred awe, reverence, holiness and wonder. I remember visiting someone in Hong Kong. We planned to go for a walk, but were late in setting out and it was beginning to get dark. He took me for a walk by a reservoir. We were on the approach road, and I remember the road being lined by trees. Bats flittered here and there. It was a bit eerie. We got to a certain point and then he stopped and said: "Well, this is where it happened." He went on to describe a spiritual experience in which he felt the presence of the "numinous" or what Rudolf Otto (an expert on Holiness) would describe as – *mysterium tremendum*. He felt sacred awe, reverence, holiness and wonder.

Come no closer! Remove the sandals from your feet, for the place on which you are standing is holy ground – *Exodus 3.5*

I fear God, yet I am not afraid of him – *Thomas Browne*

Fear the Lord and you will do everything well – *Shepherd of Hermas*

All holiness is God's holiness in us – *Anthony Bloom*

Reverence – showing respect or regarding something or someone with awe – *The Oxford Concise Dictionary*

For I am the Lord your God; sanctify yourselves therefore, and be holy, for I am holy – *Leviticus 11.44*

Holiness means living within the divine perspective – *Hugh Montefiore*

I felt deep within me that the highest point a person can attain is… Sacred Awe – *Nikos Kazantzakis*

Reverence God in *thyself;* for God is *more* in the *mind* of man, than in any part of this world besides; for we (and we *only* here) are made after the image of God – *Benjamin Whichcote*

All real joy and power of progress in humanity depend on finding something to reverence – *John Ruskin*

You shall be holy, for I the Lord your God am holy – *Leviticus 19.2*

When one meets the real thing (holiness) …it is irresistible – *C.S. Lewis*

A holy life will produce the deepest impression – *D.L. Moody*

The holiness of the saints is the restored image of God in them – *Benedicta Ward*

And when the wonder has gone out of a man he is dead – *D.H. Lawrence*

I sought the Lord, and he answered me, and delivered me from all my fears.
Look to him, and be radiant – *Psalm 34.4-5*

Wonder and love are caught, not taught; and to catch them we must be in an atmosphere where we are sure to find the germs – *Evelyn Underhill*

There is nothing that is so wonderfully created as the human soul.

There is something of God in it – *Henry Ward Beecher*

Wonder is the basis of worship – *Thomas Carlyle*

Wonder is the highest thing in man – *Johann Wolfgang von Goethe*

The first and fundamental wonder is existence itself – *W. MacNeile Dixon*

Remember the wonderful works he has done – *Psalm 105.5*

Respect for the personality of others, a strong sense of the dignity and intrinsic worth of each person – *Ordway Tead*

Without worship you shrink; it's as brutal as that – *Peter Shaffer*

The idea of God that man has in his being is the wonder of all wonders – *Rabindranath Tagore*

There is the appeal of Jesus to the imagination, to the sense of wonder – *Michael Ramsey*

That sense of wonder which is a large part of what we call worship – *Michael Ramsey*

For it was you who formed my inward parts; you knit me together in my mother's womb. I praise you, for I am fearfully and wonderfully made. Wonderful are your works; that I know very well – *Psalm 139.13-14*

Reverence for life – *Albert Schweitzer*

Christian belief in the sanctity of human life is derived from the doctrine of God as Creator. Humankind was made in God's image – *Thomas Wood*

Wonder is at the base of all true living – *G.A. Studdert Kennedy*

The most precious element in life is wonder – *D.H. Lawrence*

Be reverent towards each day. Love it, respect it, do not sully it, do not hinder it from coming to flower – *Romain Rolland*

Those who listen to me will be secure and will live at ease, without dread of disaster – *Proverbs 1.33*

Holiness – of high moral excellence – *The Concise Oxford Dictionary*

Life is sacred, that is to say, it is the supreme value to which all other values are subordinate – *Albert Einstein*

He had about him an air of awe and reverence – an aura of holiness – *Said of Anthony Bloom*

Holiness... in men, is their dei-formity; likeness to God in goodness, righteousness, and truth – *Benjamin Whichcote*

Jesus wants us to be holy as his Father is – *Mother Teresa*

The fear of the Lord is life indeed; filled with it one rests secure – *Proverbs 19.23*

He called them that they might be holy and holiness is the beauty produced by His workmanship in them – *Thomas Watson*

The serene, silent beauty of a holy life is the most powerful influence in the world next to the power of God – *Blaise Pascal*

There is no true Holiness, without Humility – *Thomas Fuller*

The way of holiness was by the gift of the Holy Spirit, and the common use of the word 'saint' waited on the outpourings of the Spirit – *W.E. Sangster*

Be silent, all people, before the Lord; for he has roused himself from his holy dwelling – *Zechariah 2.13*

We must have a real living determination to reach holiness – *Mother*

Teresa

The Christian must be consumed by the conviction of the infinite beauty of holiness – *Thomas Carlyle*

A true love of God must begin with a delight in his holiness – *Jonathan Edwards*

The secret of education is respecting the pupil – *Ralph Waldo Emerson*

But for you who revere my name the sun of righteousness shall rise, with healing in its wings – *Malachi 4.2*

Always and in every way let there be reverence – *Confucius*

Holiness is… a question of the Holy Spirit's producing His fruits in the life, reproducing those graces which were seen in perfection in the life of Christ – *F.F. Bruce*

In deeper reverence, praise – *John Greenleaf Whittier*

Holiness is…the unique experience of Presence – *John Main OSB*

All spoke well of him and were amazed at the gracious words that came from his mouth – *Luke 4.22*

To fear God is never to pass over any good thing that ought to be done – *St Gregory 1, Pope, the Great*

The fear of God kills all other fears – *Hugh Black*

Real holiness has a fragrance about it which is its own advertisement – *Father Andrew SDC*

He that leaves off prayer leaves off the fear of God – *Thomas Watson*

Peace I leave with you; my peace I give to you. I do not give to you as the world gives. Do not let your hearts be troubled, and do not let them be afraid – *John 14.27*

The older I get the more I find of wonder everywhere – *Stephen MacKenna*

The greatest insights happen to us in moments of awe – *Abraham Heschel*

He who can no longer pause to wonder and stand rapt in awe, is as good as dead; his eyes are closed – *Albert Einstein*

Making holiness perfect in the fear of God – *2 Corinthians 7.1*

The first mark of a Christian is a deep reverence for persons as destined for eternity with God – *Michael Ramsey*

Holiness is a process, a continual movement towards God – *Philip Sheldrake*

The essence of true holiness consists in conformity to the nature and will of God – *Samuel Lucas*

God made us and we wonder at it – *Spanish proverb*

The beauty of holiness has done more, and will do more, to regenerate the world and bring in everlasting righteousness than all the other agencies put together – *Thomas Chalmers*

If you want to be respected by others the great thing is to respect yourself – *Fyodor Dostoyevsky*

And to be renewed in the spirit of your minds, and to clothe yourselves with the new self, created according to the likeness of God in true righteousness and holiness – *Ephesians 4.23-24*

The more we learn about the wonders of the universe, the more clearly we are going to perceive the hand of God – *Frank Borman*

Wonder is involuntary praise – *Edward Young*

Our progress in holiness depends on God and ourselves – on God's grace and on our will to be holy – *Mother Teresa*

Wonder is essentially an "opening attitude" – an awareness that there is more to life than one has yet fathomed, an experience of new vistas in life to be explored as well as new profundities to be plumbed – *Rollo May*

To obtain the gift of Christian holiness is the work of a lifetime – *John Henry Newman*

The wonder of Creation suggests another gateway to worship: the door of Beauty – *Olive Wyon*

Be subject to one another out of reverence for Christ – *Ephesians 5.21*

There is nothing holier, in this life of ours, than the first consciousness of love, – the first fluttering of its silken wings – *Henry Wadsworth Longfellow*

That the Inward man by the Light of Grace, through possession and practice of a holy life, is to be acknowledged and live in us – *Rufus M. Jones*

Let the remembrance of all the glory wherein I was created make me more serious and humble, more deep and penitent, more pure and holy before Thee –
Thomas Traherne

No one can resist the argument of holiness, brought in a personified form before him, in its gentleness, in its sweetness, in its aspiration, in its love, in all its blossoms and fruits of peace and joy – *Henry Ward Beecher*

Holiness is the goal of every true Christian. 'Holy' means 'set apart for God'. A holy person is not gloomy and unnatural, but 'whole' and therefore happy. That is why holiness, whenever we see it in others, is always attractive – *Hugh Montefiore*

He disciplines us for our good, in order that we may share his holiness – *Hebrews 12.10*

All human love is a holy thing, the holiest thing in our experience – *W.R. Inge*

In religious matters it is holiness which gives authority; it is love, or the power of devotion and sacrifice, which goes to the heart, which moves and persuades – *Henri Frédéric Amiel*

Truth sees God: wisdom gazes on God. And these two produce a third, a holy, wondering delight in God, which is love – *Lady Julian of Norwich*

Therefore, since we are receiving a kingdom that cannot be shaken, let us give thanks, by which we offer to God an acceptable worship, with reverence and awe – *Hebrews 12.28*

Reverence thyself – *W.H. Brown*

When we look at the Ten Commandments, which are the essence and the foundation of all law, we can see that their whole meaning can be summed up in one word – *respect*, or even better *reverence* – *William Barclay*

Reverence for God and for the name of God, reverence for God's day, respect for parents, respect for life, respect for property, respect for personality, respect for the truth and for another person's good nature, respect for oneself –
William Barclay

O worship the Lord in the beauty of holiness – *J.S.B. Monsell*

If we earnestly desire holiness, self-denial must enter our lives fully after prayer – *Mother Teresa*

He that sees the beauty of holiness, or true moral good, sees the greatest and most important thing in the world – *Jonathan Edwards*

Practical holiness and entire self-consecration to God are not sufficiently attended to by modern Christians in this country – *J.C. Ryle*

Holiness is not an original extra to the process of creation but rather the whole point of it – *Donald Nicholl*

Study universal holiness of life. Your whole usefulness depends on this – *Robert Murray M'Cheyne*

Progress in holiness can best be measured… by the quality of our personal relationships – *Stephen F. Winward*

The stiff and wooden quality about our religious lives is a result of our lack of holy desires – *A.W. Tozer*

The more we appropriate God into our lives the more progress we make on the road of Christian godliness and holiness – *Madame Guyon*

Nothing can make a man truly great but being truly good and partaking of God's holiness – *Matthew Henry*

We are dealing with something for which there is only one appropriate expression, *mysterium tremendum* – *Rudolph Otto*

Each individual is infinitely precious to God and made for an eternal destiny – *Thomas Wood*

The Christian attitude to human life can only be one of reverence – *Thomas Wood*

Reverence – to be extended to every individual from the moment of conception to extreme old age and death – *Thomas Wood*

The remarkable thing about fearing God is that when you fear God, you fear nothing else, whereas if you do not fear God, you fear everything else –
Oswald Chambers

In reverence for life my knowledge passes into existence…My life carries its own meaning in itself. This meaning lies in my living out the highest idea which shows itself in my will-to-live, the idea of reverence for life. With that as a starting-point I give value to my own life and to all the will-to-live which surrounds me. I persevere in activity, and I produce values – *Albert Schweitzer*

Wonder (which is the seed of knowledge) – *Francis Bacon*

To be surprised, to wonder, is to begin to understand – *José Ortega Y Gasset*

Worship is transcendent wonder; wonder for which there is no limit or measure – *Thomas Carlyle*

The world will never starve for wonders, but only for want of wonder – *G K. Chesterton*

Men love to wonder and that is the seed of our science – *Ralph Waldo Emerson*

Philosophy begins in wonder. And, at the end, when philosophic thought has done its best, the wonder remains – *Alfred North Whitehead*

And bid them rise, awake, and walk the way, the steep white way of wonder, up to God – *G.A. Studdert Kennedy*

The wonder and curiosity which welcomes what is new, regards it not as threatening but enriching life – that wonder and curiosity is God – *H.A. Williams CR*

It is wonder that prompts the mind to examine its environment –

William Temple

All things begin in wonder, and in some wonder end – *St Augustine*

The sense of wonder. That is our sixth sense. And it is the *natural* religious sense – *D.H. Lawrence*

Christ is the most perfect image of God, into which we are so renewed as to bear the image of God, a knowledge, purity, righteousness, and true holiness – *John Calvin*

There is no greater holiness than in procuring and rejoicing in another's good – *George Herbert*

Things that are holy are revealed only by men who are holy – *Hippocrates*

Holiness involves friendship with God. There has to be a moment in our relationship with God when he ceases to be just a Sunday acquaintance and becomes a weekday friend – *Basil Hume OSB*

The perfume of holiness travels against the wind – *Indian proverb*

A man who has lost his sense of wonder is a man dead – *William of St Thierry*

We have lost the art of worship – *A.W. Tozer*

To fear God is to stand in awe of him – *Carroll E. Simcox*

To put it briefly, the holy things of God cannot truly be laid hold of except by holy persons; and holiness is the result of both divine grace and self-discipline. Both are requisite for the successful theologian – *Francis Hall*

Self-respect is the noblest garment with which a man may clothe himself, the most elevating feeling with which the mind can be inspired – *Samuel Smiles*

Reverence is the attitude which can be designated as the mother of all moral life, for in it man first takes a position towards the world which opens his spiritual eyes and enables him to grasp values – *Dietrich von Hildebrand*

A price must be paid for extreme specialization, even in holiness – *W.R. Inge*

True holiness consists in doing God's will with a smile – *Mother Teresa*

Wonder is especially proper to childhood and it is the sense of wonder above all that keeps us young – *Gerald Vann*

We must fear God through love, not love Him through fear – *Jean Pierre Camus*

Self-reverence, self-knowledge, self-control, these three alone lead life to sovereign power – *Alfred, Lord Tennyson*

Welfare is for a purpose. Christian love is for a person – *Mother Teresa*

Does not the power to contemplate involve first the power to be awed? – *Carlo Carretto*

It was through the feeling of wonder that men now and at first began to philosophize – *Aristotle*

When we experience the spiritual or divine element in our being it is not long before we become conscious of a sense of awe and wonder. The one universal element in consciousness which is fundamental to life is the element of wonder – *D.H. Lawrence*

The more man becomes irradiated with the divinity of Christ, the more, not the less, truly he is man – *Phillips Brooks*

Life in the Spirit is holiness – *Michael Ramsey*

The wondering imagination – *Michael Ramsey*

Jesus evokes the sense of wonder – *Michael Ramsey*

The most beautiful experience we can have is the mysterious – *Albert Einstein*

Everything that lives is holy – *William Blake*

> To yield reverence to another, to hold ourselves and our lives at his disposal, is not slavery; often it is the noblest state in which a man can live in this world – *John Ruskin*

7 POWER

I remember reading an account about a miner who had been converted to Christianity. He was being teased by his fellow-miners. One of them mocked him with the following repost: "I suppose you really believe he turned water into wine?" To this he gave the following answer: "I don't know about that, but I do know that in my own life he has turned beer into furniture, and that is good enough for me."

I am unable to come out with anything so dramatic like that, but I do know that in my own life I have been conscious of a power at work, which has turned my life upside down, inside out and back to front, and I am grateful for it having been so.

With God are wisdom and strength – *Job 12.13*

We are to open ourselves to power, energy, vigour, dynamism, vitality and strength

They are really always rich because they have such wealth and vital power within them – *Thomas Wolfe*

Power – a positive healing force – *Olive Wyon*

Supreme and tremendous energy and positiveness enter into the spiritual delineation of Christian character – *Henry Ward Beecher*

The voice of the Lord is powerful – *Psalm 29.4*

The force of character is cumulative – *Ralph Waldo Emerson*

His power (that of Kahlil Gibran) came from some great reservoir of spiritual life – *Claude Bragdon*

Christianity is a soul of immense power which bestows significance, beauty, and a new lightness on what we are already doing – *Pierre Teilhard de Chardin*

It was at the baptism that the Spirit came upon Jesus with power – *William Barclay*

He gives power and strength to his people – *Psalm 68.35*

The Spirit was *power*; power like a mighty rushing wind – *William Barclay*

The ultimate authority of his own spiritual experience – *Father Andrew SDC*

The power of a great personality – *Stuart Jackman*

Happy are those whose strength is in you…They go from strength to strength – *Psalm 84.5-7*

The power and the life of the Spirit were beyond mere human achievement and attainment – *William Barclay*

Energy of will may be defined to be the very central power of character in a man – *Samuel Smiles*

The vehemence and fire of the Holy Spirit – *Thomas Traherne*

Life engenders life. Energy creates energy. It is by spending oneself that one becomes rich – *Sarah Bernhardt*

Energy is Eternal Delight – *William Blake*

But as for me, I am filled with power, with the spirit of the Lord –

Micah 3.8

The knack of drawing strength from Him into our lives – *Evelyn Underhill*

All the resources of the Godhead are at our disposal – *Jonathan Goforth*

The power of man has grown in every sphere, except over himself – *Winston Churchill*

Meet the world with the fullness of your being and you shall meet God. If you wish to believe, love – *Martin Buber*

Not by might, nor by power, but by my spirit, says the Lord of hosts – *Zechariah 4.6*

The strongest man in the world is the man who stands alone – *Henrik Ibsen*

The Holy Spirit is the secret of the power in my life – *Kathryn Kublman*

The power of thought, the vast regions which it can master – *Bertrand Russell*

The night is given to us to take breath, to pray, to drink deep at the fountain of power – *Florence Nightingale*

That willingness that God shall possess, indwell, fertilize, bring forth fruit of *His* Spirit to us instead of fruits of our spirit – is the secret of all Christian power – *Evelyn Underhill*

He will baptize you with the Holy Spirit and fire – *Matthew 3.11*

Empower Yourself – Prayerfully

A cultivation of the powers of one's own personality is one of the greatest needs of life – *Randolph Bourne*

Love is dynamic and strong; the secret of moral force – *Ronald Higgins*

Happiness is the full use of your powers along lines of excellence – *John F. Kennedy*

And Jesus came and said to them, 'All authority in heaven and on earth has been given to me – *Matthew 28.18*

Concentration is the secret of strength in politics, in war, in trade, in short, in all management of human affairs – *Ralph Waldo Emerson*

Meditation – to experience the presence of Jesus within us, to experience the power of his Spirit within us – *John Main OSB*

This is the true power of God, the power of an infinite understanding – *Stuart Jackman*

I know that when with intense faith you mentally hold a person or cause or crisis in the infinite presence; a current of the power of God, starting from your own soul, acts like a dynamic force for the object for which you pray

Then Jesus, filled with the power of the Spirit, returned to Galilee – *Luke 4.14*

I desire a greatness of soul, an irradiance of mind, a deeper insight, a broader hope. Give me power of soul, so that I may actually effect by its will that which I strive for – *Richard Jefferies*

In drawing upon this power above ourselves, we take this higher power *into* ourselves; we raise ourselves above ourselves – *W.R. Inge*

Patience and Gentleness is Power – *Leigh Hunt*

Power in complete subordination to love – that is something like a definition of the Kingdom of God – *William Temple*

But you will receive power when the Holy Spirit has come upon you – *Acts 1.8*

New thought… requires a certain intellectual detachment, a certain solitary energy, a power of inwardly dominating the world and the outlook that the world engenders – *Bertrand Russell*

Contemplation strengthens – *St Bernard of Clairvaux*

Prayer is the secret of power – *Evan Roberts*

How God anointed Jesus of Nazareth with the Holy Spirit and with power – *Acts 10.38*

Right and Truth are greater than any *Power*, and all Power is limited by Right – *Benjamin Whichcote*

Christ comes with a spirit of life and power – *John Owen*

It is the divine spark in the soul of man which unites him with divine power – *Pauline Rose*

We are the wire. God is the current. Our only power is to let the current pass through us – *Carlo Caretto*

I have raised you up for the very purpose of showing my power in you – *Romans 9.17*

Real power in prayer flows only when man's spirit touches God's Spirit – *Catherine Marshall*

Knowledge is power – *Stuart Jackman*

Strength is born in the deep silence of long-suffering hearts, not amid joy – *Felicia Hemans*

The presence of a superior reasoning power revealed in the incomprehensible universe, forms my idea of God – *Albert Einstein*

If we are too busy to pray, we are too busy to have power – *R.A. Torrey*

But we have this treasure in clay jars, so that it may be made clear that this extraordinary power belongs to God and does not come from us – *2 Corinthians 4.7*

The power of God is the worship He inspires – *Alfred North Whitehead*

Man is a born child, his power is the power of growth – *Rabindranath Tagore*

The Spirit was *life*, the very centre and soul and essence of life, the very dynamic of the existence of man; the Spirit was *God*. The coming of the Spirit into a man's life was the coming of God – *William Barclay*

Place yourself in the middle of the stream of power and wisdom which flows into you as life, place yourself in the full centre of that flood, then you are without effort impelled to truth, to light, and a perfect contentment –
Ralph Waldo Emerson

The power which is sure and strong and is therefore able to be gentle and tolerant – *Stuart Jackman*

And what is the immeasurable greatness of his power for us who believe, according to the working of his great power – *Ephesians 1.19*

That inward power that resides in our will, imagination, and desires – *William Law*

The prayer of faith, has a kindling and creating power, and forms and transforms the soul into everything that its desires reach after – *William Law*

I felt myself invaded by a power – *W.H. Auden*

There are two powers in the world – the sword and the spirit, but the spirit has always vanquished the sword – *Napoleon Bonaparte*

Now to him who by the power at work within us is able to accomplish abundantly far more than all we can ask or imagine – *Ephesians 3.20*

The best antidote for a powerless Church is the influence of a praying man –
David Smithers

An inward presence and power – *Charles Gore*

The important thing is the intensity of your presence there – *Neville Cryer*

The power of grace always remains God's power, but it becomes operative in man and thus fulfils, sustains and renews human nature – *Daniel D. Williams*

There is one thing stronger than all the armies of the world; an idea whose time has come – *Victor Hugo*

He will transform the body of our humiliation so that it may be conformed to the body of his glory, by the power that also enables him to make all things subject to himself – *Philippians 3.21*

In order to obtain and hold power a man must love it. Thus the effort to get it is not likely to be coupled with goodness, but with the opposite qualities of pride, craft and cruelty – *Leo Tolstoy*

No one can do the work of God until he has the Holy Spirit, and is endued with power. It is impossible to preach the Gospel save in the power of the Spirit – *G. Campbell Morgan*

The problem of life is not to make life easier, but to make men stronger – *David Storr Jordan*

To the Church, Pentecost brought light, power, joy. There came to each illumination of mind, assurance of heart, intensity of love, fullness of power, exuberance of joy. No one needed to ask if they had received the Holy Spirit. Fire is self-evident. So is power – *Samuel Chadwick*

May you be made strong with all the strength that comes from his glorious power – *Colossians 1.11*

Let us lie low in the Lord's power, and learn that truth alone makes rich and great – *Ralph Waldo Emerson*

Prayer enlarges the heart until it is capable of containing God's gift of himself – *Mother Teresa*

God develops spiritual power in our lives through pressure of hard places

Personality is that being which has power over itself – *Paul Tillich*

A unification, co-ordination, and centralizing of the inner faculties, so that there is an increment of power revealed in the entire personality – *Rufus M. Jones*

Strength to battle with difficulties and overcome them – *Johann Wolfgang von Goethe*

Power is never good unless he be good who has it. A good name is better than wealth. No sword can slay it. No rope can bind it – *King Alfred*

A characteristic of this life (in the Spirit) is Power – *R.B. Rackham*

God's great power is in the gentle breeze, not in the storm – *Rabindranath Tagore*

There is a power which lapses into the human soul – *Mary Ward*

Beecher

Sometimes great difficulties are permitted only in order to strengthen character – *R.H. Benson*

He (Christ) stimulates us, as other men stimulate us, but we find a power coming from Him into our lives that enable us to respond... It does not happen with others – *William Temple*

Give me the strength lightly to bear my joys and sorrows – *Rabindranath Tagore*

Give me the strength to make my love fruitful in service – *Rabindranath Tagore*

Give me the strength never to disown the poor or bend my knees before the insolent might – *Rabindranath Tagore*

Give me the strength to raise my mind high above daily trifles – *Rabindranath Tagore*

And give me the strength to surrender my strength to thy will with love – *Rabindranath Tagore*

Receive his strength and power from whence life comes – *George Fox*

The capacity for religious or mystical awareness is largely a question of natural endowment – *J.A.T. Robinson*

This is the true power of God, the power of an infinite understanding, and it can only exist in a context of eternity – *Stuart Jackman*

By the exercise of a faith in the crucified, risen and glorious God-Man, as the life-giving Spirit, real power from a higher world streams into the soul – *Rufus M. Jones*

Something 'pneumatic'...comes into the person...with living, renewing, organizing power – *Rufus M. Jones*

The greatness of a man's power is the measure of his surrender – *William Booth*

Grace is power – *John Piper*

If you want to test a man's character, give him power – *Abraham Lincoln*

To be powerful you must be strong, and to have dominion you must have a genius for organization – *John Henry Newman*

True contentment is a real, even an active, virtue – not only affirmative but creative. It is the power of getting out of any situation all there is in it – *G.K. Chesterton*

There is no such thing as great talent without great will-power – *Honoré de Balzac*

The power of love – *Oliver Quick*

The power of love can only be truly apprehended from within, or rather by those in whom it already dwells – *Oliver Quick*

It is those who believe, says St Paul, that the Cross is the power of God – *Oliver Quick*

Not only the power to achieve, but the will to labour energetically and perseveringly – *Samuel Smiles*

Christians are not called to turn their backs on power but to use it responsibly – *Hugh Montefiore*

8 THE SPIRIT OF THE LORD

When I completed my two years of National Service, most of it being spent in the Far East, I went up to Balliol College, Oxford, to read for an Honours Degree in Jurisprudence (Law). As far as religion was concerned I was well and truly sitting on the fence. I was persuaded to go and hear a certain bishop preach. Sitting somewhat rebelliously in the pew I was completely overwhelmed by his appearance. He was human! He was fully alive! He was energetic! And what's more he was radiant! I had never seen a priest like this before. In the space of a few minutes I was gently hauled off the fence, and there and then made a lasting commitment.

I was never argued into Christian belief. Experiencing a genuine and sincere believer was enough for me.

Then the Lord God formed man from the dust of the ground, and breathed into his nostrils the breath of life; and the man became a living being – *Genesis 2.7*

Spirituality really means "Holy Spirit at work" – *Leon Joseph Suenens*

His ministry was fresh and vital, and made his hearers *feel* the presence and power of the Holy Spirit – *Rufus M. Jones*

He wanted everyone to share the treasure that he had brought – *George Appleton*

The spirit, alive and gifted, focusing with practical intent on the most immediate concerns, is the finest thing on earth – *Johann Wolfgang von Goethe*

I have filled him with divine spirit, with ability, intelligence, and knowledge in every kind of craft – *Exodus 31.3*

For Paul the Spirit was an experienced reality – *H. Gunkel*

The Spirit of God works deeply within us – *Martin Israel*

God is especially present in the hearts of His people, by His Holy Spirit; and indeed the hearts of holy men are temples in the truth of things – *Jeremy Taylor*

The spirit of the Lord shall rest on him, the spirit of wisdom and understanding, the spirit of counsel and might, the spirit of knowledge and the fear of the Lord – *Isaiah 11.2*

Live in a continual dependence on the Spirit of God – *Francois Fénelon*

The simple fact is that the world is too busy to give the Holy Spirit a chance to enter in – *William Barclay*

Human love is a reflection of something in the divine nature itself – *A.E. Brooke*

Transform your whole being into the magic of the Godhead through contemplation – *Clare of Assisi*

I will put my spirit within you, and you shall live – *Ezekiel 37.14*

Prayer obtains fresh and continual outpourings of the Spirit – *J.C. Ryle*

This Spirit was the Spirit of God, but also and therefore the Spirit of Jesus – *Charles Gore*

God works immediately by his Spirit in and on the wills of his saints – *John Owen*

There is no better evangelist in the world than the Holy Spirit – *D.L. Moody*

The Spirit breathes upon the word, and brings the truth to sight – *William Cowper*

I will pour out my spirit on all flesh – *Joel 2.28*

The great heresy of the Church of the present day is unbelief in this Spirit – *George MacDonald*

Meditation is the attempt to provide the soul with a proper environment in which to grow and become – *Morton T. Kelsey*

Spirituality is intellectual and moral energy raised to the highest degree – *Lilian Whiting*

We share in the divine nature through the sharing of the Spirit – *Athanasius of Alexandria*

Every time we say, "I believe in the Holy Spirit," we mean that we believe that there is a living God able and willing to enter human personality and change it – *J.B. Phillips*

And when Jesus had been baptized, just as he came up from the water, suddenly the heavens were opened to him and he saw the Spirit of God descending like a dove and alighting on him – *Matthew 3.16*

Spiritual experience is the supreme reality in man's life: in it the divine is not proven, it is simply shown – *Nicolas Berdyaev*

The Spirit was *life*, the very centre and soul and essence of life, the very dynamic of the existence of man – *William Barclay*

The direct relation of the human spirit with the divine Spirit – *Rufus M. Jones*

Spiritual Life comes from God's breath within us and from the formation of Christ within the soul - *Rufus M. Jones*

Let anyone who is thirsty, come to me, and let the one who believes in me drink.
As the scripture has said, "Out of the believer's heart shall flow rivers of living water" – *John 7.37-38*

Spirituality of life is an achievement as well as a gift –*Lilian Whiting*

Spirituality is an absolute persistence in well-doing – *Lilian Whiting*

Spirituality of life is, indeed, life raised to its highest power – *Lilian Whiting*

I believe in the surprises of the Holy Spirit – *Leon Joseph Suenens*

When he had said this, he breathed on them, and said to them, 'Receive the Holy Spirit' – *John 20.22*

To pray is to open oneself to the possibility of sainthood, to the possibility of becoming set on fire by the Spirit – *Kenneth Leech*

Prayer is the breathing in of the Holy Spirit – *Sadhu Sundar Singh*

If we are too busy to pray, we are too busy – *Anon*

God's love has been poured into our hearts through the Holy Spirit that has been given to us – *Romans 5.5*

Holiness is a question of the Holy Spirit producing those graces which were seen in perfection in the life of Christ – *F.F. Bruce*

The life of the Spirit is seen to be our life lived in accord with the Spirit of God which is our true end and happiness – *Herbert*

Waddams

Share His life and partake of the conquering power of His Spirit – *Rufus M. Jones*

Living in the power and grace and serenity (serenity amidst toil and sacrifice) of the Holy Spirit of God – *Norman Goodall*

The saint is essentially someone who communicates and radiates the character of God, his love, his joy, his peace – *Kenneth Leech*

For all who are led by the Spirit of God are children of God. For you did not receive a spirit of slavery to fall back into fear, but you have received a spirit of adoption. When we cry 'Abba! Father!' it is that very Spirit bearing witness with our spirit that we are children of God, and if children, then heirs, heirs of God and joint heirs with Christ – *Romans 8.14-17*

His mission (that of the Holy Spirit) is to bring Christ, to ensure His presence – *Frank Hallock*

We are not producing saints – *A.W. Tozer*

Those who have the gale of the Holy Spirit go forward even in sleep – *Brother Lawrence*

High contemplation is the best life on earth – *Margery Kempe*

Do not lag in zeal, be ardent in spirit, serve the Lord – *Romans 12.11*

He was an ideal pastor and true shepherd of his flock – loving them and being beloved by them. His ministry was fresh and vital, and made his hearers *feel* the presence and power of the Spirit of God – *Rufus M. Jones*

The Spirit…is not something other than God, but God in that manner of the divine Being in which he comes closest, dwells with us, acts upon us – *John Macquarrie*

Shed abroad thy Spirit in our hearts, for in that doth all the fulfilling of all thy promises consist – *Thomas Traherne*

Now we have received not the spirit of the world, but the Spirit that is from God, so that we may understand the gifts bestowed on us by God – *1 Corinthians 2.12*

The whole future of the human race depends on bringing the individual soul more completely and perfectly under the sway of the Holy Spirit – *Isaac Hecker*

Christ, together with the Father's and his own Spirit, comes to dwell in each of us, though we are many, still the Spirit is one and undivided – *St Cyril of Alexandria*

The life of the spiritual adventure – *John S. Dunne*

Holy Spirit, think through me till your ideas are my ideas – *Amy Carmichael*

Spiritual growth consists most in the growth of the root, which is out of sight – *Matthew Henry*

Happy the man whose words come from the Holy Spirit and not from himself – *St Anthony of Padua*

In proportion as we have the Spirit of Jesus we have the true knowledge of Jesus – *Albert Schweitzer*

The Spirit of God is given to the true saints to dwell in them, as his lasting abode; and to influence their hearts as a principle of new nature or as a divine supernatural spring of life and action – *Jonathan Edwards*

A general rule for the good use of time is to accustom oneself to live in a continual dependence on the Spirit of God – *Francois Fénelon*

The Eucharist is the means whereby those who once received the

Spirit in baptism are constantly renewed in the Spirit until their life's end – *Alan Richardson*

Do you not know that you are God's temple and that God's Spirit dwells in you? – *1 Corinthians 3.16*

Every advance in spiritual life has its corresponding dangers; every step that we rise nearer God increases the depth of the gulf into which we may fall – *R.H. Benson*

Our spiritual bodies will have every faculty of our earthly tabernacles, only with heightened sensitivity and wonderful new freedom – *Catherine Marshall*

My spirit has become dry because it forgets to feed on you – *St John of the Cross*

Pursue love and strive for the spiritual gifts – *1 Corinthians 14.1*

The saint is a saint because he received the Holy Spirit – *Abraham Kuyper*

Great men are they who see that spiritual is stronger than any material force – *Ralph Waldo Emerson*

The Holy Spirit has promised to lead us step by step into the fullness of life – *Leon Joseph Suenens*

What else are the laws of God written in our hearts but the very presence of the Holy Spirit – *St Augustine*

The Holy Spirit is the living interiority of God – *Romero Guardini*

Do not quench the Spirit – *1 Thessalonians 5.19*

I am a man of hope, not for human reasons, nor for any natural optimism, but because I believe the Holy Spirit is at work in the Church and in the World, even when His name remains unheard –

Leon Joseph Suenens

Only on the wings of mysticism can the spirit soar to its full height – *Alexis Carrel*

The Church's real business is the nurturing of men and women in life's final meaning, the provision – the mediation of resources for living – *Norman Goodall*

The true goal of the spiritual life is such a oneness with God that He is in us, and we in Him, so that the inner joy and power take our outer life captive and draw us away from the world – *Rufus M. Jones*

He shall fill us with his gifts – *Thomas Traherne*

For God did not give us a spirit of cowardice, but rather a spirit of power and of love and of self-discipline – *2 Timothy 1.7*

The outpouring of His Holy Spirit is really the outpouring of His love, surrounding and penetrating your little soul with a peaceful, joyful delight in His creature – *Evelyn Underhill*

Jesus was not to them (the disciples) merely a past example, or a remote Lord, but an inward presence and power – *Charles Gore*

Contemplative prayer, so that a completely new perspective is given to all that the mind has previously accepted as final truth – *Martin Israel*

The Divine Spirit works along the line of a man's own thinking power, along the channel of a man's own motive power, and wakes up in the man that which was in him – *Henry Ward Beecher*

Spirituality is the basis and foundation of human life…It must underlie everything. To put it briefly, man is a spiritual being, and the proper work of his mind is to interpret the world according to his higher nature, and to conquer the material aspects of the world so as to bring them into subjection to the spirit – *Robert Bridges*

If these spiritual realities are to become real and effective to us, it must be through the direct relation of the human spirit with the divine Spirit – the inward spiritual Word of God. 'He who will see the truth must have God for eyes' – *Rufus M. Jones*

The Holy Spirit is… the manifest Energy of God in the world. He is, moreover, the indwelling Strengthener, who enables man to live righteously in God's sight; the Guide who leads us into truth; the Revealer of the truths of God; the Consoler in our distresses, the Encourager in our tribulations. Our Lord in His promise of the special coming of the Spirit stresses His personal and loving attributes – *Carroll E. Simcox*

The Holy Spirit carries on the work of the Saviour – *Jean Pierre Camus*

Divine knowledge flows to the receptive human soul in the practice of contemplative prayer – *Martin Israel*

There is no human power that can replace the power of the Spirit – *Lewi Pethrus*

The Holy Spirit… illuminated me with His gifts – *Martin Luther*

The gospel of the Holy Spirit – *Jean-Pierre de Caussade SJ*

Prayer is the acid test of devotion – *Samuel Chadwick*

To live according to the spirit is to think, speak and act according to the virtues that are in the spirit, and not according to the sense and sentiments which are in the flesh – *St Francis de Sales*

He is rich in spirit who has his riches in his spirit, or his spirit in his riches; he is poor in spirit who has no riches in his spirit, nor his spirit in his riches – *St Francis de Sales*

After their baptism in the Holy Spirit Christians walk in newness of life, the life of the new creation, the life of the age to come – *Alan Richardson*

Our vocation is to live in the Spirit, not to be more and more remarkable animals but to be the sons and companions of God in eternity – *Anthony Bloom*

When I have learned to do the Father's will, I shall have fully realized my vocation on earth – *Carlo Carretto*

This indwelling Holy Spirit teaches us how to pray deeply in the heart. He leads us beyond our idols constructed above God to live in the mystery of the circular movement of the Father, Son and Spirit into three relationships – *George A. Maloney*

In prayer it is better to have a heart without words, than words without a heart – *John Bunyan*

The living, inspiring Spirit of God within him – *William Law*

As the Spirit is the loving presence between God and the Son, he can be present to us only by his work of love – *George A. Maloney*

That soul is perfect which is guided habitually by the instinct of the Holy Spirit – *Isaac Hecker*

I pray that in them there may be a union based on the flesh and the spirit of Jesus Christ, Who is our everlasting life, a union of faith and love, to which nothing is preferred, but especially a union with Jesus and the Father – *St Ignatius of Antioch*

The deepest prayer which I could ever say is that which makes me One with that to which I pray – *Angelus Silesius*

Whatever we are, that we are by the divine goodness; and this goodness is specially attributed to the Holy Ghost – *Pope Leo XIII*

Prayer is the effort to live in the spirit of the whole – *Samuel Taylor Coleridge*

The soul, like the body, lives by what it feeds on – *Josiah Holland*

The man of prayer finds his happiness in continually creating, searching, being with Christ – *Roger Schultz*

The Greek word, which is translated spirit, means literally fiery breath, breath mingled with fire, and it represented, in antiquity, the notion which science represents today by the word energy. What we translate by 'Spirit of truth' signifies the energy of truth, truth as an active force. Pure love is this active force, the love that will not at any price, under any conditions, have anything to do with either falsehood or error – *Simon Weil*

Scripture is full of Christ. From Genesis to Revelation everything breathes of Him, not every letter of every sentence, but the spirit of every chapter – *F.W. Robertson*

They love with a love that glows. They serve with a faith that kindles. They serve with a devotion that consumes – *Samuel Chadwick*

The contemplation of God is promised to us as the goal of all our acts and the eternal consummation of all our joys – *St Augustine*

Prayer is and remains always a native and deep impulse of the soul of man – *Thomas Carlyle*

We must each of us be humbled by this fresh wind of the Spirit that has come to lift us up from the nadir our civilisation has reached – *George MacLeod*

We are hemmed round with mystery, and the greatest mysteries are contained in what we see and do every day – *Henri Frédéric Amiel*

The quiet working of the Holy Spirit – *Cornelius Stam*

For Paul the Spirit was the absolutely crucial matter for Christian life from beginning to end – *H. Gunkel*

Conduct as well as charisma needs to be a manifestation of the Spirit – *James D.G. Dunn*

The gift of the Holy Ghost closes the last gap between the life of God and ours… When we allow the love of God to move in us, we can no longer distinguish ours and his; he becomes us, he lives in us. It is the first fruits of the spirit, the beginning of our being made divine – *Austin Farrer*

The religion of the Spirit has an intrinsic survival value, which is quite different from the extreme survival value of the religion of authority – *W.R. Inge*

For where the Church is, there is the Spirit of God; and where the Spirit of God is, there the Church and every form of grace, for the Spirit is truth – *St Irenaeus*

The reception of the Spirit was the decisive and determinative element in the crucial transaction of conversion – *James D.G. Dunn*

The descent of the Holy Spirit at Pentecost was a change in the manner of His working, a change which may be described as both an extension and an intensification – *Frank Hallock*

Come, Holy Ghost, our souls inspire – *John Cosin*

From the beginning, the Spirit of God has been understood as God in the midst of men, God present and active in the world, God in his closeness to us as a dynamic reality shaping the lives and histories of men – *John Macquarrie*

Unless we are personally committed, the wind of the Spirit cannot blow through us – *George MacLeod*

A spiritual religion of the full and complete type will, I believe, have inward mystical depth; it will keep vitalized and intensified with its experiences of divine supplies, and of union and unification with an environing Spirit – *Rufus M. Jones*

The Holy Spirit raises us far beyond the limitations of our own understanding so that we may deeply drink of the knowledge of God – *Martin Israel*

(Our body) – a temple of the Holy Spirit – *Thomas Traherne*

Interior growth is only possible when we commit ourselves with and to others – *Jean Vanier*

I think the point of the Holy Spirit is this: a divine something in them, enabling their response to the divine above and beyond them – *Michael Ramsey*

When Christ is inwardly united to the soul and His Spirit dwells in us and reigns in us…we are risen in soul, spirit and mind with Him – *Rufus M. Jones*

We cannot be of any assistance to anyone else until we are led by the Holy Spirit – *Martin Israel*

The all important aim in Christian meditation is to allow God's mysterious and silent presence within us to become, not only a reality, but the reality in our lives; to let it become that reality *which* gives meaning and shape and purpose to everything we do; to everything we are – *John Main OSB*

When the dream in our heart is one that God has planted there, a strange happiness flows into us. At that moment all of the spiritual resources of the universe are released to help us. Our praying is then at one with the will of God and becomes a channel to the Creator's always joyous, triumphant purposes for us and our world – *Catherine Marshall*

Prayer is not us trying to grab hold of God. Prayer is to recognize God coming to us – *Stephen Verney*

Contemplation is to open our whole personality to God so that he can take possession of our emotions, our thinking and our will – *Stephen Verney*

Contemplation is nothing else but a secret, peaceful, and loving infusion of God, which, if admitted, will set the soul on fire, with the Spirit of love – *St John of the Cross*

He who has learned to pray has learned the greatest secret of a holy and happy life – *William Law*

Prayer is the most important thing in my life. If I should neglect prayer for a single day I should lose a great deal of the fire of faith – *Martin Luther*

Meditation is that exercise of the mind by which it recalls a known truth, as some kinds of creatures do their food, to be ruminated upon till all the valuable parts be extricated – *George Horne*

The current cultural trend toward spirituality affirms a truth echoed down through the centuries that we are somehow incomplete, somehow unfulfilled without God – *Luis Palau*

Deeds, and not fine speeches, are the proof of love – *Spanish proverb*

Before Christ has been *with* them; now through the agency of the Holy Spirit, He is to be *in* them; His Presence and action is central – *Frank Hallock*

True religion…is a reception and assimilation of the Life of God within the soul of man – *Rufus M. Jones*

Meditation is the concentration of the mind on God and his qualities – *L.T. Lalvani*

However well of Christ you talk and preach, unless He lives within He is beyond your reach – *Angelus Silesius*

We ascend to the heights of contemplation by the steps of the active life – *St Gregory 1, Pope, the Great*

Those who draw water from the wellspring of meditation know that God dwells close to their hearts – *Toyohiko Kagawa*

The Spirit of God is given to the true saints to dwell in them, as his proper and lasting abode – *Jonathan Edwards*

Thou, O Spirit, that dost prefer before all Temples th'upright heart and pure – *John Milton*

The unconverted do not like to hear much about the Holy Spirit – *Robert Murray M'Cheyne*

Man is a spiritual being, and the proper work of his mind is to interpret the world according to his higher nature – *Robert Bridges*

The inward area is the first place of loss of true Christian life, of true spirituality – *Francis A. Schaeffer*

A Christian is spiritual when he sees everything from God's viewpoint – *A.W. Tozer*

Read to refill the wells of inspiration – *Harold J. Ockenga*

Sanctify yourselves and you will sanctify society – *St Francis of Assisi*

Mankind are earthen jugs with spirits in them – *Nathaniel Hawthorne*

Prayer is the effort to live in the spirit of the whole – *Samuel Taylor Coleridge*

Teach me to pray; pray thyself in me – *Francois Fénelon*

God draws us out by breathing himself in – *P.T. Forsythe*

Prayer from the heart can achieve what nothing else can in the world – *Mohandas K. Gandhi*

9 LOVE

In 1963, I went on an official Oxford University Expedition to Nepal. During the Expedition we visited a Tibetan Refugee Camp, just outside Pokhora in Western Nepal. This camp was run almost single-handedly by a Swiss nurse from the Red Cross – Sister Matilda. She held a surgery each day in a makeshift dispensary. She ran a school for the children. She had set up workshops. Cotton was being spun, clothes made, rugs woven, Tibetan boots were manufactured, all under her careful supervision. She had also cultivated a piece of land, where several varieties of vegetables and crops were growing. She had adopted a two year old Tibetan boy, Dowa, whose parents had been killed. Whenever he saw her his face lit up and was radiant and this in turn was reciprocated. At every level of Sister Matilda's life, costly love was being metered out. Love, in her understanding, was a very practical activity

You shall love the alien as yourself – *Leviticus 19.34*

Love is the fulfilment of all our works – *St Augustine*

Love…is the supreme badge of any true Christianity – *Rufus M. Jones*

Human love is a reflection of something in the divine nature itself –
A.E. Brooke

The greatest thing that can happen to any human soul is to become utterly filled with love, and self-sacrifice is love's natural expression – *William Temple*

Whoever loves much, does much – *St Thomas à Kempis*

I love those who love me – *Proverbs 8.17*

He who is filled with love is filled with God himself – *St Augustine*

If you want to be loved, be lovable – *Ovid*

To love is to be vulnerable – *C.S. Lewis*

Only through love can we attain communion with God – *Albert Schweitzer*

True love rests in the depths of the heart – *Francois Fénelon*

Love your enemies and pray for those who persecute you, so that you may be children of your Father in heaven – *Matthew 5.44-45*

The single desire that dominated my search for delight was simply to love and be loved – *St Augustine*

Live love, let love invade you – *Carlo Carretto*

Love one another in truth and purity, as children impulsively, uncalculatingly – *Edward Wilson*

You shall love the Lord your God with all your heart, and with all your soul, and with all your mind and with all your strength…You shall love your neighbour as yourself – *Mark 12.30-31*

Guts comes next to love; anyway, love without them is a flimsy, sentimental thing

Only love enables humanity to grow, because love engenders life and it is the only form of energy that lasts forever – *Michel Quoist*

The sole secret is a hearty love of God, and the only way of attaining that love is by loving – *St Francis de Sales*

Not where I breathe, but where I love, I live – *Robert Southwell*

A soul enkindled with love in a gentle, meek, humble, and patient soul – *St John of the Cross*

I give you a new commandment, that you love one another. Just as I have loved you, you also should love one another – *John 13.34*

To be capable of giving and receiving mature love is as sound a criterion as we have for the fulfilled personality – *Rollo May*

Every work of love brings a person face to face with God – *Mother Teresa*

Our love is the best thing we have – *Richard Sibbes*

Those who love deeply never grow old; they may die of old age, but they die young – *Sir Arthur Wing Pinero*

He who loves, trusts – *Italian proverb*

They who have my commandments and keep them are those who love me; and those who love me will be loved by my Father, and I will love them and reveal myself to them – *John 14.21*

Spread love everywhere you go: First of all in your own house…let no one ever come to see you without leaving better and happier – *Mother Teresa*

Love is superior to all extraordinary gifts – *Charles Hodge*

The will to love God is the whole of religion – *Francois Fénelon*

Our only business is to love and delight ourselves in God – *Brother Lawrence*

Our work is the love of God – *John of Ruysbroeck*

Those who love me will keep my word, and my Father will love them, and we will come to them and make our home with them – *John 14.23*

We adore in order to love, to absorb into our own being the being of God – *Kenneth Leech*

When evening comes you will be examined in love – *St John of the Cross*

To love another person is to see the face of God – *Victor Hugo*

We are all born for love…It is the principle of existence, and its only end – *Benjamin Disraeli*

As the Father has loved me, so I have loved you; abide in my love – *John 15.9*

Love Yourself – Wholeheartedly

The course of true love never did run smooth – *William Shakespeare*

It is by loving and by being loved that one can come nearer to the soul of another – *George MacDonald*

The soul is shrivelled up and buried in a grave that does not love – *Thomas Traherne*

No one has greater love than this, to lay down one's life for one's friends – *John 15.13*

Love is a rich, strong, manly, vigorous expression of the whole round of Christian character – the Christ-like nature in its fullest development – *Henry Drummond*

Love is a great teacher – *St Augustine*

The love of God is a hard love. It demands total self-surrender – *Albert Camus*

Pursue love and strive for the spiritual gifts – *1 Corinthians 14.1*

Life is not a holiday but an education. And the one eternal lesson for us all is how better we can love – *St Augustine*

Love is the beauty of the soul – *St Augustine*

The love problem is part of mankind's heavy toll of suffering, and nobody should be ashamed that he must pay his tribute – *C.G. Jung*

Love, and *then* what you will, do – *St Augustine*

By love may He be gotten and holden; but by thought never – *The Cloud of Unknowing*

The fruit of the Spirit is…love – *Galatians 5.22*

The stream of love that flows constantly between Jesus and his Father. This stream of love is the Holy Spirit…we should become as open as possible to this stream of love – *John Main OSB*

Nothing is sweeter than love, nothing stronger, nothing higher, nothing broader; nothing is more lovely, nothing richer, nothing better in heaven or in earth –
St Thomas à Kempis

But God, who is rich in mercy, out of the great love with which he loved us…made us alive, together with Christ – *Ephesians 2.4-5*

Real love… is powerful enough to transform you in a moment, and offer you more joy than any material possession could – *Barbara DeAngelis*

Love to God is the slowest development to mature in the soul. No man ever learned to love God with all his heart, and his neighbour as himself, in a day – *Henry Ward Beecher*

Charity (love) means nothing else than to love God for himself above all creatures, and to love one's fellow men for God's sake as one loves oneself – *The Cloud of Unknowing*

Love means to love the unlovable, or it is no virtue at all – *G.K. Chesterton*

To love God is the greatest of virtues; to be loved by God is the greatest of all blessings – *Portuguese proverb*

And to know the love of Christ that surpasses knowledge, so that you may be filled with all the fullness of God – *Ephesians 3.19*

God thou art Love! I build my faith on that – *Robert Browning*

The great enduring realities are love and service – *Helen Keller*

Happiness is a great love and much serving – *Olive Schreiner*

It is always springtime in the heart that loves God – *John Vianney*

Love is whispered by the Holy Spirit in the heart – *Bishop Lumsden Barkway*

Beloved, let us love one another, because love is from God; everyone who loves is born of God and knows God – *1 John 4.7*

Love is the best motivation and finally the only valid one. It is dynamic and strong; the secret of moral force – *Ronald Higgins*

Love is the greatest of risks; the giving of myself – *Jean Vanier*

One loving heart sets another on fire – *St Augustine*

To love as Jesus loves; this is not only the Lord's precept, it is our vocation – *René Voillaume*

The first step in personhood is to allow ourselves to be loved. To know ourselves loved is to have the depths of our capacity to love opened up – *John Main OSB*

Every approach unto God by ardent love and delight is transfiguring – *John Owen*

Beloved, since God loved us so much, we also ought to love one another… God lives in us, and his love is perfected in us – *1 John 4.11-12*

The love of our neighbour is the only door out of the dungeon of self – *George MacDonald*

The emotionally crippled person is always the product of a love gone wrong

The true love of God which comes from this sight of His beauty causes a spiritual and holy joy in the soul; a joy in God, and exulting in Him – *Jonathan Edwards*

That man becomes a more powerful centre from which the love of God can radiate – *Grace Cooke*

We can all experience God whenever and wherever we encounter love – *John Main OSB*

Someone has called bereavement "loving in a new key"– *J. Neville Ward*

Love is a condition in which the happiness of another person is essential to your own – *Robert Heinlein*

So we have known and believe the love that God has for us. God is love, and those who abide in love abide in God and God abides in them – *1 John 4.16*

Beware you are not swallowed up in books! An ounce of love is worth a pound of knowledge – *John Wesley*

The most effective remedy for self-love and self-absorption is the habit of humble listening – *Emma Herman*

The secret of being loved is in being lovely; and the secret of being lovely is in being unselfish – *Josiah Holland*

In real love you want the other person's good. In romantic love, you want the other person – *Margaret Anderson*

The love of a man and a woman gains immeasurably in power when placed under divine restraint – *Elizabeth Elliot*

We are shaped and fashioned by what we love – *Johann Wolfgang von Goethe*

Love cures people – both the one who gives it and the one who receives it – *Karl Menninger*

If you genuinely desire union with the unspeakable love of God, then you must be prepared to have your "religious" world shattered – *Rowan Williams*

Love is the abridgment of all theology – *St Francis de Sales*

Theology is but an appendix to love, and an unreliable appendix! – *Toyohiko Kagawa*

It is not a matter of thinking a great deal, but of loving a great deal, so do whatever arouses you most to love – *St Teresa of Avila*

Agape (love) means understanding, redeeming good will for all persons – *Martin Luther King*

Temperance is love in training – *D.L. Moody*

The first duty of love is to listen – *Paul Tillich*

You can never establish a personal relationship without opening up your own heart – *Paul Tournier*

Charity is the pure gold which makes us rich in eternal wealth – *Jean Pierre Camus*

True Christianity is love in action – *David O. McKay*

When we love, it is Christ loving through us – *Leon Joseph Suenens*

We cannot help conforming ourselves to what we love – *St Francis de Sales*

The love which we bear to others remains the mark of the authenticity of our contemplation – *Roger Schultz*

Where there is no love, pour love in, and you will draw love out – *St John of the Cross*

Loving relationships are a family's best protection against the challenges of the world – *Bernie Wiebe*

Proficiency in meditation lies not in thinking much, but in loving much. It is a way of seeking the divine companionship, the 'closer walk' – *Richardson Wright*

Living in our selfishness means stopping at human limits and preventing our transformation into Divine Love – *Carlo Carretto*

The great tragedy of life is not that men perish, but that they cease to love – *W. Somerset Maugham*

The highest love of all finds its fulfilment not in what it keeps, but in what it gives – *Father Andrew SDC*

You give but little when you give of your possessions. It is when you give of yourself that you truly give – *Kahlil Gibran*

For even as love crowns you so shall he crucify you. Even as he is for your growth so is he for your pruning – *Kahlil Gibran*

There is no surprise more magical than the surprise of being loved; it is God's finger on man's shoulder – *Charles Morgan*

We should take pains to be polite to those whom we love. Politeness preserves love, is a kind of sheath to it – *Mark Rutherford*

Love it is – not conscious – that is God's regent in the human soul, because it can govern the soul as nothing else can – *Henry Ward Beecher*

When you love you should not say "God is in my heart"; but rather, "I am in the heart of God:" And think not you can direct the course of love, for love, if it find you worthy, directs your course – *Kahlil Gibran*

Love is eager, sincere and kind; it is glad and lovely; it is strong, patient and faithful; wise, long-suffering and resolute; and it never seeks its own ends, for where a man seeks his own ends, he at once falls out of love – *St Thomas à Kempis*

Love all God's creation, the whole of it and every grain of sand. Love every leaf, every ray of God's light! Love the animals, love the plants, love everything, if you love everything, you will perceive the divine mystery in things. And once you have perceived it, you will begin to comprehend it ceaselessly more and more every day – *Fyodor Dostoyevsky*

Give me such love for God and men, as will blot out all hatred and bitterness – *Dietrich Bonhoeffer*

We are put on earth a little space that we may learn to bear the beams of love – *William Blake*

'Love', wrote a survivor of the Ravensbruck concentration camp, 'is larger than the walls which shut it in' (Corrie ten Boom). This was certainly true of the growing Christian movement in the Acts of the Apostles – literally! – *Richard Bewes*

Whoever loves true life, will love true love – *Elizabeth Barrett Browning*

Love is the fulfilment of the law and should be everyone's rule of life – *Carlo Carretto*

Love is an instinctive force present in every person from birth to death – *Smiley Blanton*

Lack of love makes people depressed, anxious and without zest for life. They remain lonely and unhappy without friends or work they care for, their life a barren treadmill, stripped of all creative action and joy – *Smiley Blanton*

Love will teach us all things – *Fyodor Dostoevsky*

Let all find compassion in you – *St John of the Cross*

A blaze of divine and holy love – *Jonathan Edwards*

Love begets love – *Latin proverb*

One word frees us of all the weight and pain of life. That word is love – *Sophocles*

Long-suffering is love enduring – *D.L. Moody*

Friendship is in loving rather than in being lov'd – *Robert Bridges*

Christ cannot live his life today in this world without our mouth, without our eyes, without our going and coming, without our heart. When we love, it is Christ loving through us – *Leon Joseph Suenens*

There is no living in love without suffering – *St Thomas à Kempis*

To love is to wish the other's highest good – *R.H. Benson*

Love must be learned again and again – *Katherine Anne Porter*

God forces no one, for love cannot compel, and God's service, therefore, is a thing of perfect freedom – *Hans Denk*

Pity melts the mind to love – *John Dryden*

The end of love is no other thing than the union of the lover and the thing loved – *St Francis de Sales*

It is not only by the imitation of Christ, but by actual union with Him that love becomes and remains the driving force of the soul – *R.H. Benson*

Man is never nearer the Divine than in his compassionate moments – *Joseph Hertz*

The most satisfying thing in life is to have been able to give a large part of oneself to others – *Pierre Teilhard de Chardin*

Jesus did not come to explain away suffering or remove it. He came to fill it with His presence - *Paul Claudel*

Christianity taught men that love is worth more than intelligence – *Jacques Maritain*

Let your religion be less of a theory and more of a love affair – *G.K. Chesterton*

To love is to be willing to put the beloved in the first place and oneself in the second place – *Norman Pittenger*

In Love and divinity what is most worth saying cannot be said – *Coventry Patmore*

Example is not the main thing in influencing others – it is the only thing – *Albert Schweitzer*

To love God is something greater than to know him – *St Thomas Aquinas*

God does not love us because we are valuable. We are valuable because God loves us – *Fulton J. Sheen*

To believe in God is to love him – *Miguel de Unamuno*

The acts of contemplation are four; to seek after God, to find Him, to feel His sacred touch in the soul, and to be united with Him and to enjoy Him – *Archbishop Ullathorne*

Seek in reading and thou shalt find in meditation; knock in prayer and it shall be opened to thee in contemplation – *St John of the Cross*

Love's secret is always to be doing things for God and not to mind because they are such very little ones – *F.W. Faber*

All is well with him who is beloved of his neighbours – *George Herbert*

Love is like death – it kills the self-willed me, it breaks its stranglehold and sets the Spirit free – *Angelus Silesius*

The greatness of contemplation can be given to none but that love – *St Gregory 1, Pope, the Great*

We become contemplatives when God discovers Himself in us – *Thomas Merton*

A sermon is a proclamation of the generous love of God in Christ, or it is not a Christian sermon – *Norman Pittenger*

The soul that walks in love neither tires others or grows tired – *St John of the Cross*

Whoever preaches with love preaches effectively – *St Francis de Sales*

And he alone is great who turns the voice of the wind into a song, made sweeter by his own loving – *Kahlil Gibran*

Happy the man who is able to love all men alike – *St Maximus the Confessor*

"Come with me into the desert." There is something much greater than human action: prayer; and it has a power much stronger than the works of men: love. And I went into the desert – *Carlo Carretto*

He alone loves the Creator perfectly who manifests a pure love for his neighbour – *The Venerable Bede*

To make Love the ruling power of my life, the only power. To be kind, gentle, considerate and unselfish – *Edward Wilson*

The whole purpose of spiritual unfoldment is for the individual man so to train himself that he becomes a more powerful centre from which the love of God can radiate – *Grace Cooke*

Make love your aim – *1 Corinthians 14.1 (RSV)*

Love once kindled in the soul, is the mother of all heroic actions…the man who has lighted his life from Christ's love is constant in trials, patient in sufferings, courageous in assaults, prudent in difficulties, victorious and triumphant in action – *Rufus M. Jones*

Love is the noblest frailty of the mind – *John Dryden*

Let us think of the love of God, which we shall feel in its full tide upon the soul – *F.W. Robertson*

Love knows how to abound and overflow – *Rufus M. Jones*

All that heals, cultivates, protects, and inspires – all this is a part of love – *Smiley Blanton*

True love always involves renunciation of one's personal comfort – *Leo Tolstoy*

Duty does not have to be dull. Love can make it beautiful and fill it with life – *Thomas Merton*

Love him totally who gave himself totally for your love – *Clare of Assisi*

The great secret of morals is love – *Percy Bysshe. Shelley*

Religion is nothing else but love to God and man – *William Penn*

Joy is love exalted; peace is love in repose; long-suffering is love enduring; gentleness is love in society; goodness is love in action; faith is love on the battlefield, meekness is love in school; and temperance is love in training –
D. L. Moody

Love is the most universal, most tremendous, and the most mysterious of the cosmic forces – *Pierre Teilhard de Chardin*

Love is life. All, everything that I understand, I understand only because I love – *Leo Tolstoy*

To love someone deeply gives you strength. Being loved by someone deeply gives you courage – *Lao tzu*

Charity means love. It is called *Agape* in the New Testament to distinguish it from *Eros* (sexual love), *Storge* (family affection) and *Philia* friendship). So there are four kinds of love, all good in their proper place, but *Agape* is the best because it is the kind of love God has for us and is good in all circumstances – *C.S. Lewis*

Increase my capacity for love and decrease my impulse to throw stones, actual or mental – *George Appleton*

We are able to love others only when we love ourselves – *Brent*

Barlow

The moments when you really live are the moments when you have done things in the spirit of love – *Henry Drummond*

You learn love by loving – *St Francis de Sales*

Love is an act of faith, and whoever is of little faith is also of little love – *Erich Fromm*

Love never claims, it ever gives; love never suffers, never resents, never revenges itself. Where there is love there is life – *Mohandas K. Gandhi*

The test of love is how one relates not to saints and scholars but to rascals – *Abraham Heschel*

The most precious possession that ever comes to a man in this world is a woman's heart – *Josiah G. Holland*

Love of men necessarily arises out of love of God – *John Hooper*

The greatest happiness of life is the conviction that we are loved – loved for ourselves, or rather, loved in spite of ourselves – *Victor Hugo*

To love another person is to help them love God – *Søren Kierkegaard*

Love is the only force capable of transforming an enemy into a friend – *Martin Luther King*

When you love someone you love him as he is – *Charles Péguy*

True love's the gift which God has given to man alone beneath the heaven – *Sir Walter Scott*

Love is the greatest thing that God can give us, for Himself is love: and it is the greatest thing we can give to God – *Jeremy Taylor*

The thing I mean is love, Christian love, or compassion. If you feel this, you have a motive for existence, a reason for courage, an imperative necessity for intellectual honesty – *Bertrand Russell*

Love does not consist in gazing at each other, but in looking outward together in the same direction – *Antoine de Saint-Exupéry*

10 JOY

In 1968, having been ordained for three years, I went on a six month secondment to Ibadan, a city in the Western State of Nigeria, to look after a Church whilst the regular priest returned to England for long leave. At the time Nigeria was in the middle of a bitter civil war, with the breakaway state of "Biafra." Fortunately for me, most of the fighting was 300 miles away.

It was in Nigeria that I learnt a lot about joy, even though the country was going through a difficult time. Every so often I would come across a Nigerian and feel that this particular person had just been feasting with the gods. He, or she, was brimming and overflowing with joy.

C.S. Lewis in his book *Surprised by Joy* opened my eyes to a dynamic source of joy – namely something to be found in the depth of ourselves. Thinking about joy I came to see that "Joy" is one of the fruits of the Spirit, and a part of our inheritance, when life is lived in supernatural regard.

For the joy of the Lord is your strength – *Nehemiah 8.10*

The fullness of joy is to see God in all things – *Lady Julian of Norwich*

Joy, rather than happiness, is the goal of life – *Rollo May*

Study always to have joy – *St Francis of Assisi*

Desire joy and thank God for it. Renounce it, if need be, for other's sake. That's joy beyond joy – *Robert Browning*

To be simply ensconced in God is true joy – *C.C. Colton*

In your presence there is fullness of joy – *Psalm 16.11*

The joy of Jesus lifts up life to be celebrated – *Henri J.M. Nouwen*

Man cannot live without joy, therefore when he is deprived of true spiritual joy it is necessary that he become addicted to carnal pleasures – *St Thomas Aquinas*

Joy rises in me, like a summer's morn – *Samuel Taylor Coleridge*

Joy is prayer - Joy is strength - Joy is love… A joyful heart is the normal result of a heart burning with love – *Mother Teresa*

My heart and my flesh sing for joy to the living God – *Psalm 84.2*

Many people hardly believe any more in the possibility of a truly joy-filled life – *Henri J.M. Nouwen*

Joy is the triumph of *life*; it is the sign that we are living our true life as spiritual beings – *W.R. Inge*

Life in the dimension of Spirit is a mystery rooted in the joy of being – *John Main OSB*

To be a joy-bearer and a joy-giver – *Janet Erskine Stuart*

The mainspring of life is in the heart. Joy is the vital air of the soul – *Henri Frédéric Amiel*

This is the day that the Lord has made; let us rejoice and be glad in it – *Psalm 118.24*

Joy can be real only if people look upon their life as a service, and have a definite object in life outside themselves and their perennial happiness – *Leo Tolstoy*

The fulness of joy is in God's immediate presence – *Richard Baxter*

Joy is the holy fire that keeps our purpose warm and our intelligence aglow – *Helen Keller*

Resolve to keep happy, and your joy and you shall form an invincible host against difficulty – *Helen Keller*

Every joy, great or small, is akin and always a refreshment – *Johann Wolfgang von Goethe*

A joyful heart is life itself, and rejoicing lengthens one's life span – *Ecclesiasticus 30.22*

The joy which a man finds in his work and which transforms the tears and sweat of it into happiness and delight – that joy is God – *Harry Williams CR*

Real joy comes not from ease of riches or from the praise of men, but from doing something worthwhile – *Sir Wilfred Grenfell*

One filled with joy preaches without preaching – *Mother Teresa*

Well done, good and trustworthy slave…enter into the joy of your master – *Matthew 25.21*

Joy is the affect which comes when we use our powers – *Rollo May*

The joy that Jesus offers his disciples is his own joy, which flows from his intimate communion with the One who sent him – *Henri J.M. Nouwen*

This joy is a divine gift that does not leave us during times of illness, poverty, oppression or persecution – *Henri J.M. Nouwen*

All true joy has an eternal and Divine soul and goal – *W.R. Inge*

I have said these things to you so that my joy may be in you, and that your joy may be complete – *John 15.11*

When we rejoice in our fullness, then we can part with our fruits with joy – *Rabindranath Tagore*

Joy is the experience of knowing that you are unconditionally loved – *Henri J.M. Nouwen*

To enjoy God in his beauty and loveliness – *Michael Ramsey*

But now I am coming to you, and I speak these things in the world so that they may have my joy made complete in themselves – *John 17.13*

For in the depth is truth; and in the depth is hope; and in the depth is joy – *Paul Tillich*

The surest mark of a Christian is not faith, or even love, but joy – *Samuel Schoemaker*

We have within ourselves enough to fill the present day with joy, and overspread the future years with life – *William Wordsworth*

And the disciples were filled with joy and with the Holy Spirit – *Acts 13.52*

Value Yourself – Joyfully

I asked God for all things, that I might enjoy life. God gave me life, that I might enjoy all things – *found on the body of a Confederate soldier*

The religion of Christ is the religion of joy – *Octavius Winslow*

Rejoice in the Lord always; again I will say, Rejoice – *Philippians 4.4*

Joy is everywhere; it is in the earth's green covering of grass – *Rabindranath Tagore*

Joy is in the blue serenity of the sky – *Rabindranath Tagore*

Joy is in the reckless exuberance of Spring – *Rabindranath Tagore*

Joy is in the severe abstinence of grey winter – *Rabindranath Tagore*

Joy is in the acquisition of knowledge – *Rabindranath Tagore*

You received the word with joy inspired by the Holy Spirit – *1 Thessalonians 1.6*

The richer the creation, the deeper the joy – *W.R. Inge*

Eternal joy is the end of the ways of God – *Paul Tillich*

The message of all religions is that the kingdom of God is peace and joy. And it is the message of Christianity – *Paul Tillich*

He gives himself to them to be their joy, their treasure, their never-ending bliss – *Richard Challoner*

Although you have not seen him, you love him; and even though you do not see him now, you believe in him and rejoice with an indescribable and glorious joy – *1 Peter 1.8*

The joy of achievement is the recognition of a task understood and done – *W.R. Inge*

Till you can sing and rejoice and delight in God, as misers do in gold, and kings in sceptres, you never enjoy the world – *Thomas Traherne*

Joy is the infallible sign of the presence of God – *Leon Bloy*

Enjoy the bright and happy things of life – *Oliver Bell Bunce*

Silence is the perfect herald of joy – *William Shakespeare*

Be absolutely determined to enjoy what you do – *Gerry Sikorski*

Joy dwells with God; it descends from him and seizes spirit, soul and body – *Dietrich Bonhoeffer*

To be able to find joy in another's joy, that is the secret of happiness – *George Bernanos*

The enjoyment of God is the only happiness with which our souls can be satisfied – *Jonathan Edwards*

We are all strings in the concert of his joy – *Jacob Boehme*

The joy that Jesus gives is the result of our disposition being at one with his own disposition – *Oswald Chambers*

Joy is never in our power, and pleasure is. I doubt whether anyone who has tasted joy would ever, if both were in his power, exchange it for all the pleasure in the world – *C.S. Lewis*

One joy dispels a hundred cares – *Oriental proverb*

Joy is the heavenly o'kay of the inner life of power – *Agnes Sanford*

What brings joy to the heart is not so much the friend's gift as the friend's love – *St Ailred of Rievaulx*

If there is joy in the world, surely the man of pure heart possesses it – *St Thomas à Kempis*

How good is man's life, the mere living! How fit to employ all the heart and the soul and senses for ever in joy! – *Robert Browning*

Joy is the signal that we are spiritually alive and active – *W.R. Inge*

To try to create something worth creating, as our life's work, is the way to understanding what joy is in this life – *W.R. Inge*

Joy is the echo of God's life within us – *Joseph Marmion*

Those who bring sunshine to the lives of others cannot keep it from themselves – *J.M. Barrie*

Happiness is the practice of the virtues – *St Clement of Alexandria*

Christian Joy is the flag which is flown high from the castle of the heart when the King is in residence there – *P. Rainmy*

These little thoughts are the rustle of leaves: they have their whisper of joy in my mind – *Rabindranth Tagore*

This glory and honour wherewith man is crowned ought to affect every person that is grateful, with celestial joy; and so much the rather because it is every man's proper end and sole inheritance – *Thomas Traherne*

Joy is the sentiment that is born in a soul, conscious of the good it possesses.
The good of our intelligence is truth; the more this truth is abundant and luminous, the deeper is our inward joy – *D. Columbia Marmion*

The Christian joy and hope do not arise from an ignoring of the evil in the world, but from facing it at its worst. The light that shines for ever in the Church breaks out of the veriest pit of gloom – *William Temple*

Our faith is faith in what the synoptic gospels call 'the Kingdom of God' and the Kingdom of God is simply God's power enthroned in our hearts. This is what makes us light of heart and it is what Christian joy is all about – *John Main OSB*

If a man has sought first and chiefly the soul's treasure – goodness, kindness, gentleness, devoutness, cheerfulness, hope, faith, and love – he will extract more joy from the poorest furniture and outfitting of life than otherwise he would get from the whole world – *Henry Ward Beecher*

'The fruit of the spirit is love – joy.' So the opaque Christian is a slander on God. The thing which the church has been so much afraid of – joy, cheerfulness, hopefulness, gentleness, sweetness, overflowing manhood – this is one of the fruits of the Spirit. Love and joy are put first – *Henry Ward Beecher*

There are some people who have the quality of richness and joy in them and they communicate it to everything they touch. It is first of all a physical quality; then it is a quality of the spirit. With such people it makes no difference if they are rich or poor; they are really always rich because they have such wealth and vital power within them that they give everything interest, dignity, and a warm colour – *Thomas Wolfe*

Joy is distinctly a Christian word and a Christian thing. It is the reverse of happiness. Happiness is the result of what happens of an agreeable sort. Joy has its springs deep down inside, and that spring never runs dry, no matter what happens. Only Jesus gives that joy. He had joy, singing its music within, even under the shadow of the cross. It is an unknown word and thing except as He has sway within – *Samuel Gordon*

Joy is in the living flesh that animates our bodily frame – *Rabindranath Tagore*

Where joy has grasped a man it grows greater, carries him away, opens closed doors – *Dietrich Bonhoeffer*

Love offers you more joy than any material possession could – *Babara DeAngelis*

Christian joy is a gift of God flowing from a good conscience – *Philip Neri*

This is the true joy in life, the being used for a purpose, recognized by yourself as a mighty one, the being thoroughly worn out before you are thrown in the scrap heap; the being a force of Nature instead of a feverish selfish little clod of ailments and grievances complaining that the world will not devote itself to making you happy – *George Bernard Shaw*

An aspiration is a joy for ever, a possession as solid as a landed estate, a fortune which we can never exhaust and which gives year by year a revenue of pleasurable activity – *Robert Louis Stevenson*

The joy of the Lord, the joy that is strength, the joy that no man taketh from us, the joy wherewith we joy before God, the abundant joy of faith and hope and love and praise – this it is that gathers like a radiant, fostering, cheerful air around the soul that yields itself to the grace of God, to do His holy, loving Will – *Francis Paget*

Mark then, how joy springs out at once as the unfailing token of the Holy Spirit's presence, the first sign that He is having His own way with a man's heart – *Francis Paget*

Joy's soul lies in doing – *William Shakespeare*

Joy is for all men. It is of the soul, or the soul's character: it is the wealth of the soul's whole being when it is filled with the spirit of Jesus, which is the spirit of eternal love – *Horace Bushnell*

Thou shalt ever joy at eventide if you spend the day fruitfully – *St Thomas à Kempis*

Joy is the perfect poise of the human figure, noble and upright – *Rabindranath Tagore*

Joy is in living – *Rabindranath Tagore*

Joy is in the exercise of all our powers – *Rabindranath Tagore*

Clothe yourselves with cheerfulness, which always finds favour with God and is acceptable to him – *Shepherd of Hermas*

To see God is the promised goal of all our actions and the promised height of all our joys – *St Augustine*

This is the secret of joy. We shall no longer strive for our own way; but commit ourselves, easily and simply, to God's way, acquiesce in his will and in so doing find our peace – *Evelyn Underhill*

Joy is not in things, it is in us – *Richard Wagner*

Joy is the serious business of heaven – *C.S. Lewis*

Every revelation of truth felt with interior savour and spiritual joy is a secret whispering of God in the ear of a pure soul – *Walter Hilton*

In joy one not only feels secure, but something goes out from oneself, a warm positive effluence of love – *Richard Hooker*

Where can we find a joy so real, so deep, so pure, so lasting? There is every element of joy – deep, ecstatic, satisfying, sanctifying joy in the gospel of Christ – *Octavius Winslow*

Joy was in fact the most characteristic result of all Jesus' activity amongst the poor and oppressed – *Albert Nolan*

He enjoys true leisure who has time to improve his soul's estate – *Henry David Thoreau*

Religion might be defined as the power which makes us joyful about the things that matter – *G.K. Chesterton*

There is a joy which knows nothing of sorrow, need and anxiety of the heart – *Rollo May*

Joy is the emotion which accompanies our fulfilling our natures as human beings – *Dietrich Bonhoeffer*

Rejoice always – *1 Thessalonians 5.16*

Joy, the Greek word is *chara*, and the characteristic of this word is that it most often describes that joy which has a basis in religion, and whose real foundation is God…It is a joy whose basis is God –

William Barclay

We must learn to make God our only joy and satisfaction – *Ruth Burrows*

Joy in the Lord. It is the joy experienced by those who, come what may, are beginning to know God, to enjoy God in his beauty and loveliness, and to be exposed to his energies – *Michael Ramsey*

It is not only the joy of a sure faith that God reigns supreme; it is the joy of a practical fellowship with the one who is joy and pours joy into lives which are united with him – *Michael Ramsey*

We could never learn to be brave and patient if there were only joy in the world – *Helen Keller*

Let us dwell together so that your joy may be mine, and my joy complete – *Rex Chapman*

Christ is not only a remedy for your weariness and trouble, but he will give you an abundance of all contrary, joy and delight – *Jonathan Edwards*

There is a joy which is not given to the ungodly, but to those who love Thee for Thine own sake, whose joy Thou Thyself art – *St Augustine*

And this is the happy life, to rejoice to Thee, of Thee, for Thee; this it is, and there is no other – *St Augustine*

Man is fond of counting his troubles but he does not count his joys. If he counted them up as he ought to, he would see that every lot has enough happiness provided for it – *Fyodor Dostoyoevsky*

Know that joy is rarer, more difficult, and more beautiful than sadness. Once you make this all-important discovery, you must embrace joy as a moral obligation – *André Gide*

Eternal joy is not to be reached by living on the surface. It is rather attained by breaking through the surface, by penetrating the deep things of ourselves, of our world, and of God – *Paul Tillich*

Joy is love exalted – *D.L. Moody*

Shared joy is double joy and shared sorrow is half-sorrow – *Swedish proverb*

Joy is the life of man's life – *Benjamin Whichcote*

Where our work is, there let our joy be – *Tertullian*

If there is joy in the world, surely the man of pure heart possesses it – *St Thomas à Kempis*

Joy is the passage from a lesser to a greater perfection – *Baruch Spinoza*

11 PEACE

I did my curacy as a Minor Canon at Bradford Cathedral and worked there for four years, which included a secondment to Nigeria for six months. As part of my duties I was a part-time Hospital Chaplain at the Bradford Royal Infirmary, and used to visit 100 patients each week.

I remember one patient in particular. He was dying of cancer and knew it. I was struck by his appearance. He had a calm, serene disposition and quiet demeanour. He had come to terms with the fact that he was shortly to die, and I was impressed by his faith and peace of mind.

He was troubled by a row in the ward between a patient and a nurse. This had somehow tarnished the atmosphere, so he set about trying to sort it out. He first of all became friendly with the patient, and got to know him well. He then befriended the nurse and later reconciled the two. He was delighted with the outcome, especially as the peaceful atmosphere of the ward was restored.

Peace is supremely important, and many of us can be instruments of peace, wherever we are.

The Lord lift up his countenance upon you, and give you peace –
Numbers 6.26

Blessedness gives us peace of mind in the midst of outward trials –
Francois Fénelon

Peace is such a precious jewel that I would give anything for it but truth – *Matthew Henry*

A harvest of peace is produced from a seed of contentment – *Indian proverb*

Peace – which no experience in life can ever take from us – *William Barclay*

Agree with God, and be at peace; in this way good will come to you – *Job 22.21*

If we have no peace, it is because we have forgotten that we belong to each other – *Mother Teresa*

Peace is before all else an interior thing, belonging to the spirit – *Pope John XXIII*

Peace cannot be attained through violence, it can only be attained through understanding – *Ralph Waldo Emerson*

Live in peace yourself and then you can bring peace to others – a peaceable man does more good than a learned one – *St Thomas à Kempis*

Men of peace are usually brave – *Benjamin Spock*

It isn't enough to talk about peace. One must believe in it. And it isn't enough to believe in it. One must work at it – *Eleanor Roosevelt*

I will both lie down and sleep in peace; for you alone, O Lord, make me lie down in safety – *Psalm 4.8*

The basis of international peace is, above all, truth – *Pope John XXIII*

That peace which is found in the spirit and the inner life is well worth our care for in that peace lies the satisfaction of all our wants –

John Tauler

You touched me, and I am inflamed with love of your peace – *St Augustine*

Those of steadfast mind you keep in peace – in peace because they trust in you – *Isaiah 26.3*

Peace does not dwell in outward things, but within the soul – *Francois Fénelon*

This inner peace is so valuable, nothing in life should ever be allowed to take its place – *John Tauler*

Peace is not an absence of war, it is a virtue, a state of mind, a disposition for benevolence, confidence, justice – *Baruch Spinoza*

Blessed are the peacemakers, for they will be called children of God – *Matthew 5.9*

Shalom (peace) was all that makes for wholeness and prosperity – *James D.G. Dunn*

Peace, feeling the presence of the living God – *D.H. Lawrence*

Where there is peace, God is – *George Herbert*

Who except God can give you peace? Has the world ever been able to satisfy the heart? – *Gerard Majella*

Peace I leave with you; my peace I give to you. I do not give to you as the world gives. Do not let your hearts be troubled, and do not let them be afraid – *John 14.27*

Peace is always beautiful – *Walt Whitman*

Lord, make me an instrument of thy peace – *St Francis of Assisi*

Peace is growth and expansion, fertility in husbandry and family, health and strength throughout life – *J. Pedersen*

The peace of the contemplative is at once the most beautiful and the most fruitful act of man – *Stephen Mackenna*

There is an experience of being in pure consciousness which gives lasting peace to the soul – *Bede Griffiths OSB*

But nothing will deprive you of peace – *Francois Fénelon*

I have said this to you, so that in me you may have peace. In the world you face persecution. But take courage. I have conquered the world – *John 16.33*

Peace in the sense of inward spiritual calm – the serenity of a secure relationship with God, which is sustained by grace through all kinds of tribulation and pressures – *James D.G. Dunn*

The beauty of thy peace – *John Greenleaf Whittier*

Peace, quiet, joy – the apanage of simple and humble souls – *Father Yelchaninov*

In Thy will is our peace – *Dante Alighieri*

Peace lies in the hearts and minds of all people – *John F. Kennedy*

Jesus came and stood among them and said, 'Peace be with you' *John 20.19*

Peace, the central feeling of all happiness – *William Wordsworth*

It is understanding that gives an ability to have peace – *Harry S. Truman*

Peace here below consists not in an exemption from suffering, but a voluntary acceptance of it – *Francois Fénelon*

There is never any peace for those who resist God – *Francois Fénelon*

Peace can only be manifested in society when there is peace within the human heart – *Bede Griffiths OSB*

If it is possible, so far as it depends on you, live peaceably with all – *Romans 12.18*

The good news they (the first Christians) proclaimed was the gospel of peace – *James D.G. Dunn*

You have made us for yourself and our hearts find no peace until they rest in you – *St Augustine*

God's will is our peace and there is no other peace – *Father Andrew SDC*

We must pursue peaceful ends through peaceful means – *Martin Luther King*

(Peace) is the tranquillity of order – *St Augustine*

Let us then pursue what makes for peace and for mutual edification – *Romans 14.19*

Nothing can bring you peace but yourself – *Ralph Waldo Emerson*

Peace's fundamental condition – is a loving and filial dependence on the will of God – *Pope John XXIII*

This peace a man should allow nothing to take from him, whatever betide, come weal or woe, honour or shame – *John Tauler*

I love peace, but I love truth even more – *Latin proverb*

Make us children of quietness, and heirs of peace – *St Clement of Alexandria*

The fruit of the Spirit is…peace – *Galatians 5.22*

Peace may be translated "Harmony". Harmony with one's self is integrity; harmony with life itself is gratitude; harmony with people is brotherhood; harmony with God is faith. All this adds up to the meaning of peace. It is the gift of Christ – *Oscar Blackwelder*

Peace is love in repose – *D.L. Moody*

He is happiest, be he king or peasant, who finds peace in his home – *Johann Wolfgang von Goethe*

Keep your heart in peace; let nothing in this world disturb it; everything has an end – *St John of the Cross*

There is a deep peace that grows out of illness and loneliness and a sense of failure – *Frank C. Laubach*

And the peace of God which surpasses all understanding, will guard your hearts and your minds in Christ Jesus – *Philippians 4.7*

In peace the Kingdom of God is discovered and His righteousness is found – *John Tauler*

He only is advancing in life, whose heart is getting softer, his blood warmer, his brain quicker, and his spirit entering into living peace – *John Ruskin*

If the basis of peace is God, the secret of peace is trust – *J.B. Figgis*

We should have much peace if we would not busy ourselves with the sayings and doings of others – *St Thomas à Kempis*

Keep on doing the things that you have learned and received and heard and seen in me, and the God of peace will be with you – *Philippians 4.9*

Peace within makes beauty without – *English proverb*

Nothing can bring you peace but the triumph of principle – *Ralph*

Waldo Emerson

He gave his disciples peace, but not peace as the world gives – *T.S. Eliot*

Peace is not made at the council tables, or by treaties, but in the hearts of men – *Herbert Hoover*

When Christ came into the world, peace was sung; and when He went out of the world, peace was bequeathed – *Francis Bacon*

A great many people are trying to make peace, but that has already been done. God has not left it for us to do; all we have to do is to enter into it – *D. L. Moody*

And let the peace of Christ rule in your hearts, to which indeed you were called in the one body – *Colossians 3.15*

I am a child of peace and am resolved to keep the peace for ever and ever, with the whole world, inasmuch as I have concluded it at last with my own self –
Johann Wolfgang von Goethe

People are always expecting to get peace in heaven; but you know whatever peace they get there will be ready made. Whatever making of peace *they* can be blest for, must be on earth here –
John Ruskin

To thee, O God, we turn for peace…but grant us too the blessed assurance that nothing shall deprive us of that peace, neither *ourselves*, nor our foolish, earthly desires, nor my wild longings, nor the anxious cravings of my heart –
Søren Kierkegaard

A soul divided against itself can never find peace. Peace cannot exist where there are contrary loyalties. For true peace there has to be psychological and moral harmony. Conscience must be at rest –

Hubert van Zeller

May the God of peace himself sanctify you entirely; and may your spirit and soul and body be kept sound and blameless – *1 Thessalonians 5.23*

In India the great example of the power of peace was seen in Mahatma Gandhi whose inner peace influenced the whole nation. Work for peace must first of all be a work within ourselves – *Bede Griffiths OSB*

No man has touched the essential characteristic of Christianity, and no man has entered into the interior spirit of Christianity, who has not reached to a certain extent that peace which Christ said He gave to His disciples, and which at times they declared to be past all understanding – *Henry Ward Beecher*

Now may the Lord of peace himself give you peace at all times in all ways.
The Lord be with all of you – *2 Thessalonians 3.16*

The peace of the rational soul is the ordered agreement of knowledge and action – *St Augustine*

Christ alone can bring lasting peace – peace with God – peace among men and nations – and peace within our hearts – *Billy Graham*

Every good man in whom religion rules is at peace and unity with himself – *John Smith the Platonist*

Blessed are the single-hearted, for they shall have abundance of peace – *St Thomas à Kempis*

He who knoweth how to suffer will enjoy much peace. Such a one is a conqueror of himself and lord of the world, a friend of Christ, and an heir of Heaven – *St Thomas à Kempis*

Charity gives peace to the soul. For whoever loves God above all things rests his heart in the eternal peace – *Archbishop Ullathorne*

Never give in! Never give in! Never, never, never, never – in anything great or small, large or petty – never give in except to convictions of honour and good sense – *Winston Churchill*

Thy peace shall be in much patience – *St Thomas à Kempis*

Blessed are the simple, for they shall enjoy much peace – *St Thomas à Kempis*

If we wish to have true peace, we must give it a soul. The soul of peace is love. It is love that gives life to peace, more than victory or defeat, more than self-interest or fear or weariness or need. The soul of peace is love which for us believers comes from the love of God and expresses itself in love for men – *Pope Paul VI*

To think well is to serve God in the interior court: To have a mind composed of divine thoughts, and set frame, to be like Him within – *Thomas Traherne*

There are many things that are essential to arriving at true peace of mind, and one of the most important is faith, which cannot be acquired without prayer – *John Wooden*

No man is peaceful without rejoicing – *Isaac of Nineveh*

In peace there's nothing so becomes a man as modest stillness and humility – *William Shakespeare*

Until he extends the circle of his compassion to all living things, man will not himself find peace – *Albert Schweitzer*

I feel within me a peace above all earthly dignities; a still and quiet conscience – *William Shakespeare*

The peaceful are the strong – *Oliver Wendall Holmes*

Peace is rarely denied to the peaceful – *Friedrich von Schiller*

Peace cannot be kept by force, It can only be achieved by understanding – *Albert Einstein*

In the Bible the word *peace, shalom,* never means the absence of trouble. Peace means everything that makes for our highest good. – *William Barclay*

It is the peace which no sorrow, no danger, no suffering can make less – *William Barclay*

It is the peace which is independent of outward circumstance – *William Barclay*

It is only the religion of Jesus that can give us peace. This sets us at peace with ourselves; it subdues our passions, and regulates our desires; it consoles us, with the hope of everlasting good; it gives us the joy of the holy Spirit; it enables us to be happy; it gives us peace of mind in the midst of outward trials; and as the source from where it springs is inexhaustible…it is to the righteous a treasure that can never fail – *Francois Fénelon*

True peace is the possession of the favour of God – *Francois Fénelon*

Desire only the will of God, seek him alone, and you will find peace; you shall enjoy it in spite of the world – *Francois Fénelon*

We are not at peace with others because we are not at peace with ourselves, and we are not at peace with ourselves because we are not at peace with God –
Thomas Merton

Peace is our final good – *St Augustine*

His face wore the utter peace of one whose life is hid in God's own heart – *Hamilton King*

Five great enemies to peace inhabit with us, namely, avarice, ambition, envy, anger, and pride. If these enemies were to be banished, we should infallibly enjoy perpetual peace – *Petrarch*

The wise man looks inside his heart and finds eternal peace – *Hindu proverb*

12 PATIENCE

I used to visit the occupants of two blocks of high rise flats in Bradford as a part of my duties at the Cathedral. On one of these visits I met Doreen. She was in her late thirties. She was a paraplegic, with hardly any legs, and a hunchback. She had great difficulties with one of her arms, which hung loosely from her shoulder. Numerous operations had failed to remove the roots of a troublesome abscess. The arm looked to be held to the shoulder by skin. Life had not been easy for Doreen. She had been like this from birth. She was kept going by the patience of Job.

We became friends, and I used to visit her on a regular basis. Each visit was a challenge. She was well endowed with Yorkshire directness and very much a no-nonsense person. In this situation I valued my Yorkshire roots. There were no easy answers for her. Any false utterance on my part was quickly demolished by caustic invective.

I learnt a lot about patience from Doreen in these visits. Not surprisingly, "patience" is one of the fruits of the Spirit. It is often found in unusual places, and in unusual people!

Be still before the Lord, and wait patiently for him – *Psalm 37.7*

Patience is not passive; on the contrary, it is active: it is concentrated strength – *Anon*

The saint watches, longs, and expects. He watches unto prayer and longs with a growing intensity; has patience in the dark and faith to believe that his eyes will behold it – *W.E. Sangster*

True patience grows with the growth of love – *St Gregory 1, Pope, the Great*

Whoever is slow to anger has great understanding – *Proverbs 14.29*

Possess your soul with patience – *John Dryden*

The patient man is already experiencing a deep and healthful purging – *St Thomas à Kempis*

I worked with patience, which means almost power – *Elizabeth Barrett Browning*

One of the principal parts of faith is patience – *George MacDonald*

But those who wait for the Lord shall renew their strength, they shall mount up with wings like eagles, they shall run and not be weary, they shall walk and not faint – *Isaiah 40.31*

Patient endurance is godlike – *Henry Wadsworth Longfellow*

Patience and application will carry us through – *Thomas Fuller*

Our hard task is this: to have patience with the patience of God – *W.E. Sangster*

Not only are the saints brave: *They are patient – W.E. Sangster*

Patience is the companion of wisdom – *St Augustine*

Those who are patient stay calm until the right moment, and then cheerfulness comes back to them – *Ecclesiasticus 1.23*

Patience with others is Love – *Adel Bestavros*

Patience with self is Hope – *Adel Bestavros*

Patience with God is Faith – *Adel Bestavros*

Patience will achieve more than force – *Edmund Burke*

The greatest power is often simple patience – *Joseph Cossman*

But as for that in the good soil, these are the ones who, when they hear the word, hold it fast in an honest and good heart, and bear fruit with patient endurance – *Luke 8.15*

Adopt the pace of nature; her secret is patience – *Ralph Waldo Emerson*

Patience is very necessary for one: for I perceive that many things in this life do fall out as we would not – *St Thomas à Kempis*

Patience is bitter, but it has a sweet fruit – *German proverb*

Patience and diligence, like faith remove mountains – *William Penn*

Be patient in suffering – *Romans 12.12*

To be patient with self is an almost incalculable blessing – *F.W. Faber*

Patience is more worth than miracles doing – *Margery Kempe*

Patience is power; with time and patience the mulberry leaf becomes silk – *Chinese proverb*

Love is patient; love is kind…It bears all things, believes all things, hopes all things, endures all things. Love never ends – *1 Corinthians 13.4, 7-8*

Patience has been found to be a remedy for every sorrow – *Publilius Syrus*

To know how to wait is the great secret of success – *Xavier de Moistre*

An ounce of patience is worth a pound of brains – *Dutch proverb*

A truly patient person bears all – *St Thomas à Kempis*

Have patience with all things, but chiefly have patience with yourself – *St Francis de Sales*

The fruit of the Spirit is…patience – *Galatians 5.22*

The secret of patience is "doing something else in the meantime" – *W.E. Sangster*

How poor are they that have not patience – *William Shakespeare*

The exercise of patience involves a continual practice of the presence of God – *F.W. Faber*

Patience is the grace of God – *E.B. Pusey*

Unwearying patience is of the greatest power – *Jeremy Drexelius*

Clothe yourselves with compassion, kindness, humility, meekness and patience – *Colossians 3.12*

Each man can learn something from his neighbour: at least he can learn to have patience with him, to live and let live – *Charles Kingsley*

We have need of patience with ourselves and with others – *E.B. Pusey*

Patience is the queen of virtues – *St John Chrysostom*

One moment of patience may ward off great disaster, one moment of impatience may ruin a whole life – *Chinese proverb*

Encourage the faint-hearted, help the weak, be patient with all of them – *1 Thessalonians 5.14*

Everything comes if a person will only wait – *Benjamin Disraeli*

Patience bears with others because it loves them – *St Gregory 1,*

Pope, the Great

Patience and time do more than strength or passion – *Jean de la Fontaine*

The fruit of the Spirit is longsuffering. It is the courage which *endures* – *W.E. Sangster*

Be patient, therefore, beloved, until the coming of the Lord. The farmer waits for the precious crop from the earth, being patient with it until it receives the early and late rains. You also must be patient – *James 5.7-8*

Patient waiting is often the highest way of doing God's will – *Jeremy Collier*

Patient endurance attains all things – *St Teresa of Avila*

Patience is the finest and worthiest part of fortitude – and the rarest too – *John Ruskin*

As an example of suffering and patience, beloved, take the prophets who spoke in the name of the Lord. Indeed we call blessed those who showed endurance – *James 5.10-11*

Don't lose heart; great people and mighty nations have learned a great deal, when they practise patience – *Johann Wolfgang von Goethe*

Patience is the touchstone of all the virtues – *St Catherine of Siena*

Endeavour is the crowning quality, and patience all the passion of great hearts – *J.R. Lowell*

Patience does not destroy pain, it helps us to bear it; it does not take it away, it makes it feel lighter – *G.G. Lynch*

He that hath patience may compass anything – *Rabelais*

We do not lose time if we bear its loss with gentleness and patience – *Francois Fénelon*

Quiet patient work often brings startling results – *Bishop Walsham How*

God is unwearied patience, a meekness that cannot be provoked – *William Law*

Patience my lord! Why it is the soul of peace – *Thomas Dekker*

Patience is needed with everyone, but first of all with ourselves – *St Francis de Sales*

Endure and dare, true heart – through patience with boldness, come we at a crown enriched with a thousand blessings – *Spanish proverb*

Obedience is the fruit of faith: patience the bloom on the fruit – *Christina Rossetti*

Genius is patience – *Sir Isaac Newton*

They should have known that he (Christ) was God. His patience should have proved that to them – *Tertullian*

Patient endurance is the perfection of charity – *St Ambrose*

All men commend patience, although few be willing to practise it – *St Thomas à Kempis*

Calumnies are answer'd best with silence – *Ben Jonson*

Sorrow and silence are strong, and patient endurance is godlike – *Henry Wadsworth Longfellow*

Faith takes up the cross, love binds it to the soul, patience bears it to the end – *Horatius Bonar*

Those things that a man cannot amend in himself or in others, he ought to suffer patiently, until God orders things otherwise – *St Thomas à Kempis*

A lot of the road to heaven has to be taken at thirty miles an hour – *Evelyn Underhill*

Found scratched on a wall at the Tower of London by prisoners: 'It is not adversity that kills, but the impatience with which we bear our adversity'

Patience – calm endurance of pain or any provocation; perseverance – *Concise Oxford Dictionary*

Endurance is nobler than strength, and patience than beauty – *John Ruskin*

I know how unbearable is suspense of mind, to have to face a situation which one cannot alter or even effect, and have to wait – *A.C. Benson*

People are always talking of perseverance, courage, and fortitude, but patience is the first and worthiest part of fortitude, and the rarest too – *John Ruskin*

I can see that patience is essential in this life, for there is much that goes against the grain. Whatever I do to ensure my peace, I find that fighting and suffering are inevitable – *St Thomas à Kempis*

Patience is the most difficult thing of all and the only thing that is worth learning. All nature, all growth, all peace, everything that flowers and is beautiful in the world depends on patience, requires time, silence, trust, and faith in long-term processes which far exceed any single lifetime – *Herman Hesse*

Beware the fury of a patient man – *John Dryden*

Where there is patience and humility, there is neither anger nor vexation – *St Francis of Assisi*

If we truly preserve patience in our souls, we are martyrs without being killed – *St Gregory1, Pope, the Great*

On the whole it is patience which makes the final difference between those who succeed, or fail, to do things – *John Ruskin*

True patience is to suffer the wrongs done to us by others in an unruffled spirit and without feeling resentment – *St Gregory 1, Pope, the Great*

Our real blessings often appear to us in the shape of pains, losses and disappointments; but let us have patience, and we soon shall see them in their proper figures – *Joseph Addison*

Patience is a necessary ingredient of genius – *Benjamin Disraeli*

The principal part of faith is patience – *George MacDonald*

Though God takes the sun out of Heaven, yet we must have patience – *George Herbert*

Patience with ourselves is a duty for Christians, and the only real humility – *Evelyn Underhill*

To forbear replying to an unjust reproach, and overlook it with a generous or, if possible, with an entire neglect of it, is one of the most heroic acts of a great soul – *R. H. Benson*

O God, make us children of quietness, and heirs of peace – *St Clement of Alexandria*

Nothing great was ever done without much enduring – *St Catherine of Siena*

Be long-suffering and prudent, and you will obtain the mastery over wickedness and accomplish all justice – *Shepherd of Hermas*

Patience is the root and guardian of all the virtues – *St Gregory 1,*

Pope, the Great

It takes patience to appreciate domestic bliss; volatile spirits prefer unhappiness – *George Santayana*

The future belongs to him who knows how to wait – *Russian proverb*

'Rest in the Lord, wait patiently on him and he will give thee thy heart's desire.'
The more central this thought becomes, the less difficulty you will find its outward expression, that is to say, long-suffering and gentleness in all encounters of everyday life – *Evelyn Underhill*

True waiting means waiting without anxiety – *St Francis de Sales*

The virtue of patience is the one which most assures us of freedom – *St Francis de Sales*

Prompt to move, but firm to wait – knowing things rashly sought are rarely found – *William Wordsworth*

Be of hope, suffer, be silent and patient, let nothing affright thee; all of it will have a time to end: patience brings a man everything – *Miguel de Molinos*

Patience enough to toil, until some good is accomplished – *Johann Wolfgang von Goethe*

That's the advantage of having lived sixty-five years. You don't feel the need to be impatient any longer – *Thornton Wilder*

Not a weariness or painfulness endured patiently…but it enlarges the whole soul for the endless capacity of the love of God – *E.B Pusey*

A soul enkindled with love is a gentle, meek, humble, and patient soul – *St John of the Cross*

All things come to him who waits – *Austin O'Malley*

We must wait for God, long, meekly, in the wind and wet, in the thunder and lightning, in the cold and the dark. Wait, and He will come – *F.W. Faber*

A waiting person is a patient person. The word *patience* means the willingness to stay where we are and live the situation out to the fullest in the belief that something hidden there will manifest itself to us - *Henri J.M. Nouwen*

Let patience have her perfect work. Statue under the chisel of the sculptor, stand steady to the blows of the mallet – *George MacDonald*

Patience of all the virtues blessedest, a thousand treasures for a single one – *Leopold Schefer*

It takes a long time to bring excellence to maturity – *Publilius Syrus*

Some strains are bearable and even bracing, but others are deadly – *A.C. Benson*

Life should be a voluntary overcoming of difficulties, those met with and those voluntarily created, otherwise it is just a dice-game – *A.R. Orage*

I often wish there were some index or inward monitor showing me when I had reached the limit of my power of resistance and endurance in trouble. Sometimes, I dare say, I fancy I can hold out no longer when, in reality, I am nowhere near falling – *Mark Rutherford*

To endure is greater than to dare, to tire out hostile fortune, to be daunted by no difficulty; to keep heart when all have lost it; it is to go through intrigue spotless; to forego even ambition when the end is gained – who can say this is not greatness? – *William Makepeace Thackeray*

There remain times when one can only endure. One lives on, one doesn't die, and the only thing that one can do, is to fill one's mind and time as far as possible with the concerns of other people. It doesn't bring immediate peace, but it brings the dawn nearer – *A.C. Benson*

The years should temper a man like steel, so that he can bear more and more and emerge more and more the conqueror over life. In the nature of things we must grow weaker in body, but in the divine nature of things we must grow even stronger in the faith which can endure the slings and arrows of life, and not fall – *William Barclay*

Life makes many an attempt to take away our faith. Things happen to us and others which baffle our understanding; life has its problems to which there seems to be no solution and its questions to which there is no answer; life has its dark places where there seems to be nothing to do but hold on. Faith is always a *victory*, the victory of the soul which tenaciously maintains its clutch on God – *William Barclay*

There is a spirit, which I feel, that delights to do no evil nor to revenge any wrong, but delights to endure all things, in hope to enjoy its own in the end. Its hope is to outlive all wrath and contention, and to weary out all exultation and cruelty, or whatever is of a nature contrary to itself – *James Naylor*

Perseverance, dear my lord, keeps honour bright – *William Shakespeare*

Attempt the end, and never stand to doubt, nothing's so hard, but search will find it out – *Robert Herrick*

No great cause is ever lost or ever won. The battle must always be renewed and the creed restated – *John Buchan*

For me at least there came moments when faith wavered. But there is the great lesson and the great triumph if you keep the fire burning until, by and by, out of the mass of sordid details there comes some result, be it some new generalization or be it a transcending spiritual repose – *Oliver Wendell Holmes*

We live in a very beautiful world; but few good things are to be had in it without hard work. It is not a world in which any one can expect to be prosperous if he is easily discouraged. Perseverance – earnest, steady perseverance – is necessary to success. This is no drawback. Good, solid work is as necessary to peace of mind as it is for the health of the body; in fact the two are inseparable – *Rt Hon. Lord Avebury*

Disraeli the elder held that the secret of all success consisted in being master of your subject, such mastery being attainable only through continuous application and study. Hence it happens that the men who have most moved the world have been not so much men of genius, strictly so called, as men of intense mediocre abilities, untiring workers, persevering, self-reliant and indefatigable, not so often the gifted, of naturally bright and shining qualities, as those who have applied themselves diligently to their work, in whatever line that might be – *Samuel Smiles*

13 KINDNESS

If someone was to ask me what has been the greatest influence in my life, I would have to say – kindness.

I have experienced kindness in my parents, in my long-suffering sisters, in numerous friends and several exceptional teachers, particularly my late Headmaster.

Kindness is one of the great qualities of the Gurkhas. As well as being fierce soldiers, with numerous VC's to their credit, they have many commendable qualities, such as loyalty, courage, honesty, bravery, cheerfulness – and kindness!

The Bishop who ordained me was kind-hearted and an inspiration, He kept a wise distant eye on me during my four year curacy, and gave me every possible support. For nine years I was Chaplain to University College London. Although the College is a so-called "godless" institution, I experienced a great deal of kindness and understanding at all levels, but particularly amongst the students. This has also been my experience in the twenty seven years I spent as Chaplain Fellow of University College, Oxford. Kindness, indeed, has been an enormous influence in my life

Blessed be the Lord, for he has wondrously shown his steadfast love to me – *Psalm 31.21*

A kind word is like a Spring Day – *Russian proverb*

Kindnesses, like grain, grow by sowing – *Proverb*

What wisdom can you find that is greater than kindness? – *Jean Jacques Rousseau*

Happy are those who are kind to the poor – *Proverbs 14.21*

Kindly words, sympathizing attentions, watchfulness against wounding men's sensitiveness – these cost very little, but they are priceless in their value – *F.W. Robertson*

No act of kindness, no matter how small, is ever wasted – *AEsop*

He who plants kindness gathers love – *St Basil the Great*

Kindness is the noblest weapon to conquer with – *Thomas Fuller*

Never lose a chance of saying a kind word – *William Makepeace Thackeray*

Whoever pursues righteousness and kindness will find life and honour – *Proverbs 21.21*

Be kind and merciful. Let no one ever come to you without leaving better and happier – *Mother Teresa*

Be the living expression of God's kindness – *Mother Teresa*

Kindness in your face – *Mother Teresa*

Kindness in your eyes – *Mother Teresa*

Kindness in your smile – *Mother Teresa*

Let kindness be present in your warm greeting – *Mother Teresa*

Render true judgements, show kindness and mercy to one another – *Zechariah 7.9*

Kindness is the overflowing of self upon others – *F.W. Faber*

Three things in human life are important. The first is to be kind. The second is to be kind. The third is to be kind – *Henry James*

Kindness is more important than wisdom, and the recognition of this is the beginning of wisdom – *Theodore Rubin*

He who does kindly deeds becomes rich – *Hindu proverb*

But love your enemies, do good, and lend, expecting nothing in return. Your reward will be great, and you will be children of the Most High; for he is kind to the ungrateful and the wicked – *Luke 6.35*

Properly understood, kindness is a virtue of the strong – *W.E. Sangster*

There is a grace of kind listening, as well as a grace of kind speaking – *F.W. Faber*

Kind thoughts are rarer than either kind words or kind deeds – *F.W. Faber*

Note then the kindness and the severity of God; severity towards those who have fallen, but God's kindness towards you, provided you continue in his kindness – *Romans 11.22*

Kind words do not cost much. Yet they accomplish much – *Blaise Pascal*

Be kind, for everyone you meet is fighting a harder battle – *Plato*

Constant kindness can accomplish much. As the sun makes ice melt, kindness causes misunderstanding, mistrust and hostility to evaporate – *Albert Schweitzer*

By purity, knowledge, patience, kindness, holiness of spirit, genuine love, truthful speech, and the power of God – *2 Corinthians 6.6*

Wherever there is a human being, there is an opportunity for kindness – *Seneca*

One kind word can warm three winter months – *Japanese proverb*

If you stop to be kind, you must swerve often from your path – *Mary Webb*

A part of kindness consists in loving people more than they deserve – *Joseph Joubert*

Kindness begets kindness – *Sophocles*

The fruit of the Spirit is…kindness – *Galatians 5.22*

Always repay kindness with even more kindness – *Welsh proverb*

I expect to pass through this world but once; any good thing therefore that I can do, or any kindness that I can show to any fellow creature, let me do it now; let me not defer or neglect it, for I shall not pass this way again –
attributed to Stephen Grellet

To be kind, with that true kindness which comes not from the lips but from the heart – *Elizabeth Leseur*

In the ages to come he might show the immeasurable riches of his grace in kindness towards us in Christ Jesus – *Ephesians 2.7*

Kindness is the principle of tact, and respect for others the first condition of *savoir-vivre* – *Henri Frédéric Amiel*

Neither genius, fame, nor love shows the greatness of the soul. Only kindness can do that – *Jean Baptiste Henre Lacordaire*

The secret impulse out of which kindness acts is an instinct which is the noblest part of ourselves, the most undoubted remnant of the image of God, which was given to us at the first – *F.W. Faber*

Kind hearts are more than coronets – *Alfred, Lord Tennyson*

Getting money is not all a man's business; to cultivate kindness is a valuable part of the business of life – *Samuel Johnson*

Be kind to one another, tender-hearted, forgiving one another, as God in Christ has forgiven you – *Ephesians 4.32*

Kindness has converted more sinners than zeal, eloquence, and learning – *F.W. Faber*

The heart benevolent and kind, the most resembles GOD – *Robert Burns*

Kindliness in judgment is nothing less than a sacred duty – *William Barclay*

As God's chosen ones, holy and beloved, clothe yourselves with compassion, kindness, humility, meekness, and patience – *Colossians 3.12*

It is kindness which makes life's capabilities blossom – *F.W. Faber*

Kindness has been described…as 'a constant feeling in us about our "kind"' – *F.W. Faber*

On that best portion of a good man's life - his little, nameless, unremembered acts of kindness and of love – *William Wordsworth*

Love is something more stern and splendid than mere kindness – *C.S. Lewis*

And the Lord's servant must not be quarrelsome but kindly to everyone – *2 Timothy 2.24*

The greatest thing a man can do for his heavenly Father is to be kind to some of His other children – *Henry Drummond*

A kind heart is a fountain of gladness, making everything in its vicinity freshen into smiles – *Washington Irving*

Conquer evil men by your gentle kindness – *Isaac of Nineveh*

Kind words can be short and easy to speak, but their echoes are truly endless – *Mother Teresa*

Let us be kinder to one another – *Aldous Huxley (his last words)*

Kindness in thinking creates profoundness. Kindness in giving creates love – *Lao tzu*

Kind words are the music of the world – *F. W. Faber*

Well-bred thinking means kindly and sensitive thoughts – *Francois de la Rochefoucauld*

Kindness is the quality which lifts a person out of the ruck of ordinary men… kindness lives on enthroned in the hearts of men – *William Barclay*

And let us consider how to provoke one another to love and good deeds – *Hebrews 10.24*

The compassion that you see in the kind-hearted is God's compassion; he has given it to them to protect the helpless – *Sri Ramakrishna*

Kindness is the golden chain by which society is bound together – *Benjamin Franklin*

Lead the life that will make you kindly and friendly to everyone around you, and you will be surprised what a happy life you will live – *C.M. Schwab*

Creation was divine kindness. From it as from a fountain, flow the possibilities, the powers, the blessings of all created kindness – *F.W. Faber*

Kindness is also like divine grace, for it gives man something of which neither the self nor nature can give them – *F.W. Faber*

Great people are able to do great kindnesses – *Miguel de Cervantes*

The ideals which have lighted my way – have been Kindness, Beauty and Truth – *Albert Einstein*

Life is short, and we have never too much time for gladdening the hearts of those who are travelling the dark journey with us. Oh, be swift to love, make haste to be kind! – *Henri Frédéric Amiel*

My feeling is that there is nothing in life but refraining from hurting others, and comforting those that are sad – *Olive Schreiner*

Kind thoughts are rarer than either kind words or kind deeds. They imply a great deal of thinking about others. This in itself is rare. But they imply also a great deal of thinking about others without the thoughts being criticisms.
This is rarer still – *F.W. Faber*

I have had that curiously *symbolic* and reassuring pleasure, of being entertained with overflowing and simple kindness by a family of totally unknown people – an adventure which always brings home to me the goodwill of the world –
A.C. Benson

True kindness presupposes the faculty of imagining as one's own the suffering and joy of others. Without imagination, there can be weakness, theoretical or practical philanthropy, but not true kindness – *André Gide*

And it is here that the saints serve us yet again. Kindness recovers all its apostolic quality in them. In the saint it is never sentimental: never divorced from reality; never undisciplined; never evasive. On the other hand it is ever-present…He reveals kindness *as a fruit of the Spirit*. He shows it grounded in the nature of God. It flows directly from his faith. It is supernatural love disclosing itself in costly affection towards his fellow-men…That is why it has a robustness and pertinacity unknown to the sentimental kindness of the world – *W.E. Sangster*

Kindness in giving creates love – *Lao tzu*

Deeds of kindness weigh as much as all the commandments – *The Talmud*

Loving-kindness is the better part of goodness. It lends grace to the sterner qualities of which this consists – *W. Somerset Maugham*

One of the most difficult things to give away is kindness – it is usually returned – *C. Flint*

Wise sayings often fall on barren ground; but a kind word is never thrown away – *Arthur Helps*

There is nothing so kingly as kindness, and nothing so royal as truth – *Alice Carey*

Compassion is the basis of all morality – *Arthur Schopenhaur*

One thing will always secure heaven for us – the acts of charity and kindness with which we have filled our lives – *Mother Teresa*

The genius of communication is the ability to be both totally honest and totally kind at the same time – *John Powell*

Where there is no truth there is no kindness – *Nachman of Bretslav*

All the kindness which a man puts out into the world works on the heart and the thoughts of mankind – *Albert Schweitzer*

Gentleness as the fruit of the Spirit is a strong man's treating all men with lenity, and kindness, and forbearance and patience – *Henry Ward Beecher*

By a sweet tongue and kindness you can drag an elephant with a hair – *Persian proverb*

From hour to hour, from moment to moment, we are supported, blest, by small kindnesses – *F.W. Robertson*

Join the great company of those who make the barren places of life fruitful with kindness – *Helen Keller*

But kindness works simply and perseveringly; it produces no strained relations which prejudice its working; strained relations which already exist it relaxes. Mistrust and misunderstandings it puts to flight, and it strengthens itself by calling forth answering kindness – *Albert Schweitzer*

Kindness is the coming to the rescue of others, when they need it and it is in our power to supply what they need; and this is the work of the attributes of God towards His creatures – *F.W. Faber*

Kindness adds sweetness to everything. It is kindness which makes life's capabilities blossom, and paints them with their cheering hues, and endows them with their invigorating fragrance – *F.W. Faber*

Kindness which is bestowed on the good is never wasted – *Plato*

It is not written, blessed is he that feedeth the poor, but he that considereth the poor. A little thought and a little kindness are often worth more than a great deal of money – *John Ruskin*

The art of saying appropriate words in a kindly way is one that never goes out of fashion, never ceases to please and is within the reach of the humblest –
F.W. Faber

Only those equipped from heaven are able, while bearing their own burden, to thrust their shoulder under somebody else's. It calls in those able to give it – for strength of mind as well as strength of heart – *W.E. Sangster*

Have a deaf ear for unkind remarks about others, and a blind eye for the trivial faults of your brethren – *Sir Walter Scott*

The more vigour you need, the more gentleness and kindness you must combine with it. All stiff, harsh goodness is contrary to Jesus – *Francois Fénelon*

You can never do a kindness too soon because you never know how soon it will be too late – *Ralph Waldo Emerson*

When I was young, I used to admire intelligent people. Now I admire kind people – *Abraham Heschel*

Kindness is in our power, even when fondness is not – *Samuel Johnson*

Every act of kindness and compassion done by any man for his fellow Christian is done by Christ working within him – *Lady Julian of Norwich*

If I can put one touch of rosy sunset into the life of any man or woman, I shall feel that I have worked with God – *John MacDonald*

Loving kindness survives death – *The Talmud*

The smile you send out returns to you – *Indian proverb*

We must be purposely kind and generous, or we miss the best part of existence.
The heart that goes out of itself, gets large and full of joy – *Horace Mann*

Great men are nearly always the kindest – *Stefan Zweig*

14 GOODNESS

Several years ago I had the privilege of meeting Jean Vanier at a university mission in Oxford. I had read several of his books, and from these I gleaned he was the son of a Governor-General of Canada, and for a career he was an officer in the Royal Navy. In later life he left the navy to study for a doctorate in philosophy, and then lectured in a Canadian university.

A significant change followed. He bought a dilapidated house in a village outside Paris and invited three handicapped people to come and live with him. This was the start of L'Arche – a mixed community of handicapped and able-bodied people which came into being in 1964. Since then L'Arche communities have proliferated in many different parts of the world.

With this background I was curious to meet Jean Vanier. I was not disappointed. He had all the qualities which make for "Goodness." He came over as a man of great compassion and understanding, mingled with kindness and sympathy. I found his brand of goodness extremely attractive – quietly charismatic.

God saw everything that he had made, and indeed, it was very good –
Genesis 1.31

Good nature is worth more than knowledge, more than money, more than honour, to the person who possesses it, and certainly to everybody who dwells with them, in so far as mere happiness is concerned – *Henry Ward Beecher*

Goodness is something so simple: always to live for others, never to seek one's own advantage – *Dag Hammarskjőld*

Good nature is one of the richest fruits of Christianity – *Henry Ward Beecher*

Every good work in us is performed only by grace – *St Augustine*

For he is good, for his steadfast love endures for ever – *2 Chronicles 5.13*

The contemplation of the Good – *Iris Murdoch*

My whole day is a feast of doing good! – *Rachel Levin Varnhagen*

Be good yourself and the world will be good – *Hindu proverb*

Nature meant me to be, on the whole, a good man – *Charlotte Brontë*

To be good is to be in harmony with one's self – *Oscar Wilde*

O taste and see that the Lord is good; happy are those who take refuge in him – *Psalm 34.8*

All that is good, all that is true, all that is beautiful, all that is beneficent, be it great or small, be it perfect or fragmentary, natural as well as supernatural, moral as well as material, comes from God – *John Henry Newman*

You've got to actively seek good – *Halcyon Backhouse*

In goodness there are all kinds of wisdom – *Euripides*

I am larger, better than I thought, I did not know I held so much goodness – *Walt Whitman*

Depart from evil, and do good; seek peace, and pursue it – *Psalm*

34.14

Goodness is a special kind of truth and beauty. It is truth and beauty in human behaviour – *H.A. Overstreet*

That which is striking and beautiful is not always good; but that which is good is always beautiful – *Lenclos de Ninon*

There is only one way to put an end to evil, and that is to do good for evil – *Leo Tolstoy*

There is so much good in the worst of us, and so much bad in the best of us, that it little behoves any of us to talk about the rest of us – *John Brantingham*

Goodness *is* uneventful. It does not flash, it glows. It is deep, quiet, and very simple – *David Grayson*

I am the good shepherd. The good shepherd lays down his life for the sheep – *John 10.11*

In his love he clothes us, enfolds and embraces us; that tender love completely surrounds us, never to leave us. As I saw it he is everything that is good –
Lady Julian of Norwich

Goodness may be felt in the touch of a friendly hand or the look of a kindly eye – *David Grayson*

So that nothing is to be compared for value with goodness; that riches, honour, power, pleasure, learning, the whole world and all in it, are not worth having in comparison with being good – *Charles Kingsley*

All good develops from within us, growing up from the hidden depths of our being – *Thomas Merton*

You ask, 'What is the Good?' I suppose God Himself is the Good –

Charles Kingsley

Jesus said to him, "Why do you call me good? No one is good but God alone – *Mark 10.18*

I was guided by an implicit faith in God's Goodness – *Thomas Traherne*

Look around the Habitable World, how few know their own Good; or knowing it, pursue – *John Dryden*

Overcome the evil man, by goodness – *Indian proverb*

Loving-kindness is the better part of goodness. It lends grace to the sterner qualities of which this consists – *W. Somerset Maugham*

Be Good to You, Be Yourself – *Truthfully*

The good person out of the good treasure of the heart produces good – *Luke 6.45*

And man matures through work which inspires him to difficult good – *Karol Wojtyla*

To know God is to know Goodness. It is to see the beauty of infinite Love – *Thomas Traherne*

The line between good and evil passes not through states, nor between classes, nor between parties, but right through every human heart, through all human hearts – *Alexander Solzhenitsyn*

How God anointed Jesus of Nazareth with the Holy Spirit and with power; how he went about doing good – *Acts 10.38*

The inclination to goodness is imprinted deeply in the nature of man – *Francis Bacon*

Seek to achieve good in your own small corner of the world – *Herbert*

Butterfield

His form of goodness is extremely attractive – quietly charismatic – *Said of Jean Vanier*

Good is no good, but if it be spend: God giveth good for none other end – *Edmund Spenser*

He was a good man, full of the Holy Spirit and of faith – *Acts 11.24*

Goodness as a fruit of the Divine Spirit is raining satisfaction and happiness upon all around us, not studying our own welfare; a fountain out of which all the time flow streams of delight for others – *Henry Ward Beecher*

Always say to yourself this one thing, 'Good, I will become, whatever it cost me' – *Charles Kingsley*

Did it ever strike you that goodness is not merely a beautiful thing, but by far the most beautiful thing in the whole world? – *Charles Kingsley*

Do not be conformed to this world, but be transformed by the renewing of your minds, so that you may discern what is the will of God – what is good and acceptable and perfect – *Romans 12.2*

God's purpose is like a stream of goodness flowing out into the world and all its needs – *Michael Ramsey*

(Goodness) needeth not to enter into the soul, for it is there already, only it is unperceived – *Theologia Germanica*

Good in a strong many-compounded nature is of slower growth than any other mortal thing, and must not be forced – *George Meredith*

Good, the more communicated, more abundant grows – *John Milton*

Let love be genuine; hate what is evil, hold fast to what is good –

Romans 12.9

Riches, Fame, and Pleasure. With these three the mind is so engrossed that it cannot scarcely think of any other good – *Baruch Spinoza*

Goodness is love in action – *D.L. Moody*

God! Glory in His goodness – *Henry Ward Beecher*

Explore the countless springs of silent good – *William Wordsworth*

Be not simply good, but good for something – *St Thomas à Kempis*

For we are what he has made us, created in Christ Jesus for good works, which God prepared beforehand to be our way of life – *Ephesians 2.10*

The heart of a good man is the sanctuary of God in this world – *Madam Necker*

The moral good is not a goal but an inner force which lights up a man's life from within – *Nicolas Berdyaev*

We need greater virtues to sustain good than evil fortune – *Francis, Duc de La Rochefoucauld*

The greatest good is wisdom – *St Augustine*

How goodness heightens beauty! – *Hannah More*

A blessed life may be defined as consisting simply and solely in the possession of goodness and truth – *St Ambrose*

To reach something good it is very useful to have gone astray, and thus acquire experience – *St Teresa of Avila*

Goodness is not tied to greatness, but greatness to goodness – *Greek proverb*

The great instrument of moral good is the imagination – *Percy Bysshe Shelley*

It is good if a man can bring about that God sings within him – *Rabbi Elimelech of Lizhensk*

The goodness of a saint is a peculiar goodness. It flames with the numinous. It is a good which unconsciously proclaims itself. One feels it as an aura around its possessor. It is irradiant. It is *essential* goodness: goodness 'in the inward parts' – *W.E. Sangster*

Faith is a living, busy, active, powerful thing; it is impossible for it not to do us good continually – *Martin Luther*

It is very hard to be simple enough to be good – *Ralph Waldo Emerson*

An act of goodness, the least act of true goodness, is indeed the best proof of the existence of God – *Jacques Maritain*

Nothing can make a man truly great but being truly good and partaking of God's holiness – *Matthew Henry*

The saint is saint, not because he is 'good' but because he is transparent for something that is more than he himself is – *Paul Tillich*

Good order is the foundation of all good things – *Edmund Burke*

Anyone who proposes to do good must not expect people to roll stones out of his way, but must accept his lot calmly if they even roll a few more upon it –
Albert Schweitzer

There is but one unconditional commandment, which is that we should seek incessantly, with fear and trembling, so to vote and to act as to bring about the very largest total universe of good which we can see – *William James*

How God is a true, simple, perfect Good, and how He is a Light and a Reason and all virtues, and how what is highest and best, that is God, ought to be most loved by us – *Theologia Germanica*

By desiring what is perfectly good, even when we don't quite know what it is and cannot do what we would, we are part of the divine power against evil – widening the skirts of light and making the struggle with darkness narrower – *George Eliot*

But my life now, my whole life, independently of anything that can happen to me, every minute of it is no longer meaningless as it was before, but has a positive meaning of goodness with which I have power to invest it – *Leo Tolstoy*

Good men are not those who now and then do a good act, but men who join one good act to another. It is men, the whole tendency of whose lives is the production of good things, kind things, right things – *Henry Ward Beecher*

It should be part of our private ritual to devote a quarter of an hour every day to the concentration of the good qualities of our friends. When we are not *active*, we fall back idly upon defects, even of those whom we most love – *Mark Rutherford*

He (John Smith the Platonist) lived in a continuous enjoyment of God and perpetually drew nearer to the Centre of his soul's rest and always stayed God's time of advancement. His spirit was absorbed in the business and employment of becoming perfect in his art and profession – which was the art *of being a good man* – *Rufus M. Jones*

Goodness is easier to recognize than to define – *W.H Auden*

The Infinite Goodness has such wide arms that it takes whatever turns to it – *Dante Alighieri*

The power of the soul for good is in proportion to the strength of its passions. Sanctity is not the negation of passion but its order. Hence great saints have often been great sinners – *Coventry Patmore*

If we believe, everything can be transformed into our Lord – *Pierre Teilhard de Chardin*

The first condition of human goodness is something to love; the second, something to reverence – *George Eliot*

Real goodness does not attach itself merely to this life – it points to another world – *Daniel Webster*

Natural reason is a good tree which God has planted in us; the fruits which spring from it cannot but be good – *St Francis de Sales*

There is no higher religion than human service. To work for the common good is the highest creed – *Albert Schweitzer*

The Gospel was not good advice but good news – *W.R. Inge*

All things work together for good if one will but trust God – *R.H. Benson*

To love is to wish the other's highest good – *R.H. Benson*

Our prayers should be for blessings in general, for God knows best what is good for us – *Socrates*

Seek the first possible opportunity to act on every good resolution you make – *William James*

Nature requires the saint since he alone knows the miracle of transformation; growth and development, the very highest and most sustained incarnation, never weary him – *Friedrich Nietzche*

The essence of Christianity is goodness. Its founder was the absolute personification of this characteristic – *E. Daplyn*

Whatever you are be a good one – *Abraham Lincoln*

He does most in God's great world who does his best in his own little world – *Thomas Jefferson*

A man of integrity, and good nature can never be concealed, for his character is wrought into his countenance – *Marcus Aurelius*

Never was good work done without much trouble – *Chinese proverb*

He who would do good to another must do it in minute particulars – *William Blake*

Whoever finds Jesus, finds a rich treasure, and a good above every good – *St Thomas à Kempis*

Be not simply good, but good for something – *Henry David Thoreau*

The good is what preserves and enhances life – *Albert Schweitzer*

A saint is one who makes goodness attractive – *A.E. Houseman*

The more vigour you need, the more gentleness and kindness you must combine with it. All stiff hard goodness is contrary to Jesus – *Francois Fénelon*

Example is not the main thing in influencing others – it is the only thing – *Albert Schweitzer*

It takes courage for a man to listen to his own goodness and act upon it – *Pablo Casals*

In God's Goodness I trust to make me good, for I am sure He wishes to see me good more than I do myself – *Charles Kingsley*

What, then, is the service rendered, to the world by Christianity? The proclamation of good news – *Henri Frédéric Amiel*

He fills their whole souls with himself, the overflowing source of all good – *Richard Challoner*

Where a man chooses as his 'good' he is in fact choosing to remain at the animal level when he has capacity for more – *William Temple*

God is the creator of laughter that is good – *Philo*

Goodness must be joined with knowledge. Mere goodness is not much use, as I have found in life. One must cultivate the fine discriminating quality which goes with spiritual courage and character – *Mohandas K. Gandhi*

It is our privilege, as God's children, to help this stream of goodness to reach other people, becoming like channels – *Michael Ramsey*

Our good actions, can be channels of God's goodness – *Michael Ramsey*

Saints are persons who make it easier for others to believe in God – *Nathan Soderblom*

We do ourselves the most good doing something for others – *Horace Mann*

It has done me good to be somewhat parched by the heat and drenched by the rain of life – *Henry Wadsworth Longfellow*

Blessed is he who does good to others and desires not that others should do good to him – *Giles of Assisi*

Good men use the world in order to enjoy God – *St Augustine*

Good is that which makes for beauty – *Aldous Huxley*

A good conscience is a continual Christmas – *Benjamin Franklin*

In the rush and noise of life, as you have intervals, step home within yourselves and be still. Wait upon God, and feel his good presence; this will carry you evenly through your day's business – *William Penn*

The source and foundation of goodness and nobility of character is faith in Jesus Christ – *Alexander Maclaren*

A tree is known by its fruits; a man by his deeds. A good deed is never lost – *St Basil the Great*

Do what you can, and do it solely for God's glory – *Meister Eckhart*

15 FAITHFULNESS

When I was ordained in 1965, I had a fear about the future. I felt I would be keen and enthusiastic for the first twelve years of ministry, and then would end up just going through the motions. I was wrong on both counts. After only four years I entered a period of time in which I felt to be going through the motions.

A new way beckoned forward through the discovery of a book – *The Choice is Always Ours* – an Anthology by Dorothy Berkley Phillips, first published in 1960. This remarkable book opened up an outline of faith of enormous dimensions. Founded on the Bible and the writings of many theologians, faith moved on to include the insights of some poets, playwrights, novelists, scientists, philosophers, theologians, historians, politicians, economists, statesmen, psychologists, artists and musicians. Side by side with this newly found faith has been the practice of a simple form of contemplation. Through this practice, described in the Introduction, I entered a state of faithfulness which still goes forward for me after almost fifty years of practice.

Know therefore that the Lord your God is God, the faithful God – *Deuteronomy 7.9*

Our life is grounded in faith, with hope and love besides – *Lady Julian of Norwich*

Faith is a living bold trust in God's grace – *Martin Luther*

Faith is an act of self-consecration, in which the will, the intellect, and the affections all have their place – *W.R. Inge*

Faith is not the holding of correct doctrines, but personal fellowship with the Living God – *William Temple*

The saints of God are sealed inwardly with faith, but outwardly with good works – *John Boys*

Believe in the Lord your God and you will be established – *2 Chronicles 20.20*

Faith is kept alive in us, and gathers strength, from practice more than from speculation – *Joseph Addison*

Relying on God has to begin all over again every day as if nothing had yet been done – *C.S. Lewis*

Faith is an active creative force – *J.H. Oldham*

The faithful person lives constantly with God – *St Clement of Alexandria*

The steadfast love of the Lord never ceases, his mercies never come to an end; they are new every morning; great is your faithfulness – *Lamentations 3.22-23*

The only way to learn strong faith is to endure great trials – *George Müller*

While faith makes all things possible, it is love that makes all things easy – *Evan Hopkins*

The secret behind getting more faith, is to get to know God more – *Lester Sumrall*

In Christian tradition faith…combines a certitude with an equal acknowledgement of mystery – *Keith Clements*

A STILL MORE EXCELLENT WAY

Feed your faith and starve your doubts to death – *Andrew Murray*

But the righteous live by their faith - *Habakkuk 2.4*

Faith is a kind of winged intellect. The great workmen of history have been men who believed like giants – *Charles H. Parkhurst*

We live in an age which asks for faith, pure faith, naked faith, mystical faith – *William Johnston*

Faith in Christ is a way of life, a following, an allegiance – *Edward Wilson*

Though they do not see me with bodily eyes, yet with the spirit they will believe the things I have said – *2 Esdras 1.37*

He who lives up to a little faith shall have more faith – *Thomas Brooks*

God has made for us two kinds of eyes; those of flesh, and those of faith – *St John Chrysostom*

Well done, good and trustworthy slave; you have been trustworthy in a few things, I will put you in charge of many things; enter into the joy of your master – *Matthew 25.23*

Strong Son of God, immortal Love, whom we, that have not seen thy face, by faith and faith alone, embrace, believing where we cannot prove – *Alfred, Lord Tennyson*

It is faith among men that holds the moral elements of society together – *William Maxwell Evarts*

Faith is the highest passion in a human being – *Søren Kierkegaard*

Faith, as Paul saw it, was a living flaming thing – *A.W. Tozer*

Faith is not a refuge from reality. It is a demand that we face reality, with all the difficulties, opportunities and implications – *Evelyn Underhill*

All things can be done for the one who believes – *Mark 9.23*

I do not want merely to possess a faith; I want a faith that possesses me – *Charles Kingsley*

Faith is a matter of spiritual manhood. It is a matter of maturity – *P.T. Forsyth*

Faith is a way of renewing strength in Him and of becoming a participator in His divine nature – *Rufus M Jones*

I hold by faith what I cannot grasp with the mind – *St Bernard of Clairvaux*

Faith is the realization of an invisible presence of truth – *Henry Ward Beecher*

Whoever is faithful in a very little is faithful also in much – *Luke 16.10*

Faith today is difficult. This is an indisputable sign of our times – *Carlo Carretto*

The fruit of our faith is the fulfilment of our hope – *Diana Benze*

Faith is a kind of spiritual sight, an in-seeing into realities – *George Appleton*

God thou art Love! I build my faith on that – *Robert Browning*

God is faithful, and he will not let you be tested beyond your strength – *1 Corinthians 10.13*

Faith is required of you, and a sincere life, not a lofty intellect nor a delving into the mysteries of God – *St Thomas à Kempis*

I learned really to practice mustard seed faith, and positive thinking, and remarkable things happened – *Sir John Walton*

Faith as an original experience of the life of the Spirit – *Nicolas Berdyaev*

Faithfulness in carrying out present duties is the best preparation for the future – *Francois Fénelon*

The supreme venture of faith – *Norman Pittenger*

For we walk by faith, not by sight – *2 Corinthians 5.7*

Faith is the key to the treasury, the key of the abyss of divine wisdom – *Jean Pierre de Caussade SJ*

The disease with which the human mind now labours is want of faith – *Ralph Waldo Emerson*

A mature person has faith in himself which becomes stronger as it is fortified by his faith in God – *Leonard Wedel*

Faith always shows itself in the whole personality – *Martyn Lloyd-Jones*

For in Christ Jesus you are all children of God through faith – *Galatians 3.26*

Faith is the sight of the inward eye – *Alexander Maclaren*

A faithful friend is an image of God – *French proverb*

Faith is not something we can achieve; it is something achieved within us by God – *Alister McGrath*

Faith in the fatherly love of God – *Henri Frédéric Amiel*

Faith has need of the whole truth – *Pierre Teilhard de Chardin*

The fruit of the Spirit is…faithfulness – *Galatians 5.22*

Faith is often strengthened right at the place of disappointment – *Rodney McBride*

Ultimately, faith is the only key to the universe. The final meaning of human existence, and the answers to the questions on which all our happiness depends cannot be found in any other way – *Thomas Merton*

All effort is in the last analysis sustained by faith that it is worth making – *Ordway Tead*

By faith we are convinced that fellowship is possible with our fellow man and with God – *B.F. Westcott*

If we are faithless, he remains faithful – for he cannot deny himself – *2 Timothy 2.13*

Faith is just that total reliance of human weakness on divine grace which allows the Spirit to operate most effectively within the human condition – *James D.G. Dunn*

Faith is not a once-done act, but a continuous gaze of the heart at the Triune God – *A.W. Tozer*

Discipline is the secret of holiness. You must learn to discipline yourself for the purpose of godliness – *Joy Adams*

The best discipline, maybe the only discipline that really works – is self-discipline – *Walter Kiechell 111*

Say to yourself, "I am loved by God more than I can either conceive or understand." Let this fill all your soul and never leave you. You will see that this is the way to find God – *Henri de Tourville*

Now faith is the assurance of things hoped for, the conviction of things not seen – *Hebrews 11.1*

Believe in God with all your might, for hope rests on faith, love on hope, and victory on love – *Lady Julian of Norwich*

The deep secret of the mystery of faith lies in the fact that it is a 'baptism' in the death and sacrifice of Christ. We can only give ourselves to God when Christ, by His grace, dies and rises again spiritually within us – *Thomas Merton*

Faith, like light, should always be simple, and unbending; while love, like warmth, should beam forth on every side, and bend to every necessity of our brethren – *Martin Luther*

Belief is a truth held in the mind. Faith is a fire in the heart – *Joseph Addison*

Looking to Jesus the pioneer and perfecter of our faith – *Hebrews 12.2*

Faith sees by ears – *English proverb*

All work that is worth anything is done by faith – *Albert Schweitzer*

He who is faithful over a few things is a lord of cities. It does not matter whether you preach in Westminster Abbey, or teach a ragged class, so you be faithful.
The faithfulness is all – *George MacDonald*

Men of integrity, by their very existence, rekindle the belief that as a people we can live above the level of moral squalor – *John Gardner*

Christian faith is like a grand cathedral, with divinely pictured windows. Standing without, you can see no glory, nor can imagine any, but standing within, every ray of light reveals a harmony of unspeakable splendours – *Nathaniel Hawthorne*

The only faith that wears well and holds its colour in all weathers is that which is woven of conviction and set with the sharp mordant of experience – *J.R. Lowell*

Faith is a certitude without proofs…Faith is a sentiment, for it is a hope; it is an instinct, for it precedes all outward instruction – *Henri Frédéric Amiel*

Faith is loyalty to some inspired teacher, some spiritual hero – *Thomas Carlyle*

Faith is consecration in overalls – *Evelyn Underhill*

Faith is a power, pre-eminently, of holding fast to an unseen power of goodness – *Matthew Arnold*

Faith consists in the belief that we are loved – *Alexandra Vinet*

Religious faith does not consist in supposing that there is a God; it consists in personal trust in God rising to personal fellowship with God – *William Temple*

It is faith that is expected of you and honest living, not profound understanding and deep knowledge of the mysteries of God – *St Thomas à Kempis*

One in whom persuasion and belief had ripened into faith, and faith become a passionate intuition – *William Wordsworth*

It is neither *necessary*, nor indeed *possible* to understand any matter of Faith; farther than it is Revealed – *Benjamin Whichcote*

Reason saw not till *Faith* sprung the Light – *John Dryden*

To abandon religion for science is merely to fly from one region of faith to another – *Giles and Melville Harcourt*

Faith in Christ was not primarily a matter of doctrinal or intellectual belief, but a way of life, a following, an allegiance – *Edward Wilson*

The life of faith is a continually renewed victory over doubt, a continually renewed grasp of meaning in the midst of meaninglessness – *Lesslie Newbigin*

Nothing in life is more wonderful than faith – the one great moving force which we can neither weigh in the balance nor test in the crucible – *Sir William Osler*

Like all human knowledge, the knowledge of faith is also fragmentary. Only when faith remains aware of this does it remain free from arrogance, intolerance, and false zeal – *Hans Küng*

To have faith is to meet the world with the conviction that in spite of all its ambiguities and its downright evils, there can be discerned in it the reality of love and a ground of hope – *John Macquarrie*

Proofs are the last thing looked for by a truly religious mind which feels the imaginative fitness of its faith and knows instinctively that, in such a manner, imaginative fitness is all that can be required – *George Santayana*

It is better to be faithful than famous – *Theodore Roosevelt*

God did not call us to be successful, but to be faithful – *Mother Teresa*

The life of faith does not earn eternal life; it is eternal life. And Christ is its vehicle – *William Temple*

Faith and works should travel side by side, step answering to step, like the legs of men walking. First faith, and then works; and the faith again, and then works again – until you can scarcely distinguish which is the one and which is the other – *William Booth*

It is by believing in roses that one brings them to bloom – *French proverb*

It is necessary to the happiness of a man that he is mentally faithful to himself – *Thomas Payne*

A simple, childlike faith in a Divine Friend solves all the problems that come to us by land or sea – *Helen Keller*

Faith means believing the unbelievable, or it is no virtue at all – *G.K. Chesterton*

Faithfulness in little things is a big thing – *St John Chrysostom*

Faith is to believe what we do not see, and the reward of this faith is to see what we believe – *St Augustine*

Faith is the bird that sings while dawn is still dark – *Rabindranath Tagore*

Faith makes the uplook good, the outlook bright, the internal favour favourable, and the future glorious – *Raymond Edman*

Faith is not knowledge or certainty – *George Appleton*

A living faith is not something you have to carry, but something which carries you – *J.H. Oldham*

O Lord my God, give me understanding to know you, diligence to seek you, wisdom to fear you, and a faithfulness that may finally embrace you – *St Thomas Aquinas*

I do not pray for success, I ask for faithfulness – *Mother Teresa*

A person consists of his faith. Whatever is his faith, even so is he – *Indian proverb*

Faith embraces many truths which seem to contradict each other – *Blaise Pascal*

Faith is an attitude of the person. It means you are prepared to stake yourself on something being so – *Michael Ramsey*

Trust the past to God's mercy, the present to God's love and the future to God's providence – *St Augustine*

The only sufficient ground of faith is the authority of God Himself as he addresses me in His Word – *Emil Brunner*

I see heaven's glories shine and faith shines equal – *Emily Brontë*

To us also, through every star, through every blade of grass, is not God made visible if we will open our minds and our eyes? – *Thomas Carlyle*

All I have seen teaches me to trust the Creator for all I have not seen – *Ralph Waldo Emerson*

Believe that you have it (faith), and you have it – *Erasmus*

It is cynicism and fear that freeze life; it is faith that thaws it out, releases it, sets it free – *Harry Emerson Fosdick*

Faith fills a man with love for the beauty of its truth, with faith in the truth of its beauty – *St Francis de Sales*

When I cannot enjoy the faith of assurance, I live by the faith of adherence – *Matthew Henry*

The ultimate ground of faith and knowledge is confidence in God – *Charles Hodge*

Take the first step in faith. You don't have to see the whole staircase, just take the first step – *Martin Luther King*

In actual life every great enterprise begins with and takes its first step forward in faith – *August Wilhelm von Schlegel*

One of the most essential qualities of a faith - that is to attempt great things for God and to expect great things from God, is holy audacity – *A.B. Simpson*

The smallest seed of faith is better than the largest fruit of happiness – *Henry David Thoreau*

16 GENTLENESS

I was in my last year at Theological College. We felt the Church of England at the time was at a low ebb, and were making the mistake of being hyperactive, in an attempt to get things moving. We rushed here, there, and everywhere, and got nowhere. Fatigue set in. The future looked bleak.

We had a short visit from a black South African priest. He spoke very little and there was no trace at all of him being in a hurry. On the contrary he was very relaxed and gentle. A quiet confidence emanated from him. I remember observing him and thinking "Yes, he's got the grace of God in him." The sight of him enabled me to relax and be reassured. I am sure he had no idea of the power and influence that was radiating from him. In those few days we got a real insight into gentleness. We were in the presence of someone who had let go, in order to make room for the love of God to operate in his life. Through him we got a glimpse of the glory of God in action.

A soft answer turns away wrath – *Proverbs 15.1*

Be gentle to all and stern with yourself – *St Teresa of Avila*

Show yourself humble in all things – *St Thomas à Kempis*

True humility is contentment – *Henri Frédéric Amiel*

True humility, the highest virtue, mother of them all – *Alfred, Lord*

Tennyson

I dwell in the high and holy place, and also with those who are contrite and humble in spirit – *Isaiah 57.15*

Humility like darkness reveals the heavenly lights – *Henry David Thoreau*

An humble able man is a jewel worth a kingdom – *William Penn*

Humility… is the ground-work of Christian virtues – *Charlotte Brontë*

Learn to humble yourself, you who are but earth and clay – *St Thomas à Kempis*

All paths open up before me because I walk in humility – *Johann Wolfgang von Goethe*

Take my yoke upon you, and learn from me; for I am gentle and humble in heart, and you will find rest for your souls – *Matthew 11.29*

Gentleness as the fruit of the Spirit is a strong man's treating all people with lenity, and kindness, and forbearance, and patience – *Henry Ward Beecher*

He is gentle that doth gentle deeds – *Geoffrey Chaucer*

Unto the humble He revealeth His secrets, and sweetly draweth nigh and inviteth him unto Himself – *St Thomas à Kempis*

There is no true and constant gentleness without humility – *Francois Fénelon*

I myself, Paul, appeal to you by the meekness and gentleness of Christ – *2 Corinthians 10.1*

Nothing is so strong as gentleness, nothing so gentle as real strength –

St Francis de Sales

The source of humility… is the habit of realizing the presence of God – *William Temple*

Humility rests upon the disclosure of the consummate wonder of God – *Thomas Kelly*

The fruit of the Spirit is…gentleness – *Galatians 5.23*

The humility of the saints comes from the vision of the glory, the majesty, the beauty of God – *Anthony Bloom*

The humble man, because he sees himself as nothing, can see other things as they are – *Iris Murdoch*

That something hidden away in my nature, like a treasure in a field, is Humility – *Oscar Wilde*

Humility is the recognition on your part and mine of our mind and spirit's need of God – *Alistair MacLean*

If anyone is detected in a transgression, you who have received the Spirit should restore such a one in a spirit of gentleness – *Galatians 6.1*

Humility contains in itself the answer to all the great problems of the life of the soul – *Thomas Merton*

It is only persons of firmness that can have real gentleness– *Francis, Duc de La Rochefoucauld*

Humble thyself in all things – *St Thomas à Kempis*

The gentle mind by gentle deeds is known – *Edmund Spenser*

Let your gentleness be known to everyone – *Philippians 4.5*

It's so easy to laugh, it's so easy to hate. It takes strength to be gentle and kind – *Stephen Morrissey*

Life is a long lesson in humility – *J. M. Barrie*

True humility is not an abject, grovelling self-despising spirit but it is a right estimate of ourselves as God sees us – *Tyron Edwards*

Pride makes us artificial and humility makes us real – *Thomas Merton*

The only wisdom we can hope to acquire is the wisdom of humility – humility is endless – *T.S. Eliot*

Clothe yourselves with compassion, kindness, humility, meekness and patience – *Colossians 3.12*

Humility is that holy place in which God bids us make the sacrifice of ourselves – *A Desert Father*

If you plan to build a tall house of virtues, you must first lay deep foundations of humility – *St Augustine*

I am persuaded that love and humility are the highest attainments in the school of Christ – *John Newton*

Pursue righteousness, godliness, faith, love, endurance, gentleness – *1 Timothy 6.11*

Christian humility is based on the sight of self, the vision of Christ, and the realization of God – *William Barclay*

We must view humility as one of the most essential things that characterizes true Christianity – *Jonathan Edwards*

There is no true and constant gentleness without humility – *Francois Fénelon*

Humility comes from the constant sense of our own creatureliness – *R.C. Trench*

And the Lord's servant must not be quarrelsome but kindly to everyone, an apt teacher, patient, correcting opponents with gentleness – *2 Timothy 2. 24-25*

Humility is not a grace that can be acquired in a few months: it is the work of a life-time - *Francois Fénelon*

Great peace is with the humble man, but in the heart of a proud man are always envy and anger – *St Thomas à Kempis*

There is certainly something in angling – that tends to produce a gentleness of spirit and a pure serenity of mind – *Washington Irving*

I believe the first test of a truly great man is his humility – *John Ruskin*

Humility is a grace in the soul. It is indescribable wealth, a name and a gift from God – *John Climacus*

Let gentleness my strong enforcement be – *William Shakespeare*

He who is gentle remembers good rather than evil, the good one has received rather than the good one has done – *Aristotle*

Humility is the virtue by which a man recognizes his own unworthiness because he really knows himself – *St Bernard of Clairvaux*

Without humility there can be no humanity – *John Buchan*

Humble yourselves therefore under the mighty hand of God, so that he may exalt you in due time. Cast all your anxieties on him, because he cares for you – 1 *Peter 5. 6-7*

Gentleness does more than violence – *Jean de la Fontaine*

Gentleness is love in society – *D.L. Moody*

The human mind is so constructed that it resists vigour and yields to gentleness – *St Francis de Sales*

Humility is nothing more than an accurate self-assessment, an awareness of oneself as one really is – *The Cloud of Unknowing*

Humility is a strange flower; it grows best in winter weather, and under storms of affliction – *Samuel Rutherford*

In the husband wisdom, in the wife gentleness – *English proverb*

If you are humble, nothing will touch you, neither praise nor disgrace, because you know what you are – *Mother Terasa*

Good manners and soft words have brought many a difficult thing to pass – *AEsop*

For faith is the beginning and the end is love, and God is the two of them brought together into unity. After these come whatever makes up a Christian gentleman – *St Ignatius of Antioch*

If you would reap praise, sow the seeds; gentle words and helpful deeds – *Benjamin Franklin*

A real gentleman is a combination of gentle strength and strong gentleness – *George Monaghan*

It is in worship, worship given to God because He is God, that man will most learn the secrets of real humility – *William Temple*

The Holy Ghost flows into the soul as fast as she is poured forth in humility and so far as she has gotten the capacity. He fills all the room he can find – *Meister Eckhart*

There must be feelings of humility, not from nature, but from penitence, not to rest in them, but to go on to greatness – *Blaise Pascal*

You will find Angling to be like the virtue of humility, which has a calmness of spirit, and a world of other blessings upon it – *Izaac Walton*

A contented mind is a continual feast – *English proverb*

The noblest mind the best contentment has – *Edmund Spenser*

A mind content, both Crown and Kingdom is – *Robert Greene*

Great wealth and content seldom live together – *Thomas Fuller*

Content will never dwell but in a meek and quiet soul – *Izaac Walton*

We only see in a lifetime a dozen faces marked with the peace of a contented spirit – *Henry Ward Beecher*

How seldom a face in repose is a face of serene content – *W.E. Sangster*

To be content with little is difficult; to be content with much, impossible – *Old Proverb*

The rarest feeling that ever lights the human face is the contentment of a loving soul – *Henry Ward Beecher*

Content is Wealth, the Riches of the Mind; and happy He who can that Treasure find – *John Dryden*

In order to be content men must also have the possibility of developing their intellectual and artistic powers to whatever extent accord with their personal characteristics and abilities – *Albert Einstein*

Those who face that which is actually before them, unburdened by the past, undistracted by the future, these are they who live, who make the best use of their lives; these are those who have found the sense of contentment –
Alban Goodier SJ

The smile that you send out returns to you – *Indian wisdom*

True humility is begotten by the worship of superiority, and chiefly by the worship of God – *Mark Rutherford*

Humility is the only key to faith, with which the spiritual life begins; for faith and humility are inseparable – *Thomas Merton*

The one who humbles himself – swims in the attributes of God, whose power, magnificence, greatness, and eternity have, through love, through humility, become our own – *Thomas Merton*

Let your dealing with those who begin with be so gentle, convincing, and winning, that the report of it may be an encouragement to others to come – *Richard Baxter*

Faithful service in a lowly place is true spiritual greatness – *D. Jackman*

It is right to be contented with what we have but never with what we are – *J. Mackintosh*

Your gentleness shall force more than your force moves us to gentleness – *William Shakespeare*

What is it to be a gentleman? The first to thank and the last to complain – *Serbian proverb*

It is the final test of a gentleman – his respect for those who can be of no possible service to him – *William Phelps*

He was the first gentleman of recorded history and the greatest gentleman who ever lived – *Irvin Cobb*

There is a politeness of the heart, and it is allied to love. It produces the most agreeable politeness of outward behaviour – *Johann Wolfgang von Goethe*

Content thyself to be obscurely good – *Joseph Addison*

True humility makes no pretence of being humble, and scarcely ever utters words of humility – *St Francis de Sales*

Love makes all hearts gentle – *English proverb*

Gentleness is invincible – *Marcus Aurelius*

Gently deal with souls untaught – *St Aidan*

Humility is pride in God – *Austin O'Malley*

There is something in humility which strangely exalts the heart – *St Augustine*

The more noble, the more humble – *John Ray*

The fruits of humility are love and peace – *Hebrew proverb*

Gentle to others, to himself severe – *Samuel Rogers*

The humility of Christ is not the moderation of keeping one's exact place in the scale of being, but rather that of absolute dependence on God, an absolute trust in him with the consequent ability to move mountains. The secret of the meekness and the gentleness of Christ lies in his relation to God – *H. Richard Niebuhr*

In peace there's nothing so becomes a man as modest stillness and humility – *William Shakespeare*

Unto the humble he revealeth His secrets, and sweetly draweth nigh and inviteth him unto Himself – *St Thomas à Kempis*

It is almost a definition of a gentleman to say he is one who never inflicts – *John Henry Newman*

It is only through the mystery of self-sacrifice that a man may find himself anew – *C.G. Jung*

Spirituality of life is justice and gentleness – *Lilian Whiting*

If thou wouldst become a pilgrim on the path of love, the first condition is that thou become as humble as dust – *Al Ansari*

This is the mark of Christianity: you are to be dead, that is, dead to the spirit and temper of the world, and live a new life in the Spirit of Jesus Christ – *William Law*

A soft, meek, patient, humble, tranquil spirit; the first true gentleman that ever breathed – *Thomas Dekker*

Not a weariness or painfulness endured patiently …but it enlarges the whole soul for the endless capacity of the love of God – *E.B. Pusey*

He who can preserve gentleness amid pains and peace amid worry and multitude of affairs, is almost perfect – *St Francis de Sales*

When you encounter difficulties and contradictions, do not try to break them, but bend them with gentleness and time – *St Francis de Sales*

Whosoever therefore grounds his virtue in humility, he shall never err – *John of Rysbroeck*

Gentle is that gentle does – *English proverb*

A soul enkindled with love is a gentle, meek, humble, and patient soul – *St John of the Cross*

Vanquish an angry man by gentleness – *Indian proverb*

True humility lies in seeing one's own unworthiness, giving oneself up to God, not doubting for a moment that he can perform the greatest results, for us and in us – *Francois Fénelon*

The reason why God is so great a lover of humility is because he is the great lover of truth. Now humility is nothing but truth, while pride is nothing but lying – *Vincent de Paul*

Men of courage, men of sense and men of letters are frequent, but a true fine gentleman is what one seldom sees – *Richard Steele*

17 SELF-CONTROL

We had a tragedy in our Oxford College. One evening a graduate student had too much to drink. His accommodation was two miles away in an annexe in North Oxford and his friends felt he was in no condition to cycle back to his abode. They took him to a room in College, and locked him in, trying to make sure he didn't attempt the journey.

He came too, some time later, and was furious to find himself imprisoned in this room. He opened the window and jumped out into the Fellows Garden. Unfortunately he mistakenly thought he was on the ground floor whereas in reality he was on the third floor. He was lucky to survive, but he did suffer permanent damage to his spine and from then onwards this affected the way he walked.

Self-control is difficult for all of us. Perhaps the contents of this topic may aid us in our life-long struggle to be self-controlled.

Set a guard over my mouth, O Lord; keep watch over the door of my lips – *Psalm 141.3*

No man is free who is not a master of himself – *Epictetus*

To enjoy freedom we have to control ourselves – *Virginia Woolf*

A mature person is one who is able to control his impulses – *Leonard Wedel*

If Passion drives, let Reason hold the Reins – *Benjamin Franklin*

Without discipline, there's no life at all – *Katharine Hepburn*

Those who guard their mouths preserve their lives – *Proverbs 13.3*

Conquer your passions and you conquer the whole world – *Hindu proverb*

To conquer self is the best and noblest victory – *Plato*

Rule your passions, or they will rule you – *Horace*

The best discipline, maybe the only discipline that really works is self-discipline – *Walter Kiechell 111*

One who is slow to anger is better than the mighty, and one whose temper is controlled than one who captures a city – *Proverbs 16.32*

Real glory springs from the silent conquest of ourselves – *Joseph P. Thompson*

Self-control is the mother of spiritual health – *John Climacus*

Control your appetites before they control you – *John Climacus*

It's not the mountain we conquer but ourselves – *Sir Edmund Hillary*

All the graces of a Christian spring from the death of self – *Madame Guyon*

Put a knife to your throat if you have a big appetite – *Proverbs 23.2*

Temperance is simply a disposition of the mind which sets bounds to the passions – *St Thomas Aquinas*

The I, the Self and the like must all be given up and done away – *Theologia Germanica*

All the activity of man in the works of self-denial has no good in itself, but is only to open an entrance for the only one Good, the light of God to operate upon us – *William Law*

We must learn to detach ourselves from all that is capable of being lost, to bind ourselves absolutely only to what is absolute and eternal – *Henri Frédéric Amiel*

Those who determine not to put self to death will never see the will of God fulfilled in their lives – *Sadhu Sundar Singh*

Life is a city breached, without walls, in one who lacks self-control – *Proverbs 25.28*

The power of man has grown in every sphere, except over himself – *Winston Churchill*

He who reigns within himself, and rules passions, desires, and fears, is more than a king – *John Milton*

I have conquered an empire but I have not been able to conquer myself – *Peter the Great*

There has never been, and cannot be, a good life, without self-control – *Leo Tolstoy*

A fool gives full vent to anger, but the wise quietly holds it back – *Proverbs 29.11*

Discipline is the secret of godliness. You must learn to discipline yourself for the purpose of godliness – *John Adams*

Intemperance is evident in one who thinks too much, too quickly, about too many subjects – *R.E.C. Browne*

We should thank God for beer and Burgundy by not drinking too much of them – *G.K. Chesterton*

A small but always persistent discipline is a great force; for a soft drop falling persistently hollows out hard rock – *Isaac of Nineveh*

Be on your guard so that your hearts are not weighed down with dissipation and drunkenness and the worries of this life, and that day does not catch you unexpectedly, like a trap – *Luke 21.34-35*

Temperance is quietness of mind in which concentration makes for profound lucid thinking – *R.E.C. Browne*

All forms of intemperance contain a neurotic element and arise from causes best described as spiritual – *R.E.C. Browne*

We must die to the narrow self in order to be raised to the wider and richer self – *Rufus M. Jones*

But I punish my body and enslave it, so that after proclaiming to others I myself should not be disqualified – *1 Corinthians 9.27*

There can be intemperance in work just as in drink – *C.S. Lewis*

The spiritual combat in which we kill our passions in order to put on the new man is the most difficult of all the arts – *Abba Nilus*

He, that has no government of himself, has no Enjoyment of himself – *Benjamin Whichcote*

However vast a man's spiritual resources, he is capable of but one great passion – *Blaise Pascal*

To go beyond the bounds of moderation is to outrage humanity – *Blaise Pascal*

For God did not give us a spirit of cowardice, but rather a spirit of power and of love and of self-discipline – *2 Timothy 1.7*

The true value of a human being is determined primarily by the measure and the sense in which he has attained liberation from the self – *Albert Einstein*

What we desire is often more than we require – *A.C. Benson*

Shun youthful passions and pursue righteousness – *2 Timothy 2.22*

No man really ever prospers in this world who violates the law of temperance or the law of God in the great matter of purity – *Henry Ward Beecher*

Religion is a restraint on man's passions and appetites, and so promotes his prosperity – *Henry Ward Beecher*

Let us take our bloated nothingness out of the paths of the divine circuits – *Ralph Waldo Emerson*

Let us lie low in the Lord's power, and learn that truth alone makes rich and great – *Ralph Waldo Emerson*

If any think they are religious, and do not bridle their tongues but deceive their hearts, their religion is worthless – *James 1.26*

Be charitable and indulgent to everyone but thyself – *Joseph Joubert*

Anything which increases the authority of the body over the mind is an evil thing – *Susannah Wesley*

Love it is – not conscious – that is God's regent in the human soul, because it can govern the soul as nothing else can – *Henry Ward Beecher*

The intemperate talk too much to too many people, taking too many into their confidence – *R.E.C. Browne*

Temperance is love in training – *D.L. Moody*

You must make every effort to support your faith with goodness, and goodness with knowledge, and knowledge with self-control, and self-control with endurance –

A STILL MORE EXCELLENT WAY

2 Peter 1.5-6

Do not give too much way to thy passions, if thou dost expect happiness – *Henry Fielding*

Take heed lest Passion sway – *John Milton*

To grow old is to pass from passion to compassion – *Albert Camus*

He conquers who overcomes himself – *Latin proverb*

We regard intemperance in any area of living as being inconsistent with the Christian life – *Moravian Covenant for Christian Living*

Let your temperance be known because the truth can only be spoken and done by temperate men – *R.E.C. Browne*

The discipline of desire is the background of character – *John Locke*

What is difficult is to control the tongue, to act with integrity, to show forth the fruit of the Spirit – *R.C. Sproul*

Listening is a conscious, willed action, requiring alertness and vigilance, by which our whole attention is focused and controlled – *Mother Mary Clare SLG*

There is a sufficiency in the world for man's need but not for man's greed – *Mohandas K. Gandhi*

Greed has three facets: love of things, love of fame, and love of pleasure; and these can be attacked directly with frugality, anonymity, and moderation – *Paul Martin*

We must be anchored in self-discipline if we are to venture successfully in freedom – *Harold E. Kohn*

No indulgence of passion destroys the spiritual nature so much as respectable selfishness – *George MacDonald*

Cast all your cares on God; that anchor holds – *Alfred, Lord Tennyson*

He has not learned the lesson of life who does not every day surmount a fear – *Ralph Waldo Emerson*

It is a help to have something to do, and not to creep about in a dim fatiguing dream of anxiety – *A.C. Benson*

I know well the feeling of being all tense with business and worry. The only cure is the old one …whenever you have too much to do, don't do it" – *A.C. Benson*

Anxiety usually comes from strain, and strain is caused by too complete a dependence on ourselves, on our own devices, our own plans, our own idea of what we are able to do – *Thomas Merton*

It was Jesus' conviction that worry is banished when God becomes the dominant power in our lives… Jesus says that worry can be defeated when we acquire the art of living one day at a time – *William Barclay*

Anger is never without a Reason, but seldom with a good one – *Benjamin Franklin*

To be angry, is to revenge the faults of others upon ourselves – *Alexander Pope*

Call for the grandest of all earthly spectacles – what is *that*? Call for the grandest of all human sentiments, what is *that*? It is that man should forget his anger before he lies down to sleep – *Thomas de Quincey*

To be angry…is what any man can do and easy: but to do these to the right person, in due proportion, at the right time, with a right object, and in the right manner, this is not as before what any man can do nor is it easy – *Aristotle*

Ennui, perhaps, has made more gamblers than avarice, more

drunkards than thirst, and perhaps, as many suicides as despair. It's only cure is the pursuit of some desirable object – *C.C. Colton*

Half the spiritual difficulties that men and women suffer arise from a morbid state of health – *Henry Ward Beecher*

More people are destroyed by unhappiness than by drink, drugs, disease, or even failure. There must be something about sadness which attracts or people would not accept it so readily into their lives – *Hubert van Zeller*

For there is no despair so absolute as that which comes with the first moments of our first great sorrow, when we have not yet known what it is to have suffered and be healed, to have despaired and to have recovered hope – *George Eliot*

Then black despair, the shadow of a starless night, was thrown over the world in which I moved alone – *Percy Bysshe Shelley*

Drunkenness ... is merely temporary suicide; the happiness that it brings is merely negative, a momentary cessation of unhappiness – *Bertrand Russell*

All excess is ill; but drunkenness is the worst sort. It destroys health, dismounts the mind, and unmans man. It reveals secrets, is quarrelsome, lascivious, impudent, dangerous, and mad. In fine he that is drunk is not a man – *William Penn*

Our passions are wild beasts. God grant us power to muzzle them – *Sir Walter Scott*

To control our passions, we must govern our habits, and keep watch over ourselves in the small details of everyday life – *Sir John Lubbock*

Every man is a tamer of wild beasts, and these wild beasts are his passions. To draw their teeth and claws, to muzzle and tame them, to turn them into servants and domestic animals, fuming, perhaps, but submissive – in this consists personal education – *Henri Frédéric Amiel*

Temperate temperance is best; intemperate temperance injures the cause of temperance – *Mark Twain*

Gluttony, intemperance, sluggishness induced by oversleep, and the draining of the system by an inordinate indulgence of the passions, dull the reason, and make a man slow and inefficient – *Henry Ward Beecher*

A man is to be temperate in all things – even in the practice of the virtues and specially in the practice of temperance – *R.E.C. Browne*

Temperance does not lie in not doing too much of anything, but in a general sobriety of living in which a person is controlling what can be controlled and does not attempt to control what cannot be controlled – *R.E.C. Browne*

The intemperate are too grateful, too sympathetic, too prone to give advice – *R.E.C. Browne*

To be intemperate is to have too much travelling on account of too many appointments, committees, obligations, commitments and responsibilities – *R.E.C. Browne*

The temperate man knows that a man's life, and usefulness, does not consist in the abundance of his activities; he knows also that the attempt to do too many pieces of work, at the same time, has almost the same result as if no such attempt were made – *R.E.C. Browne*

Temperance entails a ruthless selection of activities on the part of artists, scientists, philosophers, social workers, pastors and all other serious people – *R.E.C. Browne*

Anger is one of the sinews of the soul. He who lacks it hath a maimed mind – *Thomas Fuller*

Wickedness sucks in the greater part of its own venom, and poisons itself therewith – *Michel de Montaigne*

We should employ our passions in the service of life, not spend life in the service of our passions – *Richard Steele*

(Temperance) is that action whereby the soul extricates itself from the love of a lower beauty and wings its way to true stability and finds security in God! – *St Augustine*

Where is temperance to be found if not in the life of Christ? Those alone are temperate who strive to imitate his life…whose life is the mirror of temperance – *St Augustine*

Conscience is the voice of the soul as the passions are the voice of the body – *Jean Jacques Rousseau*

A movement of the soul contrary to nature in the sense of disobedience to reason, that is what the passions are – *St Clement of Alexandria*

Passions are vices or virtues in their highest powers – *Johann Wolfgang von Goethe*

All great virtues bear the imprint of self-denial – *William E. Channing*

They that deny themselves for Christ shall enjoy themselves in Christ – *John Mason*

Freedom is that faculty which enlarges the usefulness of all other faculties – *Immanuel Kant*

Liberty of spirit is a detachment of the Christian heart from all things to follow the known will of God – *St Francis de Sales*

If you are to be self-controlled in your speech you must be self-controlled in your thinking – *Francois Fénelon*

No bad man is free – *Greek proverb*

There is nothing that wastes the body like worry, and one who has any faith in God should be ashamed to worry about anything whatsoever – *Mohandas K. Gandhi*

God never ceases to speak to us, but the noise of the world without and the tumult of our passions within bewilder us and prevent us from listening to him – *Francois Fénelon*

All the troubles of life come upon us because we refuse to sit quietly for a while each day in our rooms – *Blaise Pascal*

He that overcomes his anger conquers his greatest enemy – *Latin proverb*

The best answer to anger is silence – *German proverb*

When angry, count ten before you speak; when very angry count a hundred – *Thomas Jefferson*

Complete abstinence is easier than perfect moderation – *St Augustine*

Abundance, like wants, ruins many – *Romanian proverb*

What we all want is inward rest, rest of heart and brain; the calm and strong, self-contained, self-denying character…the character in a word which is truly temperate, not in drink and food merely, but in all desires, thoughts, and actions – *Charles Kingsley*

Temperance is a readiness to pay attention to what others have to say and only talking about subjects appropriate to the occasion and relationships – *R.E.C. Browne*

Temperance is grateful and sympathetic in proportion to the occasion for gratitude or sympathy – *R.E.C. Browne*

Our passions are regular phoenixes. As the old one is consumed, straightway the new rises out of the ashes – *Johann Wolfgang von Goethe*

The passion to get ahead is sometimes born of a fear lest we get left behind – *Eric Hoffer*

The way to avoid evil is not by maiming our passions, but by compelling them to yield their vigour to our moral nature – *Henry Ward Beecher*

Anger punishes itself – *Thomas Fuller*

Self-reverence, self-knowledge, self-control, these three alone lead life to sovereign power – *Alfred, Lord Tennyson*

18 LIFE

The following passage is so important that it is going to form the entire introduction to "Life"

"The greatest danger facing all of us is that we may fail to perceive life's greatest meaning, fall short of its highest good, miss its deeper and most abiding happiness, be unable to render the most needed service, be unconscious of life ablaze with the Presence of God – and be content to have it so – that is the danger; that some day we may wake up and find that always we have been busy with the husks and trappings of life and have really missed life itself. For life without God, to one who has known the richness and joy of life with Him, is unthinkable, impossible. That is what one prays one's friends may be spared – satisfaction with a life that falls short of the best, that has in it no tingle or thrill that comes from a friendship with the Father."

The author is Bishop Phillips Brooks, an American Bishop of the nineteenth century. I think most of us get caught up with the husks and trappings of life, and clergy are just as prone to this as lay-people, and non-believers.

> Then the Lord God formed man from the dust of the ground, and breathed into his nostrils the breath of life; and man became a living being – *Genesis 2.7*

The secret of life is to be found in life itself; in the full organic, intellectual and spiritual activities of our body – *Alexis Carrel*

Man cannot find the ultimate explanation of his own being anywhere but in God himself – *Edward Sillem*

Reflect that life, like ev'ry other blessing, derives its value from its use alone – *Samuel Johnson*

Life is not a holiday, but an education. And the one eternal lesson for us all to know is how much better we can love – *Henry Drummond*

The life of the individual only has meaning insofar as it aids in making the life of every living thing nobler and more beautiful – *Albert Einstein*

I have set before you life and death…choose life – *Deuteronomy 30.19*

Human life is the expression of a spiritual existence, which we know has its glory in spiritual values and in spiritual beauty – *Father Andrew SDC*

The unexamined life is not worth living – *Socrates*

Each person must look to himself to teach him the meaning of life. It is not something to be moulded – *Antoine de Saint-Exupéry*

Unless a life is lived for others, it is not worthwhile – *Mother Teresa*

For whoever finds me (wisdom) finds life – *Proverbs 8.35*

The life of the spiritual adventure, the sense of being on a journey in time – *John S. Dunne*

Life is love – *Johann Wolfgang von Goethe*

The greatest use of life is to spend it for something that will outlast it – *William James*

Incline your ear, and come to me; listen, so that you may live – *Isaiah 55.3*

Life is sacred, that is to say, it is the supreme value to which all other values are subordinate – *Albert Einstein*

To live as fully, as completely as possible, to be happy and again to be happy is the true aim and end of life. 'Ripeness is all' – *Llewellyn Powys*

There are real ends in life, and they are all in that realm which always belongs to us in virtue of our spiritual and intellectual capacities, and not of our animal capacities – *William Temple*

You are the salt of the earth – *Matthew 5.13*

Life is either a daring adventure or nothing – *Helen Keller*

The devastating richness of life – *J. Neville Ward*

If we could adapt ourselves more to the life of God within us we would be more able to adapt ourselves to the will of God as expressed all about us – *Hubert van Zeller*

There have been many lives like those of St Francis, Gandhi and Schweitzer, which have shown how great is the human potential for heroic living – *George H. Gorman*

Do not worry about your life, what you will eat or what you will drink, or about your body, what you will wear. Is not life more than food, and the body more than clothing? – *Matthew 6.25*

Make me useful, positive, appreciative, generous; make me live – *Norman W. Goodacre*

The value of life lies not in the length of days, but in the use we make of them – *Michel de Montaigne*

Everything has been figured out, except how to live – *Jean-Paul Sartre*

The mystery of life is not a problem to be solved; it is a reality to be experienced – *J.J. van der Leeuw*

For the gate is narrow and the road is hard that leads to life, and there are few who find it – *Matthew 7.14*

Humour is mankind's greatest blessing – *Mark Twain*

Creative life is always on the yonder side of convention – *C.G. Jung*

There must be more to life than having everything – *Maurice Sendak*

Not a May-Game is this man's life; but a battle and a march, a warfare with principalities and powers – *Thomas Carlyle*

He who has learned to pray has learned the greatest secret of a holy and happy life – *Llewelyn Powys*

For what will it profit them if they gain the whole world but forfeit their life? – *Matthew 16.26*

Is life so wretched? Isn't it rather your hands which are too small, your vision which is muddied? You are the one who must grow up – *Dag Hammarskjöld*

Hard conditions of life are indispensable to bring out the best in human personality – *Alexis Carrel*

He lives most who thinks most; feels the noblest; acts the best – *P.J. Bailey*

The web of our life is of a mingled yarn, good and ill together – *William Shakespeare*

I am the bread of life. Whoever comes to me will never be hungry, and whoever believes in me shall never be thirsty – *John 6.35*

The highest revelation is that of God in man – *Ralph Waldo Emerson*

The highest we have power to be – *W.E. Sangster*

Life – fullness of Personality in the widest possible Fellowship – *William Temple*

Secret prayer is the spring-time of life – *Evan Roberts*

I came that they may have life, and have it abundantly – *John 10.10*

The one thing needful for a man is to *become* – to *be* at last, and to die in the fullness of being – *Antoine de Saint-Exupéry*

The rule of life for a perfect person is to be in the image and likeness of God – *St Clement of Alexandria*

There is more to life than increasing its speed – *Mohandas K. Gandhi*

To be alive, to be man alive, to be whole man alive; that is the point – *D.H. Lawrence*

I am…the life – *John 14.6*

After all it is those who have a deep and real inner life who are best able to deal with the "irritating details of outer life" – *Evelyn Underhill*

When he is in possession of his soul, then will man be fully alive – *Henry Miller*

In him we live and move and have our being – *Acts 17.28*

The most wonderful of all things in life, I believe, is the discovery of another human being with whom one's relationship has a glowing depth, beauty and joy as the years increase. This inner progressiveness of love between two human beings is a most marvellous thing, it cannot be found by looking for it or by passionately wishing for it. It is a sort of Divine accident – *Sir Hugh Walpole*

A man can be so busy making a living that he forgets to make a life – *William Barclay*

Life …is energy of love – *William Wordsworth*

What counts is that you are fully alive in any situation – *Neville Cryer*

I have been crucified with Christ; and it is no longer I who live, but it is Christ who lives in me – *Galatians 2.19-20*

Adventure is the champagne of life – *G.K. Chesterton*

I asked God for all things, that I might enjoy life. God gave me life, that I might enjoy all things – *found on the body of a Confederate soldier*

Our life is what our thoughts make it – *Catherine of Siena*

If a person gets his attitude toward money straight, it will straighten out almost every other area in his life – *Billy Graham*

The tragedy of much modern life, is that the abandonment of the knowledge of God means that futility has taken over – *Leon Morris*

For in him the whole fullness of deity dwells bodily, and you have come to fullness of life in him – *Colossians 2.9*

Adventure is not outside a man, it is within – *David Grayson*

Living a good, decent, Christian life is what's important, live that life and the rest will follow – *Spike Milligan*

All life is growth. This is especially true of the spiritual life. It

continually grows.
To stand still, to look back is death – *Herbert Slade*

The most satisfactory thing in life is to have been able to give a large part of oneself to others – *Pierre Teilhard de Chardin*

The seed dies into a new life, and so does man – *George MacDonald*

We make a living by what we get, but we make a life by what we give – *Martin Luther King*

The majority of men exist but do not live – *Benjamin Disraeli*

All life is meeting – *Martin Buber*

The tragedy of life is what dies inside us while we live – *Albert Schweitzer*

Men of integrity, by their very existence, rekindle the belief that as a people we can live above the level of moral squalor – *John Gardner*

He who has learned to pray has learned the greatest secret of a holy and happy life – *William Law*

Theirs is an endless road, a hopeless maze, who seek for goods before they seek for God – *St John Chrysostom*

Living in selfishness means stopping at human limits and preventing our transformation into Divine Love – *Carlo Carretto*

Life is its own journey; pre-supposes its own change and movement, and one tries to arrest them at one's eternal peril – *Laurens van der Post*

What makes our lives worth while is stretching towards God who is love and truth. That we reach out beyond our capacity, is at once our pain, our adventure, our hope – *Hubert van Zeller*

Life, as Christianity has always taught, as all clear-eyed observers have known,
is a perilous adventure, and a perilous adventure for men and nations it will, I fear and believe, remain – *W. MacNeile Dixon*

The true spiritual goal of life is the formation of a rightly fashioned will, the creation of a controlling personal love, the experience of a guiding inward Spirit, which keep the awakened soul steadily approximating the perfect Life which Christ has revealed – *Rufus M. Jones*

People are always blaming their circumstances for what they are. I don't believe in circumstances. The people who get on in this world are the people who get up and look for the circumstances they want, and, if they can't find them, make them – *George Bernard Shaw*

Life is a unique experience – *W. MacNeile Dixon*

We come fully to life only in meeting one another – *John S. Dunne*

I want to prepare you, to organize you for life, for illness, crisis and death…Live all you can – as complete and full a life as you can find - do as much as you can for others. Read, work, enjoy – love and help as many souls – do all this –
Friedrich von Hügel

Only a life lived for others is worth living – *Albert Einstein*

I am never better than when I am on the full stretch for God – *George Whitfield*

The quality of a person's life is in direct proportion to their commitment to excellence, regardless of their chosen field of endeavour – *Vincent Lombardi*

Happiness, I have discovered, is nearly always a rebound from hard work – *David Grayson*

Heaven is not to be looked upon only as the reward, but as the natural effect, of a religious life – *Joseph Addison*

The main object of religion is not to get a man into heaven, but to get heaven into him – *Thomas Hands*

It's not your ability, it's God's ability flowing through you – *Benny Hinn*

He became what we are that he might make us what he is – *Athanasius of Alexandria*

The aim of preaching is not the elucidation of a subject, but the transformation of a person – *Halford E. Luccock*

We must never separate what God does for us from what God does in us – *Charles Gore*

The sincere alone can recognize sincerity – *Thomas Carlyle*

The Church of Christ is not an institution; it is a new life with Christ and in Christ, guided by the Holy Spirit – *Sergius Belgakov*

There is something in man which your science cannot satisfy – *Thomas Carlyle*

If our life is not a course of humility, self-denial, renunciation of the world, poverty of spirit, and heavenly affection, we do not live the lives of Christians – *William Law*

It is one of the great principles of Christianity that all that happened to Jesus Christ must fulfil itself in the spirit and body of every Christian – *Blaise Pascal*

It is only through the mystery of self-sacrifice that a man may find himself anew – *C.G. Jung*

We are stripped bare by the curse of plenty – *Winston Churchill*

(The world is suffering) a neurosis of emptiness – *C. G. Jung*

Fundamental progress has to do with the reinterpretation of basic ideas – *Alfred North Whitehead*

Nothing is so deadening to the divine as an habitual dealing with the outsides of holy things – *George MacDonald*

Life is too short to be little – *Benjamin Disraeli*

To the inner man, to the psyche within us, whose life is warmer, nebulous and plastic, compromise seems the path of profit and justice – *George Santayana*

He would not let them take away my soul. Possessing that, I still possess the whole – *Helen Keller*

God is not an idea, or a definition that we have committed to memory, he is a presence which we experience in our hearts – *Louis Evely*

Have a heart that never hardens, and a temper that never tires, and a touch that never hurts – *Charles Dickens*

The righteousness of Jesus is the righteousness of a Godward relationship of trust, dependence, receptivity – *Michael Ramsey*

The beginning of anxiety is the end of faith, and the beginning of true faith is the end of anxiety – *George Müller*

The adventure of living has not really begun until we begin to stand on our own faith legs and claim…the resources of our God – *Catherine Marshall*

The only thing men have not learned to do is to stick up for their own instinctive feelings, against the things they are taught – *D.H. Lawrence*

To be worth anything, character must be capable of standing firm upon its feet in the world of daily work, temptation and trial, and able to bear the wear and tear of actual life. Cloistered virtues do not count for much – *Samuel Smiles*

All one's life is music, if one touches the notes rightly and in tune – *John Ruskin*

Every man has in himself a continent of undiscovered character. Happy is he who acts the Columbus to his own soul – *Sir John Stevens*

Everything that is born of God is truly no shadowy work, but a true life work. God will not bring forth a dead fruit, a lifeless and powerless work, but a living, new man must be born from the living God – *Johann Arndt*

To be alive, and not half-dead seek Jesus who is alive. Seek Him even if you seem to have lost Him. He loves you. Finding Him, you will find everything: love, peace, trust. Then life is worth living – *Roger Schultz*

The Father is our fount and origin, in whom our life and being is begun – *John of Ruysbroeck*

Realize that you must lead a dying life; the more a man dies to himself, the more he begins to live unto God – *St Thomas à Kempis*

"Eternal life" is the sole sanction for the values of this life – *Dorothy Sayers*

No wise man wants a soft life – *King Alfred*

Life is a mystery to be lived, not a problem to be solved – *Van Kaam*

The game of life is not so much in holding a good hand as in playing a poor hand well – *H.T. Leslie*

Integrity is the noblest possession – *Latin proverb*

Try not to become a man of success but rather try to become a man of value – *Albert Einstein*

There is within every soul a thirst for happiness and meaning – *St Thomas Aquinas*

To do my duty in that state of life unto which it shall please God to call me – *The Book of Common Prayer*

Real life is meeting – *J.H. Oldham*

The problem of life is not to make life easier, but to make men stronger – *David Storr Jordan*

Prayer is continual abandonment to God – *Sadhu Sundar Singh*

It is what you do with your life that counts – *Martin Luther King*

We too must have life in ourselves. We too, must like the Life himself, live. We can live in no way but that in which Jesus himself lived, in which life was made in him – *George MacDonald*

I do know that trying to be open to things that are good, and beautiful, and true, wherever they are to be found, brings me a strength that is greater than my own – *George Gorman*

You will soon break the bow if you keep it always stretched – *Phaedrus*

Life, if well used, is long enough – *Seneca*

This life, this Kingdom of God, this simplicity of absolute existence, is hard to enter. How hard? As hard as the master of salvation could find words to express the hardness – *George MacDonald*

19 LIGHT

An experience of 'healing' in Bradford affected me greatly. I was visiting a patient in hospital, during my weekly rounds. I knocked on the door and got a rather weak "come in." I met Douglas for the first time. He had just had major surgery and was recovering from the operation. He looked at me intently and asked me if I believed in faith healing? To which I replied, "Yes, if I felt the circumstances were right." He then asked me to lay hands on him and pray for healing.

I saw him the following week and he was greatly improved. We ended our session again with the laying on of hands. Eventually he made a good recovery and put it down mainly to faith healing.

I left Bradford shortly afterwards to work in London. After a year his wife rang me up to tell me Douglas had died. She didn't want me to rush up, she was feeling all right. "Douglas," she said, "died in a remarkable way." When she visited him in hospital she noticed "light" was emanating from his features. When I saw her a few days later I was taken aback by her appearance – this light was now emanating from her features.

Then God said, 'Let there be light'; and there was light" – *Genesis 1.3*

I am aware of something in myself *whose shine is my reason*...it
    seems to me that if I could grasp it, I should know all truth –
    Meister Eckhart

Christ the Light of the World shines first upon the soul, and then from within the soul upon the path of life – *William Temple*

As we let our light shine, we unconsciously give other people permission to do the same – *Nelson Mandela*

There is a Light in man which shines into his darkness, reveals his condition to him, makes him aware of evil and checks him when he is in the pursuit of it – *Rufus M. Jones*

The Light gives him a vision of righteousness, attracts him towards goodness, and points him infallibly toward Christ from whom the Light shines – *Rufus M. Jones*

The Lord make his face to shine upon you, and be gracious to you; the Lord lift up his countenance upon you, and give you peace – *Numbers 6.25-26*

Christ walked in the full light of God, we only have flashes of it – *Edward Wilson*

Open your heart to the influence of the light, which, from time to time, breaks in upon you – *Samuel Johnson*

A man should learn to detect and watch that gleam of light which flashes across his mind from within – *Ralph Waldo Emerson*

The doctrine of Christ in every man…the Light who lights every one who comes into the world – *Charles Kingsley*

You are the light of the world – but only because you are enkindled, made radiant by the One Light of the World – *Evelyn Underhill*

It is you who light my lamp; the Lord, my God, lights up my darkness – *Psalm 18.28*

Express Yourself – Radiantly

He has asked us not merely to reflect the light, but to *be* it – *Hubert van Zeller*

Jesus is the very light of God come among men; and Jesus is the light which gives men life – *William Barclay*

He who lives up to a little light shall have more light – *Thomas Brooks*

Time…is what keeps the light from reaching us. There is no greater obstacle to God than time – *Meister Eckhart*

The Lord is my light and my salvation; whom shall I fear? – *Psalm 27.1*

Of the great world of light that lies behind all human destinies – *Henry Wadsworth Longfellow*

Thou must abide within thyself; to the Light that is in thee thou must turn thee; there thou will find it and nowhere else – *Rufus M. Jones*

The real tragedy of life is when men are afraid of the light – *Plato*

What is that light whose gentle beams now and again strike through to my heart, causing me to shudder in awe yet firing me with their warmth? I shudder to feel how different I am from it; yet in so far as I am like it, I am aglow with its fire – *St Augustine*

Mind therefore, the Light that is in thee – *Rufus M. Jones*

Your word is a lamp to my feet and a light to my path – *Psalm 119.105*

The Light is that which illumines every person coming into this world – *St Augustine*

This is the light which grows in us, which urges us on to greater understanding of the beauties of people and of the universe and gradually calls us forth to wondorment and contentment – *Jean*

Vanier

Lead me from darkness to light! – *Upanishad*

Radiant personality – *W.E. Sangster*

Jesus is the Light of the World. He has taken a human nature and in that human nature has set the light of the Divine Nature, so revealing what human nature was meant for. It was meant for this great end, that in it should shine the Divine Light – *Father Andrew SDC*

Arise, shine; for your light has come, and the glory of the Lord has risen upon you – *Isaiah 60.1*

If there is light in the soul, there will be beauty in the person – *Chinese proverb*

The evening of life brings with it, its lamps – *Joseph Joubert*

God's dazzling radiance in himself – *Michael Ramsey*

All spiritual light, the light of beauty of thought, of purity of love, of goodness in people everywhere, has come from the source of light, which is God –
Father Andrew SDC

Hast never come to thee an hour, a sudden gleam divine, precipitating, bursting all these bubbles, fashions, wealth? These eager business aims – books, politics, art, amours, to utter nothingness? – *Walt Whitman*

Those who are wise shall shine like the brightness of the sky – *Daniel 12.3*

This is the light as it grows in us…to love reality – *Jean Vanier*

Now the Lord God hath opened to me by his invisible power how that every man was enlightened by the divine light of Christ – *George Fox*

An age is called Dark, not because the light fails to shine, but because people refuse to see it – *James Michener*

The more man becomes irradiated with the divinity of Christ, the more, not the less, truly he is man – *Phillips Brooks*

There is a direct in-shining, a direct in-breathing, a direct in-reaching of the Divine Soul upon the human soul – *Henry Ward Beecher*

I will light in your heart the lamp of understanding, which shall not be put out – *2 Esdras 14.25*

The fire of God fills him: I never saw his like: there lives no greater leader – *Alfred, Lord Tennyson*

The illumination, grace, and power of God the Holy Spirit – *Norman Goodacre*

The dark night of the soul through which the soul passes on its way to the Divine Light – *St John of the Cross*

My very soul was filled with celestial light – *Frances Crosby*

You are the light of the world. A city built on a hill cannot be hidden. No one after lighting a lamp puts it under a bushel basket, but on the lampstand, and it gives light to all in the house – *Matthew 5.14*

The ideals which have lighted my way…have been Kindness, Beauty and Truth – *Albert Einstein*

This Light is pure, immediate, and spiritual. It is of God, in fact it is God immanently revealed – *Rufus M. Jones*

The divine light shows the excellent loveliness of God's nature – *Jonathan Edwards*

Let your light shine before others, so that they may see your good works and give glory to your Father in heaven – *Matthew 5.16*

But whatever you have ever read or heard, concerning which there has been that inner flash, that sudden certainty, then in God's name heed it, for it is the truth – *Leslie Weatherhead*

Reason is a light which God has kindled in the soul – *Aristotle*

I arrived at Truth, not by systematic reasoning and accumulation of proofs but by a flash of light which God sent into my soul – *Al-Ghazali*

In him was life, and the life was the light of all people – *John 1.4*

This Light and Spirit, though always within us, is not, cannot be found, felt, or enjoyed but by those whose whole Spirit is turned to it – *William Law*

'The Depth of God within the Soul', the Inner Light, is the precious Pearl, the never-failing Comfort, the Panacea for all diseases, the sure Antidote even against death itself, the unfailing Guide and Way of all Wisdom – *Rufus M. Jones*

The true light, which enlightens everyone, was coming into the world – *John 1.9*

I thought the Light of Heaven was in this world: I saw it possible, and very probable, that I was infinitely beloved of Almighty God, the delights of Paradise were round about me, Heaven and earth were open to me, all riches were little things; this one pleasure being so great that it exceeded all the joys of Eden – *Thomas Traherne*

But those who do what is true come to the light – *John 3.21*

That Light whose smile kindles the Universe. That Beauty in which all things work more and *more* – *Percy Bysshe Shelley*

He was a burning and shining lamp, and you were willing to rejoice for a while in his light – *John 5.35*

The Spirit in man is the candle of the Lord, lighted by God, and lighting men to God – *Benjamin Whichcote*

Light – mental illumination, elucidation, enlightenment, vivacity in a person's face, especially in the eyes, illumination of the soul by divine truth – *The Concise Oxford Dictionary*

I am the light of the world. Whoever follows me will never walk in darkness but will have the light of life – *John 8.12*

A great floodlight of hope into our valleys of trouble – *Charles Hembree*

Illuminate – light up, give spiritual or intellectual light; to throw light upon (subject); shed lustre upon, light up, spiritually; brighten, elucidate – throw light upon, explain Enlighten – instruct, inform, (person on subject); give light to (person); free person from prejudice or superstition – *The Concise Oxford Dictionary*

While you have the light, believe in the light, so that you may become children of light – *John 12.36*

Irradiated with the light of the presence of Jesus Christ – *William Barclay*

A candle lights others and consumes itself – *Jewish proverb*

Fill me, Radiancy divine – *Charles Wesley from the hymn – Christ, whose glory fills the skies*

The only light upon the future is faith – *Isaac Hecker*

Be aglow with the Spirit – *Romans 12.11 (RSV)*

As far as we can discern, the sole purpose of human existence is to kindle a light in the darkness of mere being – *C.G. Jung*

To reflect God in all that is, both here and now, my heart must be a mirror empty, bright and clear – *Angelus Silesius*

Example is always more efficacious than precept – *Samuel Johnson*

Example is the school of mankind, and they will learn at no other – *Edmund Burke*

He is the reflection of God's glory and the exact imprint of God's very being – *Hebrews 1.3*

I think that the purpose and cause of the Incarnation was that God might illuminate the world by his wisdom and excite it to the love of Himself – *Peter Abelard*

What in me is dark illumine, what is low raise and support – *John Milton*

There is a God within us, and we glow when He stirs us – *Ovid*

Those who have once been enlightened, and have tasted the heavenly gift, and have shared in the Holy Spirit, and have tasted the goodness of the word of God and the powers of the age to come – *Hebrews 6.4-5*

Something fiery and star-like gleamed from his eyes and the majesty of Godhead shone from his countenance – *St Jerome*

Those who bring sunshine to the lives of others cannot keep it from themselves – *J.M. Barrie*

The man who has lighted his life from Christ's love, is constant in trials, patient in sufferings, courageous in assaults, prudent in difficulties, victorious and triumphant in action – *Rufus M. Jones*

In order that you may proclaim the mighty acts of him who called you out of darkness into his marvellous light – *1 Peter 2.9*

His eye (that of Jacob Boehme) fell by chance upon the surface of a polished pewter dish which reflected the bright sunlight, when suddenly he felt himself environed and penetrated by the Light of God, and admitted into the innermost ground and centre of the universe – *Rufus M. Jones*

God is nearer unto every man than himself, because He penetrates the most inward and intimate parts of men and is the Light of the inmost spirit – *Rufus M. Jones*

Lead kindly Light, amid the encircling gloom, lead Thou me on – *John Henry Newman*

It is written, "For God is light" – not the light seen by these eyes of ours, but that which the heart sees upon hearing the words, "He is Truth" – *St Augustine*

It would scarcely be necessary to expound doctrine if our lives were radiant enough.
If we behaved like true Christians, there would be no pagans – *Pope John XXIII*

Where the ray of God's light shall fall upon my path, there will I walk and in his strength perform without inquietude the work that his providence shall set me – *Francois Fénelon*

20 TRUTH

A reminder of the Genesis story of the creation of humankind. As a consequence of the divine inbreathing we are born with a seed or spark of *truth* in the depths of our being. The consequences of this were fully worked out in the life of Christ – hence Jesus' words "I am the truth." Jesus also knew this inner truth was part of our heritage, and promised his disciples – "you will know the truth, and the truth will make you free." In a resurrection appearance in the upper room Jesus stood among them and said: "Peace be with you,"…and when he had said this he breathed on them and said to them, "Receive the Holy Spirit." and before long the lives of the disciples were changed.

Paul realized what Christ had experienced, we can all in some measure also experience. Hence he used this intriguing phrase of his own experience: "As the truth of Christ is in me…"

A relatively modern writer, Rufus Jones wrote concisely on this: "To find the Truth we must break through the outward shell of words and phrases which house it, and by *experience and practice* discover the "inward beauty, life and loveliness of Truth."

This is where contemplation on "Truth" comes in enabling us to grow in Truth.

Now I know that you are a man of God, and that the word of the Lord in your mouth is truth – *1 Kings 17.24*

Rather than love, than money, than fame, give me truth – *Henry David Thoreau*

The desire for truth is the desire for God – *John Macquarrie*

The ultimate ground of faith and knowledge is confidence in God – *Charles Hodge*

Whoever lives true life, will love true love – *Elizabeth Barrett Browning*

You desire truth in the inward being; therefore teach me wisdom in my secret heart – *Psalm 51.6*

The friend of Truth obeys not the multitude, *but the Truth* – *Rufus M. Jones*

Truth… loves to be centrally located – *Herman Melville*

What do we mean when we speak of a man of integrity? One who will be true to the highest he knows; who will never betray the truth or trifle with it – *George Appleton*

Truth is precious and divine – *Samuel Butler*

(Truth) must be loved for its own sake – *Michel de Montaigne*

Consider how I love your precepts; preserve my life according to your steadfast love – *Psalm 119.159*

Say not, "I have found the truth", but rather, 'I have found a truth' – *Kahlil Gibran*

In the usefulness of truth lies the hope of humanity – *Norman Douglas*

Truth is whatever delights the higher in you – *Alistair MacLean*

Where truth is, there is God – *Miguel de Cervantes*

But the Lord is the true God; he is the living God and the everlasting King – *Jeremiah 10.10*

The pursuit of truth and beauty is a sphere of activity in which we are permitted to remain children all our lives – *Albert Einstein*

Truth is whatever makes you or me one with the mind of God – *Alistair MacLean*

We need to recognize God's truth, no matter whose mouth it comes out of – *Elizabeth Elliott*

And the Word became flesh and lived among us…full of grace and truth – *John 1.14*

Love of truth asserts itself in the ability to find and appreciate what is good wherever it be – *Johann Wolfgang von Goethe*

I think the most important quality in a person connected with religion is absolute devotion to the truth – *Albert Schweitzer*

Truth does not lie beyond humanity, but it is one of the products of the human mind and feeling – *D.H. Lawrence*

Truth is whatever summons your spirit to do battle in her service – *Alistair MacLean*

But it is not enough to possess a truth; it is essential that the truth should possess us – *Maurice Maeterlinck*

Grace and truth came through Jesus Christ. No one has ever seen God. It is God the only Son, who is close to the Father's heart, who has made him known – *John 1.17-18*

Truth is given, not to be contemplated, but to be done. Life is an action - not a thought – *F.W. Robertson*

Be so true to thyself, as thou be not false to others – *Francis Bacon*

And you will know the truth, and the truth will make you free – *John 8.32*

Truth is always the strongest argument – *Sophocles*

Time is precious, but truth is more precious than time – *Benjamin Disraeli*

Be Yourself – Truthfully

We are to answer for any truth we have understood – *Anthony Bloom*

I am…the truth – *John 14.6*

Truth lies in character. Christ did not simply *speak* truth: He *was* truth: true through and through, for truth is a thing, not of words, but of Life and Being – *F.W. Robertson*

Dare to be true – *George Herbert*

Let us rejoice in the Truth, wherever we find its lamp burning – *Albert Schweitzer*

When the Spirit of truth comes, he will guide you into all the truth – *John 16.13*

The great Easter truth is not that we are able to live newly after death, but that we are able to be new here and now by the power of the resurrection – *Phillips Brooks*

The spirit of truth and the spirit of freedom – *they* are the pillars of society – *Henrik Ibsen*

The Spirit breathes upon the Word and brings the truth to sight – *William Cowper*

"I cannot hear what you say for listening to what you are. Truth and preaching are both "truth through personality" – *William Barclay*

Sanctify them in the truth; your word is truth. As you have sent me into the world, so I have sent them into the world. And for their sakes I sanctify myself, so that they also may be sanctified in truth – *John 17.17-19*

The truth which Jesus brings enables us to get our scale of values right; it is in His truth that we see what things are really important and what things are not – *William Barclay*

The inward beauty, life and loveliness of Truth – *Rufus M. Jones*

The commandment of absolute truthfulness is really only another name for the fullness of discipleship – *Dietrich Bonhoeffer*

But speaking the truth in love, we must grow up in every way into him who is the head, into Christ – *Ephesians 4.15*

Truth has a quiet breast – *William Shakespeare*

Truth is the most valuable thing we have – *Mark Twain*

Truth is the highest thing that men may keep – *Geoffrey Chaucer*

Ethical axioms are found and tested not very differently from the axioms of science. Truth is what stands the test of experience – *Albert Einstein*

Let all of us speak the truth to our neighbours, for we are members of one another – *Ephesians 4.25*

I thirst for truth, but shall not drink it till I reach the source – *Robert Browning*

The only way to speak the truth is to speak it lovingly – *Henry David Thoreau*

All truth is precious, if not all divine – *William Cowper*

A true life work – *Johann Arndt*

A loving heart is the truest wisdom – *Charles Dickens*

We know the truth, not only by the reason, but also by the heart – *Blaise Pascal*

Stand therefore, and fasten the belt of truth around your waist – *Ephesians 6.14*

Truth is the foundation of all knowledge and the cement of all societies – *John Dryden*

Regard the utterance of truth in our age, as of equal value with that which is recorded in the Scriptures

Christ is the key which unlocks the golden doors into the temple of Divine truth – *A.W. Pink*

It is truth alone that enables any soul to glorify God – *John Owen*

The Holy Spirit has promised to lead us step by step into the fullness of truth – *Leon Joseph Suenens*

Faith has need of the whole truth – *Pierre Teilhard de Chardin*

The Bible is an inexhaustible fountain of all truths. The existence of the Bible is the greatest blessing which humanity ever experienced – *Immanuel Kant*

Justice is truth in action – *Benjamin Disraeli*

The only significance of life consists in helping to establish the Kingdom of God; and this can only be done by means of the acknowledgement and profession of the truth by each one of us – *Leo Tolstoy*

My religion is based on truth and non-violence. Truth is my God and non-violence is the means to reach Him – *Mohandas K. Gandhi*

God offers to every mind its choice between truth and repose. Take which you please - you can never have both – *Ralph Waldo Emerson*

Truth is like a lighted lamp in that it cannot be hidden away in the darkness because it carries its own light – *Edward Wilson*

The gospel story, whether historically true or not, could still be regarded as a parable; that is, as a working model, cast in fictitious form, of the way things really are – *Sydney Carter*

The arrogance of supposing that, what could not be clearly expressed could be cheerfully discarded, has impoverished religion and made lonely men of the mystics and seers – *W.E. Sangster*

When man is, with his whole nature, loving and willing the truth, he is then a live truth. But this he has not originated in himself. He has seen it, and striven for it, but not originated it. The one originating living, visible truth, embracing all truths in all relations, is Jesus Christ. He is true; he is the live Truth – *George MacDonald*

Only God is, only God knows, only God can do anything. This is the truth, and with the help of my faith I discover this more deeply every day – *Carlo Carretto*

Truth is not only violated by falsehood; it may be equally outraged by silence – *Henri Frédéric Amiel*

Doing the truth – *Paul Tillich*

Being the truth – *Paul Tillich*

Truth which is merely told is quick to be forgotten; truth which is discovered lasts a lifetime – *William Barclay*

Truth is not limited to the Scriptures, but it is limited by the Scriptures – *J. Grant Howard*

We do not err because truth is difficult to see. It is visible at a glance. We err because this is more comfortable – *Alexander Solzhenitsyn*

A man can't be always defending the truth; there must be a time to feed on it – *C.S. Lewis*

The essence of man lies in this, in his marvellous faculty for seeking truth, seeing it, loving it, and sacrificing himself to it – Truth, that over all who possess it spreads the magic breath of its puissant health – *Giuseppe Prizzolini*

Seven years of silent inquiry are needful for a man to learn the truth, but fourteen in order to learn how to make it known to his fellow men – *Plato*

Truth never yet fell dead in the streets; it has such an affinity with the soul of man, the seed however broadcast will catch somewhere and produce its hundredfold – *Theodore Parker*

The best evidence of our having the truth is our walking in the truth – *Matthew Henry*

God is Truth. To be true, to kill every form of falsehood, to live a brave, true, real life – that is to love God – *F.W. Robertson*

Any human can penetrate to the kingdom of truth, if only he longs for truth and perpetually concentrates all his attention upon its attainment – *Simone Weil*

Every revelation of truth felt with interior savour and spiritual joy is the secret whispering of God in the ear of a pure soul – *Walter Hilton*

The name of God is Truth – *Hindu proverb*

Everything which concerns religion occurs in the realm of the soul and is the outcome of direct relations between the human spirit and the Divine Spirit – *Rufus M. Jones*

Truth has a quiet breast – *William Shakespeare*

The fundamental question to which every man has consciously or unconsciously to give an answer is: "To what am I to give my life? Am I to give it to a career? Am I to give it to the amassing of material possessions? Am I to give it to pleasure? Am I to give it to the obedience and to the service of God?" – *William Barclay*

True contentment is a real, even an active, virtue – not only affirmative but creative. It is the power of getting out of any situation all there is in it – *G.K. Chesterton*

The aim of the superior man is truth – *Confucius*

In the end truth will conquer – *John Wycliffe*

The simplest and most necessary truths are always the last believed – *John Ruskin*

Truth in a word, is whatever cleanses you – *Alistair MacLean*

Preaching is truth through personality – *Phillips Brooks*

The assent to truth is by three steps, humility, compassion, and in the ecstasy of contemplation – *St Bernard of Clairvaux*

God is not only true, but Truth itself – *Pope Leo XIII*

Vain hope to make people happy by politics – *Thomas Carlyle*

He who begins by loving Christianity better than truth will proceed by loving his own sect or church better than Christianity and end in loving himself better than all – *Samuel Taylor Coleridge*

All I have seen teaches me to trust the Creator for all I have not seen – *Ralph Waldo Emerson*

A Church which abandons the truth abandons itself – *Hans Küng*

Subdue untruthful men by truthfulness – *Indian proverb*

Truth is the perfect correlation of mind and reality; and this is actualised in the Lord's person. If the gospel is true and God is, as the Bible declares, a living God, the ultimate truth is not a system of propositions grasped by a perfect intelligence, but a personal being apprehended in the only way in which persons are ever fully apprehended, that is, by love – *William Temple*

It takes two to speak the truth – one to speak the truth, the other to hear – *Henry David Thoreau*

Where I found truth, there I found my God, who is truth itself – *St Augustine*

Truth is lived, not taught – *Herman Hesse*

The truth is a reality which we can hardly bear – *Hugh Montefiore*

21 HOPE

A few weeks after joining the 2nd Gurkhas in Singapore as part of my National Service I was appointed cross country running officer. We used to train in the early morning and evening to avoid the heat of the day.

One evening we went on a training run. We were some way from the barracks when our star runner tripped over a root, and fell badly on the side of a monsoon drain. To my great horror a huge gash appeared just below his knee and blood was gushing out. I had not been faced with this sort of situation before and was hoping against hope that I would do the right thing. Before I could work out what best to do, the group beat me to it and took spontaneous action – a consequence of their training. One of them pinched the gash with his fingers and held them there, stopping the flow of blood. The others formed a human stretcher and carried him back to the barracks on their shoulders. We headed for the medical centre, and the doctor did the rest.

Sometimes we find ourselves in seemingly impossible situations. It is then that we fall back on hope. Contemplating on "hope" may well equip us with hope.

Let your steadfast love, O Lord, be upon us, even as we hope in you –
 Psalm 33.22

If it were not for hope, the heart would break – *Thomas Fuller*

He that lives in hope dances without music – *George Herbert*

We hope to see family life everywhere secure and stable, happy and unselfish, with sex fulfilling its true use in lifelong marriage. We hope to see chastity, honesty and compassion prevail – *Michael Ramsey*

The Christian hope is hope in the power of God – *William Barclay*

The Christian hope is that God's way is the best way, that the only happiness, the only peace, the only joy, the only true and lasting rewards are to be found in the way of God – *William Barclay*

Hope in God; for I shall again praise him, my help and my God – *Psalm 42.5*

Whatever enlarges hope will also exalt courage – *Samuel Johnson*

Great hopes make great men – *Thomas Fuller*

We hope to see races free from injustice to one another, for racial strife is a denial of the divine image in man – *Michael Ramsey*

But I will hope continually, and will praise you yet more and more – *Psalm 71.14*

Entertain him with hope – *William Shakespeare*

We hope to see nations so using the earth's resources and economic structures that all may have enough to eat, instead of some being affluent while others starve – *Michael Ramsey*

Hope in action is charity, and beauty in action is goodness – *Miguel de Unamuno*

Happy are those…whose hope is in the Lord their God – *Psalm 146.5*

The virtue of hope is an orientation of the soul towards a transformation after which it will be wholly and exclusively love – *Simone Weil*

Christian Hope is the consecration of desire, and desire is the hardest thing of all to consecrate. That will only happen as you begin to think how lovely the life according to Christ is – *William Temple*

Prisoners of hope – *Zechariah 9.12*

Ah! If man would but see that hope is from within and not from without – that he himself must work out his own salvation – *H. Rider Haggard*

The future is as bright as the promises of God – *Adoniram Judson*

A religious hope does not only bear up the mind under her sufferings, but makes her rejoice in them – *Joseph Addison*

If you do not hope you will not find what is beyond your hopes – *St Clement of Alexandria*

The word which God has written on the brow of every man is Hope – *Victor Hugo*

We have obtained access to this grace in which we stand; and we boast in our hope of sharing the glory of God – *Romans 5.2*

Courage is like love; it must have hope for nourishment – *Napoleon Bonaparte*

Hope is lived and it comes alive, when we go outside of ourselves and, in joy and pain take part in the lives of others – *Jürgen Moltmann*

At bottom, everything depends upon the presence or absence of one single element in the soul - hope – *Henri Frédéric Amiel*

To hope till Hope creates from its own wreck the thing it contemplates –
Percy Bysshe Shelley

And hope does not disappoint us, because God's love has been poured into our hearts through the Holy Spirit that has been given to us – *Romans 5.5*

The ability to hope is the greatest gift that God could make to man – *Carlo Carretto*

Every blade of grass, each leaf, each separate floret and petal, is an inscription of hope – *Richard Jefferies*

For when hope does awaken, an entire life awakens along with it. One comes fully to life – *John S. Dunne*

Rejoice in hope – *Romans 12.12*

The venture of hope – *Hans Küng*

We must accept finite disappointment, but we must never lose infinite hope – *Martin Luther King*

May the God of hope fill you with all joy and peace in believing, so that you may abound in hope by the power of the Holy Spirit – *Romans 15.13*

Before the rain stops we hear a bird. Even under the heavy snow we see snowdrops – *Shunryg Suzuki*

Anything that is found to stimulate hope should be seized upon and made to serve. This applies to a book, a film, a broadcast, or a conversation with someone who can impart it – *Hubert van Zeller*

Practice hope. As hopefulness becomes a habit, you can achieve a permanently happy spirit – *Norman Vincent Peale*

To them God chose to make known how great among the Gentiles are the riches of the glory of this mystery, which is Christ in you, the hope of glory –
Colossians 1.27

Something will turn up – *Benjamin Disraeli*

Hope is itself a species of happiness, and, perhaps, the chief happiness which this world affords – *Samuel Johnson*

The natural flights of the human mind are not from pleasure to pleasure, but from hope to hope – *Samuel Johnson*

Hope springs eternal in the human breast: Man never is, but always to be blest – *Alexander Pope*

We who have taken refuge might be strongly encouraged to seize the hope set before us. We have this hope, a sure and steadfast anchor of the soul –
Hebrews 6.18-19

Our imagination is the only limit to what we can hope to have in the future – *Charles F. Kettering*

All human wisdom is summed up in two words – wait and hope – *Alexander Dumas*

Hope is the struggle of the soul, breaking loose from what is perishable, and attesting her eternity – *Herman Melville*

The utmost we can hope for in this life is contentment – *Joseph Addison*

Blessed be the God and Father of our Lord Jesus Christ! By his great mercy he has given us a new birth into a living hope through the resurrection of Jesus Christ from the dead – *1 Peter 1.3*

I am a man of hope because…I believe the Holy Spirit – *Leon Joseph Suenens*

The true basis of the soul's hope in God is God's hope for the soul – *Evelyn Underhill*

Hope is one of the principle springs that keep mankind in motion – *Thomas Fuller*

He who has health has hope; and he who has hope has everything – *Arab proverb*

Nothing worth doing is completed in our life-time; therefore we must be saved by hope – *Reinhold Niebuhr*

Set all your hope on the grace that Jesus Christ will bring you when he is revealed – *1 Peter 1.13*

What oxygen is to the lungs, such is hope for the meaning of life – *Emil Brunner*

I am a man of hope, not for human reasons, nor for any natural optimism, but because I believe the Holy Spirit is at work in the Church and in the World, even when His name remains unheard – *Leon Joseph Suenens*

Optimism is the faith that leads to achievement, but nothing can be done without hope – *Helen Keller*

I live on hope and that I think do all who come into this world – *Robert Bridges*

So, when dark thoughts my boding spirit shroud, Sweet Hope, celestial influence round me shed – *John Keats*

Optimism means faith in men, in the human potentiality; hope means faith in God in His omnipotence – *Carlo Carretto*

Hope is the best possession. None are completely wretched but those who are without hope; and few are reduced so low as that – *William Hazlitt*

"Hope", says St Thomas Aquinas, "is a divine infused quality of the soul, whereby with certain trust we expect those good things of the life eternal which are to be attained by the grace of God" – *W.R. Inge*

He is a God who does not make empty promises for the hereafter nor trivialize the present darkness, futility and meaninglessness, but who himself in the midst of darkness, futility and meaninglessness invites us to the venture of hope –
Hans Küng

Oh, how good a thing it is that the great God who has placed us in this world – where amid so much that is beautiful, there still exists vast bestowal among men of grief, disappointment and agony – has planted in our bosoms, the great sheet-anchor, Hope – *Walt Whitman*

Hope is a completely confident expectation, that sureness and certitude with which the awakened soul aims at God and rests in God. It is the source of that living peace, that zest and alertness, that power of carrying on, which gives its special colour to the genuine Christian life – *Evelyn Underhill*

Love means to love that which is unlovable, or it is no virtue at all; forgiving means to pardon the unpardonable, or it is no virtue at all; faith means believing the unbelievable or it is no virtue at all. And hope means hoping when things are hopeless, or it is no virtue at all – *G.K. Chesterton*

Hope to the last. Always hope. Never leave off hoping; it don't answer. It's always something to know you've done the most you could. But don't leave off hoping, or it's no use doing anything. Hope, hope, to the last – *Charles Dickens*

To most of us the future seems unsure; but then it always has been; and we who have seen great changes must have great hopes – *John Masefield*

Theirs is an endless road, a hopeless maze, who seek for goods before they seek for God – *St John Chrysostom*

Hope means expectancy when things are otherwise hopeless – *G.K Chesterton*

Hope disposes the believer towards change. Hope is oriented toward what is coming tomorrow. In hope we count on the possibilities of the future and we do not remain imprisoned in the institutions of the past – *Jürgen Moltmann*

To help all created things, that is the measure of our responsibilities; to be helped by all, that is the measure of our hope – *Gerald Vann*

No man is able of himself to grasp the supreme good of eternal life; he needs divine help. Hence there is here a two-fold object, the eternal life we hope for, and the divine help we hope by – *St Thomas Aquinas*

Hope is the only good that is common to all men; those who have nothing else possess hope still – *Thales*

We hope to see war, and the possibility of war, banished – *Michael Ramsey*

The Christian hope is the certainty that it is better to stake one's life on God than to believe the world – *William Barclay*

The most vital movement mortals feel is hope, the balm and lifeblood of the soul – *John Armstrong*

Hope is grief's best music – *H.G. Bohn*

Patience is the art of hoping – *Luc de Vauvenargues*

It is hope that gives the real perfume of life – *Samuel Smiles*

Hope saves a man in the midst of misfortunes – *Menander of Athens*

Those who keep speaking about the sun while walking under a cloudy sky are messengers of hope, the true saints of our day – *Henri J.M. Nouwen*

Notwithstanding the sight of all our miseries, which press upon us and take us by the throat, we have an instinct which we cannot repress, and which lifts us up – *Blaise Pascal*

Everything that is done in the world is done by hope. No husbandman would sow a grain of corn if he hoped not it would grow up and become seed…Or no tradesman would set himself to work if it did not hope to reap benefit thereby – *Martin Luther*

There is no medicine like hope, no incentive so great; and no tonic so powerful as expectation of something tomorrow – *Orisen Marden*

I rejoice in the hope of the glory to be revealed – *Samuel Rutherford*

Hope is a waking dream – *Aristotle*

If seeds in the black earth can turn into such beautiful roses, what might not the heart of man become in its long journey towards the skies? – *G.K. Chesterton*

If we were logical, the future would be bleak indeed. But we are more than logical. We are human beings, and we have faith, and we have hope – *Jacques Cousteau*

Totally without hope one cannot live. To live without hope is to cease to live – *Fyodor Dostoyevsky*

All earthly delights are sweeter in expectation than in enjoyment; all spiritual pleasures, more in fruition than in expectation – *Owen Feltham*

Where there is no hope, there can be no endeavour – *Samuel Johnson*

Hope enough to remove all anxious fears concerning the future –

Johann Wolfgang von Goethe

Hope is the first thing to take some form of action – *Vincent McHaf*

22 GRACE

I was intrigued with the phrase from the Prologue of St John's Gospel – "from his fullness we have all received, *grace upon grace.*" In Greek this literally means "*grace instead of grace.*" What does this strange phrase mean?

It means that for every situation we find ourselves in, a different kind of grace is available. When we are very young, a certain kind of grace is appropriate. When we are older, possibly at university, a different kind of grace is at one's disposal. When we are middle-aged and pre-occupied with a career and family duties and responsibilities, another form of grace is within one's reach. When we are old, with failing health and troubled by various aches and pains, a different kind of grace is on hand. Seen this way, these different forms of grace are extremely valuable.

I have found a verse in 2 Corinthians to be supremely important as I have gone through life. These are some reported words of Christ: "My grace is sufficient for you; for power is made perfect in weakness." Back this up with contemplation on the material in "Grace" and we can end up well equipped for life.

I will be gracious to whom I will be gracious, and will show mercy on whom I will show mercy – *Exodus 33.19*

God gives us grace, but leaves it to us to become new creatures – *Anthony Bloom*

The greater the perfection to which a soul aspires after, the more dependent it is upon divine grace – *Brother Lawrence*

He discovered the central significance of the new birth through a creative work of Grace within – *Rufus M. Jones*

The Lord make his face to shine upon you, and be gracious to you – *Numbers 6.25*

Grace was in all her steps, Heav'n in her Eye, in every gesture dignity and love – *John Milton*

Costly grace is the treasure hidden in the field; for the sake of it a man will gladly go and sell all that he has – *Dietrich Bonhoeffer*

The Lord waits to be gracious to you – *Isaiah 30.18*

And when grace comes and your soul is penetrated by the spirit, you shouldn't pray or exert yourself, but remain passive – *John Osborne*

The chief characteristic of the new people of God gathered together by Jesus is their awareness of the boundlessness of God's grace – *Joachim Jeremias*

Accept Yourself – Gracefully

And the Word became flesh and lived among us, and we have seen his glory, the glory as of a father's only son, full of grace and truth – *John 1.14*

It clearly seems that man by grace is made like unto God, and a partaker in His divinity, and that without grace he is like unto the brute beasts – *Blaise Pascal*

The power of grace always remains God's power but it becomes operative in man and thus fulfils, sustains, and renews human nature – *Daniel D. Williams*

When once our grace we have forgot, nothing goes right – *William Shakespeare*

From his fullness we have all received, grace upon grace – *John 1.16*

Christian graces are natural faculties which have blossomed under the influence of divine love – *Henry Ward Beecher*

Give us grace to bear both our joys and our sorrows lightly – *A.C. Benson*

Grace is the free, undeserved goodness and favour of God to mankind – *Matthew Henry*

Laughter is the closest thing to the grace of God – *Karl Barth*

The grace of which the plenitude is in His Son Jesus Christ – *D. Columba Marmion*

With great power the apostles gave their testimony to the resurrection of the Lord Jesus, and great grace was upon them all – *Acts 4.33*

God gives His gifts where He finds the vessel empty enough to receive them – *C.S. Lewis*

All people who live with any degree of serenity live by some assurance of grace – *Reinhold Niebuhr*

There is nothing but God's grace. We walk upon it; we breathe it; we live and die by it; it makes the nails and axles of the universe – *Robert Louis Stephenson*

The way that a man shall walk in this world is found not in himself, but in the grace of God – *St Thomas à Kempis*

Paul and Barnabas, who spoke to them and urged them to continue in the grace of God – *Acts 13.43*

Grace is indeed needed to turn a man into a saint, and he who doubts this does not know what either a saint or a man is – *Blaise Pascal*

It is not only through the qualities of native strength that God can work. Quite equally and more conspicuously He can make our weakness the opportunity of His grace – *William Temple*

The only secret of a real prayer life - "Be filled with the Spirit," who is "the Spirit of grace and supplication" – *Stuart J. Holden*

Grace is not something other than God, imparted by Him; it is the very Love of God (which is Himself) approaching and seeking entry to the soul of man – *William Temple*

We have peace with God through our Lord Jesus Christ, through whom we have obtained access to this grace in which we stand; and we boast in our hope of sharing the glory of God – *Romans 5.1-2*

Nothing is beyond my powers, if your grace gives strength to me – *St Thomas à Kempis*

But by the grace of God I am what I am, and his grace towards me has not been in vain. On the contrary, I worked harder than any of them – though it was not I, but the grace of God that is with me – *1 Corinthians 15.10*

But when He finds a soul penetrated with a lively faith, He pours into it His graces and favours plentifully – *Brother Lawrence*

A state of mind that sees God in everything is evidence of growth in grace and a thankful heart – *Charles Finney*

For you know the generous act of our Lord Jesus Christ, that though he was rich, yet for your sakes he became poor, so that by his poverty you might become rich – *2 Corinthians 8.9*

Nothing whatever pertaining to godliness and real holiness can be accomplished without grace – *St Augustine*

Cheap grace is grace without discipleship, grace without the Cross, grace without Jesus Christ, living and incarnate – *Dietrich Bonhoeffer*

I am not what I ought to be; I am not what I wish to be; I am not what I hope to be; but by the grace of God I am what I am – *John Newton*

Grace tried is better than grace, and more than grace; it is glory in its infancy – *Samuel Rutherford*

My grace is sufficient for you, for power is made perfect in weakness – *2 Corinthians 12.9*

The true divine life of grace – *Francois Fénelon*

Grace is God himself, his loving energy at work within his Church and within our souls – *Evelyn Underhill*

Grace which we derive from our ideals – *Aldous Huxley*

Grace grows better in winter – *Samuel Rutherford*

Give us grace to listen well – *John Keble*

The grace of the Lord Jesus Christ, the love of God, and the communion of the Holy Spirit be with all of you – *2 Corinthians 13.13*

Grace is always given to those ready to give thanks for it – *St Thomas à Kempis*

Courage is grace under pressure – *Ernest Hemingway*

The Christian life starts with grace, it must continue with grace, it ends with grace – *Martyn Lloyd-Jones*

A treasury of graces – *Thomas Traherne*

Grace is given to heal the spiritually sick, not to decorate heroes –

Martin Luther

A lively consciousness of grace – *Walter Hilton*

A soul can do nothing that is more pleasing to God than to communicate in a state of grace – *St Alphonius Liguori*

Let grace be the beginning, grace the consummation, grace the crown – *The Venerable Bede*

They travel lightly whom God's grace carries – *St Thomas à Kempis*

Father! replenish with Thy grace, this longing heart of mine; make it Thy quiet dwelling-place, Thy sacred inmost shrine! – *Angelus Silesius*

Since they too are also heirs of the gracious gift of life – *1 Peter 3.7*

This gift is from God and not of man's deserving. But certainly no one ever receives such a great grace without tremendous labour and burning desire – *Richard of Saint-Victor*

But O! th'exceeding grace of highest God, that loves his creatures so, and all his works with mercy doth embrace – *Edmund Spenser*

No one is suddenly endowed with all graces, but when God, the source of all grace, helps and teaches a soul, it can attain this state by sustained spiritual exercises and wisely ordered activity – *Walter Hilton*

If you knew how to annihilate self-interest and cast out all affection for the created world, then I would come, and my grace would well up abundantly within you – *St Thomas à Kempis*

And after you have suffered for a little while, the God of all grace, who has called you to his eternal glory in Christ, will himself restore, support, strengthen, and establish you – *1 Peter 5.10*

Let nobody presume upon his own powers for such exaltation or uplifting of the heart or ascribe it to his own merits. For it is certain that this comes not from human deserving but is a divine gift – *Richard of Saint-Victor*

Grace, *charis*, in its Greek religious usage means 'divine gift' or 'favour'. Thus a 'grace' was a quality or power usually bestowed by the gods, a quality that could be exhibited by a mortal. The English word 'graceful' reflects this meaning –
Daniel D. Williams

O Lord, I need your grace so much if I am to start anything good, or go on with it, or bring it to completion. Without grace, I have no power to do anything – but nothing is beyond my powers, if your grace gives strength to me –
St Thomas à Kempis

By 'grace' we do not mean some magical power of God forcibly intervening in the events of history or in the inner life of a man. We mean rather a humble presence. Grace is God's presence and solidarity with his creatures in their strivings – *John Macquarrie*

There are two main ideas in the word grace. The first is the idea of *sheer beauty*…The second idea is the idea of sheer *undeserved generosity* – *William Barclay*

There is a grace of kind listening – *F.W. Faber*

(There is) a grace of kind speaking –*F.W. Faber*

Grace is young glory – *Alexander Peden*

Musical training is a more potent instrument than any other, because rhythm and harmony find their way into the secret places of the soul, on which they mightily fasten, imparting grace, and making the soul graceful of him who is rightly educated, or ungraceful of him who is ill-educated – *Plato*

'In the time of the philosophers,' he (Al-Ghazali) writes, 'as at every other period, there existed some of these fervent mystics. God does not deprive this world of them, for they are its sustainers.' It is they who, dying to themselves, become capable of perpetual inspiration and so are made the instruments through which divine grace is mediated on those whose unregenerate nature is impervious to the delicate touches of the Spirit – *Aldous Huxley*

But the purpose of all worship is the same: to offer praise to God for his grace and glory – *Alan Richardson*

I take the love of God and self-denial to be the sum of all saving grace and religion – *Richard Baxter*

Grace keeps us from worrying because worry deals with the past, while grace deals with the present and future – *Joyce Meyer*

Music resembles poetry, in each are nameless Graces which no Methods teach, and which a Master-hand alone can reach – *Alexander Pope*

If grace perfects nature it must expand all our natures into the full richness of the diversity which God intended when he made them, and heaven will display far more variety than hell – *C.S. Lewis*

The grace of God is in courtesy – *Hilaire Belloc*

The concept of being sustained by grace – *James D. Mallory Jr*

Humbleness is always grace; always dignity – *J.R. Lowell*

The grace of contemplation is granted only in response to a longing and importunate desire – *St Gregory 1, Pope, the Great*

Prayer is the noblest and most exalted action of which man is capable through the grace of God – *Archbishop Ullathorne*

It is for this we are created: that we may give a new and individual expression of the absolute in our own peculiar character – *Isaac Hecker*

Grace does not destroy nature, it perfects it – *St Thomas Aquinas*

We cannot bridge the gap between God and ourselves through even the most intensive and frequent prayers; the gap between God and ourselves can only be bridged by God – *Paul Tillich*

We know God better through grace than through unaided reason – *St Thomas Aquinas*

There is no such way to attain to a greater measure of grace as far as man is to live up to the little grace he has – *Phillips Brooks*

Every holy thought is a gift of God, the inspiration of God, the grace of God – *St Ambrose*

We are not drawn to God by iron chains, but by sweet attractions and holy inspirations – *St Francis de Sales*

A balanced soul, alight with tranquil grace within, is not afraid to look at the darkness without – *R.H. Benson*

The more we grow in grace, the more shall we flourish in glory. Though every vessel of glory be full, yet some vessels hold more – *Thomas Watson*

God gives grace because He is a gracious God – *Johnny Foglander*

Not only does understanding the gospel of the grace of God provide a proper motive for us to share our faith, it also gives us the proper motive and means to live the Christian life effectively – *David Howard*

The renewal of our natures is a work of great importance. It is not to be done in a day. We have not only a new house to build up, but an old one to pull down – *George Whitfield*

The one thing we long to be able to pass on to men is a vast commanding sense of the grace of the Eternal – *Hugh R. Mackintosh*

Give us grace and strength to persevere – *R.L. Stevenson*

Grace is nothing else than a kind of beginning of glory in us – *quoted by E.L. Maskell*

We learn to stay in the light and love of God so that we can achieve (those gifts of grace) in us – *Norman Goodacre*

That the inward man by the Light of Grace, through possession and practice of a holy life, is to be acknowledged and live in us – *Rufus M. Jones*

Grace is something 'given', a new harmony which emerges; and it always inclines the heart to wonder – *Rollo May*

Grace is but glory begun, and glory is but grace perfected – *Jonathan Edwards*

As the earth can produce nothing unless it is fertilized by the sun, so we can do nothing without the grace of God – *John Vianney*

Happy are they who know that discipleship simply means the life which springs from grace, and that grace simply means discipleship – *Dietrich Bonhoeffer*

The burden of life is from ourselves, its lightness from the grace of Christ and the love of God – *William Ullathorne*

23 GLORY

One of my favourite quotations is about *Glory* – "The glory of God is a living Man," written many years ago by St Irenaeus. What this means is: "The glory of God is a person *fully alive*. The whole point of this book is to enable as many people as possible to become *fully alive*.

In my life I have been very fortunate in coming across two people whom I regard as having been *fully alive* – a woman and a man

The woman was Mother Teresa. I saw her when she came to England to receive her Templeton prize many years ago. One glance convinced me that the glory of God was working through her. I felt intuitively she had opened her life to receive the gifts and fruits of the Holy Spirit, in their entirety

The man is Desmond Tutu. He came to take a mission in Oxford University several years ago. I remember talking to the Chaplain of St Hilda's, asking how he was going down in this all female College. He gave a very interesting reply: "The undergraduates I know all want to marry him." Again, he was another person manifesting the gifts and fruits of the Holy Spirit in all their *glory*.

Moses said, 'Show me your glory, I pray' – *Exodus 33.18*

Place your soul in the brilliance of glory – *Clare of Assisi*

That is what gives Him the greatest glory – the achieving of great things through the weakest and most improbable means – *Thomas Merton*

When one candle is lighted…we light many by it, and when God hath kindled the Life of His glory in one man's Heart he often enkindles many by the flame of that – *Rufus M. Jones*

Entirely filled with His glory – *William Temple*

All the earth shall be filled with the glory of the Lord – *Numbers 14.21*

We best glorify Him when we grow most like to Him – *John Smith the Platonist*

Glory to God for all things – *St John Chrysostom*

Lord, make me to see glory in every place – *Michelangelo*

Aspire to all the greatness and glory of which the soul is capable – *Henry Ward Beecher*

What are human beings that you are mindful of them…Yet you have made them a little lower than God, and crowned them with glory and honour – *Psalm 8.4-5*

Do we desire glory? – let us seek it in its true place – *Francois Fénelon*

The great end of God's work which is variously expressed in Scripture, is indeed but one; and this one end is most properly and comprehensibly called "the glory of God" – *Jonathan Edwards*

I rejoice in the hope of that glory to be revealed – *Samuel Rutherford*

The glory of God is a living Man (i.e. a man fully alive) – *St Irenaeus*

The heavens are telling the glory of God; and the firmament

proclaims his handiwork – *Psalm 19.1*

How swiftly passes away the glory of this world – *St Thomas à Kempis*

Real glory springs from the silent conquest of ourselves – *Joseph P. Thompson*

And he was transfigured before them, and his face shone like the sun – *Matthew 17.2*

No path of flowers leads to glory – *Jean de la Fontaine*

Look out for a gleam of God's glory – *W.E. Sangster*

What is the freedom of the godly man? Being absolutely nothing to and wanting absolutely nothing for himself but only the glory of God in all his works – *Meister Eckhart*

So now, Father, glorify me in your own presence, with the glory that I had in your presence before the world existed – *John 17.5*

To live for the glory of God cannot remain an idea about which we think once in a while. It must become an interior, unceasing doxology – *Henri J.M. Nowwen*

There is the supreme truth that the glory of God lies in His compassion, and that God never so fully reveals His glory as when He reveals His pity – *William Barclay*

We rather glorify God by entertaining the impressions of His glory upon us – *John Smith the Platonist*

True prayer must be aflame – *E.M. Bounds*

The glory that you have given me I have given them, so that they may be one, as we are one. I in them and you in me, that they may become completely one – *John 17.22-23*

One crowded hour of glorious life is worth an age without a name – *quoted by Sir Walter Scott*

As we become forgetful of ourselves and entirely filled with His glory, the glory of His righteousness and love, we become transformed into His image…from glory to glory – *William Temple*

To God be the glory. Think how Jesus lived, prayed, worked, suffered, all to the *greater* glory of God. He sought always the Father's glory. His pure ambition was the glory of God and the Kingdom of God – *Eric Symes Abbott*

We have obtained access to this grace in which we stand; and we boast in our hope of sharing the glory of God – *Romans 5.2*

The principle that governs the universe 'became flesh and dwelt among us and we beheld His glory', and the impression was as of something that shone through Him from beyond – *William Temple*

God's glory is the whole purpose of my life – *Joseph Tissot*

When God and His glory are made our end, we shall find a silent likeness pass in upon us; the beauty of God will, by degrees, enter upon our soul – *Stephen Charnock*

Welcome one another, therefore, just as Christ has welcomed you, for the glory of God – *Romans 15.7*

The resurrection that awaits us beyond physical death will be but the glorious consummation of the risen life which already we have in Christ – *D.T. Niles*

We become transformed into His image…from glory to glory – *William Temple*

God! Glory in His goodness – *Henry Ward Beecher*

'What is the chief end of man?' 'Man's chief end is to glorify God and enjoy Him for ever' – *The Shorter Catechism of the Westminster Catechisms*

And all of us, with unveiled faces, seeing the glory of the Lord as though reflected in a mirror, are being transformed into the same image from one degree of glory to another, for this comes from the Lord, the Spirit – *2 Corinthians 3.18*

We are His glory when we follow His ways – *Florence Nightingale*

Music is a principal means of glorifying our merciful Creator – *Henry Peacham*

God is most glorified in us when we are most satisfied in him – *John Piper*

A glimpse of the glory of God in the face of Jesus Christ causes in the heart a supreme genuine love for God – *Jonathan Edwards*

In great attempts it is glorious even to fail – *Cassius*

For it is the God who said, 'Let light shine out of darkness," who has shone in our hearts to give the light of the knowledge of the glory of God in the face of Christ. But we have this treasure in earthen vessels – *2 Corinthians 4. 6-7 (RSV)*

If the glory of God is to break out in your service, you must be ready to go out into the night – *Basilea Schlink*

The greater the difficulty, the more glory in surmounting it. Skilful pilots gain their reputation from storms and tempests – *Epicurus*

So that, with the eyes of your heart enlightened, you may know what is the hope to which he has called you, what are the riches of his glorious inheritance among the saints, and what is the immeasurable greatness of his power for us who believe, according to the working of his great power – *Ephesians 1.18-19*

The glory of love is its unaccountability: it is not something rendered proportionately – such and such an excellence, so much regard for it - but is rather a divine overflow – *Mark Rutherford*

God does all for his *own* glory, by communicating good out of himself; *not* by looking for anything from his creatures; our duty is not for His sake: our duty is our perfection and happiness – *Benjamin Whichcote*

Every energetic person wants something they can count as 'glory'. There are those who get it – film stars, famous athletes, military commanders, and even some few politicians, but they are a small minority, and the rest are left to day dreams – *Bertrand Russell*

It is to God that all glory must be referred. This glory is the end of the Divine work …If God adopts us as His children; if He realises this adoption through the grace of which the plenitude is in His Son, Jesus, if He wills to make us partakers in Christ's eternal inheritance, it is for the exaltation of His glory –
D. Columba Marmion

I pray that, according to the riches of his glory, he may grant that you may be strengthened in your inner being with power through his Spirit – *Ephesians 3.16*

A glory as of an Only Begotten Son from a Father; of One who perfectly represented something and who is perfectly united with it – *William Temple*

I believe God gives a glory to every period of life. I believe that the people who are wise – the people who live with Him – learn how to take the glory from each succeeding age. If you ask those people – those who have really learned the secret – at any stage of their life, 'What is the most glorious period of their life?' they will always say: "Now! Now!" – *W.E. Sangster*

But true glory and holy joy is to glory in Thee and not in one's own self; to rejoice in Thy name, and not to be delighted in one's own virtue, not in any creature, save only for Thy sake – *St Thomas à Kempis*

He will transform the body of our humiliation so that it may be conformed to the body of his glory, by the power that also enables him to make all things subject to himself – *Philippians 3.21*

The glory of God illuminates every part of the structure of the Christian faith – *Michael Ramsey*

The cross that Jesus tells us to carry is the one that we willingly take up ourselves – the cross of self-denial in order that we might live for the glory of the Father – *Colin Urquhart*

If Christ lives in us, controlling our personalities, we will leave glorious marks on the lives we touch. Not because of our lovely characters, but because of his – *Eugenia Price*

Transform your whole being into the magic of the Godhead itself through contemplation – *Clare of Assisi*

Endurance is not just the ability to bear a hard thing, but to turn it into glory – *William Barclay*

May you be made strong with all the strength that comes from his glorious power – *Colossians 1.11*

The glory of God, and, as our only means of glorifying Him, the salvation of human souls, is the real business of life – *C.S. Lewis*

Provided that God is glorified, we must not care by whom – *St Francis de Sales*

To be ambitious of true honour and of real glory and perfection of our nature is the very principle and incentive of virtue – *Philip Sidney*

The Son is the Image of the invisible God. All things that belong to the Father He expresses as the Image; all things that are the Father's, he illumines as the splendour of His glory and manifest to us – *St Ambrose*

God made the universe and all the creatures contained therein as so many glasses wherein he might reflect his own glory – *John Smith the Platonist*

Glory is perfected grace – *Meister Eckhart*

To them God chose to make known how great among the Gentiles are the riches of the glory of this mystery, which is Christ in you, the hope of glory – *Colossians 1.27*

It is the glory of man to continue and remain in the service of God – *St Irenaeus*

By faith we know his existence, in glory we shall know his nature – *Blaise Pascal*

Anxiety, sickness, suffering, or danger, now and then, with a foregoing of the common conveniences and charities of this life, may make us pause, and cause the spirit to waver, and the soul to sink, but let this be only for a moment.
All these are nothing when compared with the glory which shall be hereafter revealed in, and for, us – *David Livingstone*

Look at everything as though you were seeing it for the first time or the last time, then your time on earth will be filled with glory – *Betty Smith*

He is the reflection of God's glory and the exact imprint of God's very being, and he sustains all things by his powerful word – *Hebrews 1.3*

Heaven is the presence of God – *Christina Rossetti*

That abundant and increasing vitality of spirit and of body which is poured into the saints from the glorified Christ, that life from the very source of life – *B.F. Westcott*

God's dazzling radiance in himself and in his manifestation in the world – *Michael Ramsey*

It is the Christian belief that man exists in order to glorify God with the glory of heaven as his goal – *Michael Ramsey*

If you are reviled for the name of Christ, you are blessed, because the spirit of glory, which is the Spirit of God is resting on you…yet if any of you suffers as a Christian, do not consider it a disgrace, but glorify God because you bear this name – *1 Peter 4.14-16*

Grace is but glory begun and glory is but grace perfected – *Jonathan Edwards*

24 BEAUTY

The Psalmist wrote: "Let the beauty of the Lord our God be upon us" (see below)

I wonder if "Beauty" is another consequence of the divine inbreathing in the Genesis story of the creation of humankind? Out of the divine bounty we all of us have a seed or spark of this beauty 'breathed' into us. If we want to see this fully worked out in a life we go to the Gospels. In them we discern a person of great moral, spiritual and intellectual beauty. Jesus worked out in his own experience of life what is meant by being made in the image and likeness of God. As such he became a pioneer, a prototype, an incarnation of beauty.

For many people today, beauty is seen as something outside us, in nature, in such things as music, poetry and art, and in the beauty of another person. As such all these can greatly enrich our lives. However we seem to have lost the awareness that the essence of beauty lies in the depths of ourselves, and rarely do we become the beauty we observe and long for. Contemplating on "Beauty" can give direct access to this beauty residing within us and enable us to become the beauty we observe.

Worship the Lord in the beauty of holiness – *1 Chronicles 16.29* (AV)

He has a daily beauty in his life – *William Shakespeare*

Beauty is the gift of God – *Aristotle*

Beauty being the best of all we know – *Robert Bridges*

One thing I asked of the Lord, that will I seek after: to live in the house of the Lord all the days of my life, to behold the beauty of the Lord – *Psalm 27.4*

The radiance of divine beauty is wholly inexpressible: words cannot describe it, nor the ear grasp it – *Abba Philimon*

Radiant beauty – *Albert Einstein*

The wonderful beauty of prayer – *John Main OSB*

Reflecting on 'beauty' can give direct access to the beauty residing within us and enable us to become the beauty we observe – *Anon*

God's fingers can touch nothing but to mould it into loveliness – *George MacDonald*

Out of Zion, the perfection of beauty, God shines forth – *Psalm 50.2*

For this love of beauty is divinely planted – *Olive Wyon*

Youth is happy because it has the ability to see beauty. Anyone who keeps the ability to see beauty never grows old – *Franz Kafka*

The being of all things is derived from the divine beauty – *St Thomas Aquinas*

And let the beauty of the Lord our God be upon us – *Psalm 90.17(AV)*

Filled with this intense and vital beauty – *Thomas Traherne*

Grow as beautiful as God meant you to be when he thought of you first – *George MacDonald*

He has made everything beautiful in its time – *Ecclesiastes 3.11(RSV)*

Beauty is truly beauty when its comrade is a modest mind – *Greek proverb*

Beauty may be said to be God's trade mark in creation – *Henry Ward Beecher*

Too late I loved you, O Beauty so ancient yet ever new! Too late I loved you! And, behold, you were within me, and I out of myself, and there I searched for you – *St Augustine*

You were the signet of perfection, full of wisdom and perfect in beauty – *Ezekiel 28.12*

It is part and parcel of every man's life to develop beauty in himself. All perfect things have in them an element of beauty – *Henry Ward Beecher*

There is in the world only one figure of absolute beauty: Christ. That infinitely lovely figure, is as a matter of course, an infinite marvel – *Fyodor Dostoyevsky*

Truth exists for the wise, beauty for the feeling heart – *Friedrich von Schiller*

Never lose an opportunity of seeing anything that is beautiful, for beauty is God's handwriting - a wayside sacrament. Welcome it in every fair face, in every fair sky, in every flower, and thank God for it as a cup of blessing –
Ralph Waldo Emerson

Let them know how much better than these is their Lord, for the author of beauty created them…For from the greatness and beauty of created things comes a corresponding perception of their Creator – *Wisdom of Solomon 13.3,5*

For when with beauty we can virtue join, we paint the semblance of a form divine – *Matthew Prior*

Though we travel the world over to find the beautiful, we must carry it with us, or we find it not – *Ralph Waldo Emerson*

This world is the world of wild storm kept tame with the music of beauty – *Rabindranath Tagore*

Nothing in human life, least of all religion, is ever right until it is beautiful – *Harry Emerson Fosdick*

What is beautiful is a joy for all seasons and a possession for all eternity – *Oscar Wilde*

Woe to you, scribes and Pharisees, hypocrites! For you are like whitewashed tombs, which on the outside look beautiful, but inside they are full of the bones of the dead and of all kinds of filth – *Matthew 23.27*

Beauty unadorned, adorned the most – *Proverb*

Beauty is but the sensible image of the Infinite. Like trust and justice it lives within us; like virtue and the moral law it is a companion of the soul – *Richard Bancroft*

As it is written, 'How beautiful are the feet of those who bring good news!' – *Romans 10.15*

If you get simple beauty and nought else, you get about the best thing God invents – *Robert Browning*

The hours when the mind is absorbed by beauty are the only hours when we really live – *Richard Jefferies*

Finally, beloved, whatever is true, whatever is honourable, whatever is just, whatever is pure, whatever is pleasing, whatever is commendable, if there is any excellence…think about these things – *Philippians 4.8*

When you reach the heart of life you shall find beauty in all things, even in the eyes that are blind to beauty – *Kahlil Gibran*

Unless men see the beauty and delight in the worship of God, they will not do it willingly – *John Owen*

I pray thee, O God, that I may be beautiful within – *Socrates*

Every bit of beauty in this world, the beauty of man, of nature, of a work of art, is a partial transfiguration of this world, a creative break-through to another – *Nicolas Berdyaev*

Let your adornment be the inner self with the lasting beauty of a gentle and quiet spirit, which is very precious in God's sight – *1 Peter 3.4*

The Beautiful is the spiritual making itself known sensuously – *Georg Hegel*

Flowers, shade, a fine view, a sunset sky, joy, grace, feeling, abundance, and serenity, tenderness, and song – here you have the element of beauty – *Henri Frédéric Amiel*

Physical beauty is the sign of an interior beauty, a spiritual and moral beauty which is the basis, the principle, and the unity of the beautiful – *Friedrich von Schiller*

Characteristics which define beauty are wholeness, harmony and radiance – *St Thomas Aquinas*

I feel more and more that the instinct for beauty (spiritual and moral as well as natural) is the most trustworthy of all the instincts, and the surest sign of the nearness of God – *A.C. Benson*

I believe that there is nothing lovelier, deeper, more sympathetic, more rational, more manly, and more perfect than the Saviour – *Fyodor Dostoyevsky*

Wisdom in its ripeness is beauty – *A.R. Orage*

A thing of beauty is a joy for ever – *John Keats*

Each conception of spiritual beauty is a glimpse of God – *Moses Mendelssohn*

Unutterable beauty – *G.A. Studdert Kennedy*

Beauty is the radiance of truth; the fragrance of goodness – *Vincent McNabb*

The sight of the beauty of divine things will cause true desires after the things of God – *Jonathan Edwards*

The true love of God which comes from this sight of His beauty causes a spiritual and holy joy in the soul, a joy in God, and exulting in Him – *Jonathan Edwards*

Every graceful action is graceful. Every heroic act is also decent and causes the place and the bystanders to shine – *Ralph Waldo Emerson*

Beauty is the mark God sets upon virtue – *Ralph Waldo Emerson*

To forgive is beautiful – *Greek proverb*

Goodness is truth and beauty in human behaviour – *H.A. Overstreet*

The most beautiful experience we can have is the mysterious. It is the fundamental emotion which stands at the cradle of true art and science – *Albert Einstein*

Beauty is something wonderful and strange that the artist fashions out of the chaos of the world in the torment of his own soul – *W. Somerset Maugham*

The beauty of Creation may become a transparent veil, half revealing and half concealing the presence of Love itself – *Olive Wyon*

The beauty of the world, as many have felt, is the strongest evidence we have of the goodness and benevolence of the Creator…It is beautiful because its Author is beautiful – *W.R. Inge*

Spirit of BEAUTY, that dost consecrate with thine own hues all thou dost shine upon of human thought or form – where art thou gone? – *Percy Bysshe Shelley*

Man comes into life to seek and find his sufficient beauty, to serve it, to win and increase it, to fight for it, to face anything and dare anything for it, counting death as nothing so long as the dying eyes still turn to it – *H.G. Wells*

There comes a moment in life…when moral beauty seems more urgent, more penetrating, than intellectual beauty; when all that the mind has treasured must be bathed in the greatness of soul, lest it perish in the sandy desert, forlorn as the river that seeks in vain for the sea – *Maurice Maeterlinck*

Man is so inclined to concern himself with the most ordinary things, while his mind and senses are so easily blunted against impressions of beauty and perfection, that we should use all means to preserve the capacity of feeling them…Each day we should at least hear one little song, read one good poem, see one first-rate picture, and if it can be arranged, utter some sensible remarks – *Johann Wolfgang von Goethe*

Spirit of Beauty, whose sweet impulses, flung like the rose of dawn across the sea, alone can flush the exalted consciousness with shafts of sensible divinity –
Light of the World, essential loveliness – *Alan Seeger*

When we ask poets and artists to tell us what they have found in God, they answer with one voice, 'We have found him in beauty. Only it is a beauty that never was on land or sea, a beauty that in its transcendent excellence makes our best handiwork seem tawdry' – *William Brown*

Ultimately we long to love the world in a form of a living, responding being; and this is essentially the longing for the incarnation – *J. Neville Ward*

The serene silent beauty of a holy life is the most powerful influence in the world, next to the might of God – *Blaise Pascal*

The sight of the beauty of divine things will cause true desires after the things of God – *Jonathan Edwards*

It is in Music, perhaps, that the soul most nearly attains the great end for which, when inspired by the Poetic Sentiment, it struggles – the creation of Supernal Beauty – *Edgar Allan Poe*

The mystics are not only themselves an incarnation of beauty, but they reflect beauty on all who with understanding approach them – *Havelock Ellis*

The most natural beauty in the world is honesty and moral truth. For all beauty is truth. True features make the beauty of the face; true proportions, the beauty of architecture; true measures, the beauty of harmony and music –
The Earl of Shaftesbury

Genius is the unreserved devotion of the whole soul to the divine, poetic arts, and through them to God; deeming all else, even to our daily bread, only valuable as it helps us to unveil the heavenly face of Beauty – *Samuel Palmer*

An ideal of beauty and love – *Alexis Carrel*

Beauty may have fair leaves, yet bitter fruit – *English proverb*

The best and most beautiful things in the world cannot be seen or even touched. They must be felt with the heart – *Helen Keller*

Now let us do something beautiful for God – *Mother Teresa*

Cheerfulness and content are great beautifiers, and are famous preservers of good looks – *Charles Dickens*

As outward beauty disappears one must hope it goes in! – *Tennessee Williams*

Jesus was the greatest religious genius that ever lived. His beauty is eternal and his reign will never end. He is in every respect unique and nothing can be compared with him – *Ernest Renan*

Jesus alone is able to offer himself as the sufficient illustration of his own doctrine. No revolution that has ever taken place in society can be compared to that which has been produced by the words of Jesus Christ – *Hensley Henson*

A radical revolution, embracing even nature itself, was the fundamental idea of Jesus – *Ernest Renan*

When a man loves the beautiful, what does he desire? That the beautiful may be his – *Plato*

What God has resolved concerning me I know not, but this at least I know: he has instilled into me a vehement love of the beautiful – *John Milton*

Praise I call the product of the singing heart. It is the inner man responding –
The moment you begin to delight in beauty, your heart and mind are raised – *Basil Hume OSB*

Humanity is never so beautiful as when praying for forgiveness or else forgiving another – *Jean Paul Richter*

The beauty of the world is Christ's tender smile for us coming through matter – *Simone Weil*

To be needed in other human lives – is there anything greater or more beautiful in this world? – *David Grayson*

What is impenetrable to us really exists, manifesting itself as the highest wisdom and the most radiant beauty – *Albert Einstein*

Ask men and women, too, and they know that their beauty comes from God.
Yet what is it that sees the beauty? What is it that can be enraptured by the loveliness of God's creation? It is the soul which appreciates the beauty. Indeed, God made men's souls so that they could appreciate the beauty of his handiwork – *St Augustine*

(God) Himself has imparted of His own to all particular beings from the fountain of beauty – Himself. For the good and beautiful things in the world could never have been what they are, save that they were made in the image of the archetype, which is truly good and beautiful – *Philo*

We do not want merely to see beauty, though God knows, even that is bounty enough. We want something else which can hardly be put into words – to be united with the beauty we see, to pass into it, to receiving it into ourselves, to bathe in it, to become part of it – *C.S. Lewis*

Unquestionably (beauty) is one of the three ultimate values, ranking with Goodness and Truth – *W.R. Inge*

We must show every child that any existence, however humble and painful it may be, becomes radiant when it is illuminated by an ideal of beauty and love – *Alexis Carrel*

What is beautiful is good, and who is good will soon also be beautiful – *Sappho*

I see and find beauty through Truth. All Truths, not merely true ideas, but truthful faces, truthful pictures, truthful songs, are highly beautiful. Whenever men begin to see Beauty in Truth, then Art will arise – *Mohandas K. Gandhi*

The aesthetic sense is very close to the religious: beauty has a great educative power. When it takes the form of sacrifice, heroism and holiness, it irresistibly attracts men towards the heights. It is this beauty which gives life its meaning, nobility and joy – *Alexis Carrel*

We are beautiful because God made us – *St Augustine*

Virtue is like a rich stone, best plain set – *Francis Bacon*

I know a man who, when he saw a woman of striking beauty, praised the Creator for her. The sight of her lit within him the love of God – *John Climacus*

There is nothing more beautiful than cheerfulness in an old face – *Jean Paul Richter*

The touch of beauty when we feel it, is not to be merely a passing delight: it is the call of God, inviting us gently and sweetly to turn to Him – *Olive Wyon*

25 CHARACTER

I have always been influenced by people of character. Two biographies, both by George Seaver, have been about men of character, and have influenced me a great deal.

The first was *Edward Wilson of the Antarctic* – the life story of the doctor, zoologist, and artist on Scott's expedition to the Antarctic. Although Scott was the official leader, the qualities of Edward Wilson's character exercised a quiet but decisive influence on the members of the expedition.

The second was *Albert Schweitzer: The Man and His Mind.* Here was portrayed the character of a man with four doctorates, in philosophy, theology, music and medicine, who went on to found, build, and run a mission hospital in a remote part of equatorial West Africa. He was described as a man of moral strength, with impressive qualities. Character continues to be an important influence in our day and age.

For the Lord does not see as mortals see; they look on the outward appearance, but the Lord looks on the heart – *1 Samuel 16.7*

He was his Maker's Image undefac'd! – *Samuel Taylor Coleridge*

An honest man's the noblest work of God – *Alexander Pope*

Happiness is not the end of life, character is – *Henry Ward Beecher*

The foundation of every noble character is absolute sincerity – *Anon*

A talent is formed in stillness, a character in the world's torrent – *Johann Wolfgang von Goethe*

O Lord, who may abide in your tent? Who may dwell on your holy hill? Those who walk blamelessly, and do what is right, and speak the truth from their heart – *Psalm 15.1-2*

Character is higher than intellect... A great soul with be strong to live, as well as strong to think – *Ralph Waldo Emerson*

Let us be true: this is the highest maxim of art and of life, the secret of eloquence and of virtue, and of all moral authority – *Hénri Frédéric Amiel*

In every man there is a loneliness, an inner chamber of peculiar life into which God only can enter – *George MacDonald*

(Jesus) – the most innocent, the most benevolent, the most eloquent and sublime character that ever has been exhibited to man – *Thomas Jefferson*

This above all to thine own self be true, and it must follow as the night the day, thou canst not then be false to any man – *William Shakespeare*

Friends, suffering, marriage, environment, study and recreation are influences which shape character. The strongest influence, if you are generous enough to yield to it, is the grace of God – *Hubert van Zeller*

A good name is to be chosen rather than great riches, and favour is better than silver or gold – *Proverbs 22.1*

Character cannot be developed in ease and quiet. Only through experiences of trial and suffering can the soul be strengthened, vision cleared, ambition inspired and success achieved – *Helen Keller*

If we will but let our God and Father work his will with us, there can be no limit to his enlargement of our existence, to the flood of life with which he will overflow our consciousness – *George MacDonald*

To shame the guise o' th' world, I will begin the fashion – the less without and more within – *William Shakespeare*

Religion is only another word for character, and it is developed in man. Religious education is a growth and requires time – *Henry Ward Beecher*

Character – in things great and small – is indicated when a man pursues with sustained follow-through what he feels himself capable of doing – *Johann Wolfgang von Goethe*

A truer, nobler, trustier heart, more loving, or more loyal, never beat within a human heart – *William Shakespeare*

As he thinketh in his heart, so is he – *Proverbs 23.7 (AV)*

In Christ was comprehended the fullest conception of greatness and nobleness of character. Every idea of true manhood is in Him – *Henry Ward Beecher*

God made us, but we have to *be* – *George MacDonald*

It is held that valour is the chiefest virtue and most dignifies the haver – *William Shakespeare*

There is no sight more beautiful than a character which has been steadfastly growing in every direction, and has come to old age rich and ripe – *Henry Ward Beecher*

There is no point so crucial of Christian character as the power to maintain love toward all men – not a love of personal attraction, but a love of benevolence, that begets a willingness to bear with them and work for them – *Henry Ward Beecher*

Supreme and tremendous energy and positiveness enter into the spiritual delineation of Christian character. Intense virtues and self-denials, bearing yokes, bearing the cross, sacrificing, crucifying, are enjoined – *Henry Ward Beecher*

Then I heard the voice of the Lord saying, 'Whom shall I send, and who will go for us?' And I said, 'Here am I; send me!' – *Isaiah 6.8*

The man who loves his fellow is infinitely more alive than he whose endeavour is to exalt himself above his neighbour – *George MacDonald*

Quality and power of emotion are the noblest elements of character, and reason and knowledge and experience work to and for that which is the essential thing – namely, emotion, out of which comes disposition – *Henry Ward Beecher*

Our characters are shaped by our companions and by the objects to which we give most of our thoughts and with which we fill our imaginations. We cannot always be thinking even about Christ, but we can refuse to dwell on any thoughts which are out of tune with Him. We can, above all, quite deliberately turn our minds towards Him at any time when those thoughts come in – *William Temple*

The business of life is not to get as much as you can, but to do justly, and love mercy, and walk humbly with your God – *George MacDonald*

The character I admire is a character that is a rod of iron to itself and a well-spring of tenderness and pity for others; a character that forces itself to be happy in itself, blames no one but itself, and compels itself to clear away obstacles from the path to happiness for every organism it encounters – *John Cowper Powys*

You will know them by their fruits. Are grapes gathered from thorns, or figs from thistles? – *Matthew 7.16*

People's characters are tested in three ways: by the circumstances in which they live, by the people whom they meet, and by the experience of their own failures. Their characters are tested by the degree in which these things draw forth from them love and not bitterness, a humble penitence and dependence upon God and not despair – *Father Andrew SDC*

The crown of life is character –*Samuel Smiles*

The glory of Christ is character – *Samuel Smiles*

It is the character of a good man to be able to deny and disown himself, and to make a full surrender of himself unto God; forgetting himself, and minding nothing but the will of his Creator; triumphing in nothing more than in his own nothingness, and in the allness of the Divinity. But indeed this, his being nothing, is the only way to be all things; this, his being nothing, the truest way of possessing all things – *John Smith the Platonist*

What do we mean when we speak of a man of integrity? One who will be true to the highest he knows; who will never betray the truth or trifle with it; one who will never make a decision from self-regarding motives; one who will never yield to the persuasion of friends or the presence of critics unless either conforms to his own standards of right and wrong; one who will face the consequences of his attitudes, decisions and actions, however costly they may be; one who will not be loud in self-justification, but quietly confident and humbly ready to explain – *George Appleton*

The crown and glory of life is character. It is the noblest possession of a man, constituting a rank in itself, and an estate in the general good-will; dignifying every station, and exalting every position in society. It exercises a greater power than wealth, and secures all the honour without the jealousies of fame. It carries with it an influence which always tells; for it is the result of proved honour, rectitude, and consistency – qualities which, perhaps more than any other, command the general confidence and respect of mankind. Character is human nature in its best form. It is moral order embodied in the individual. Men of character are not only the conscience of society, but in every well-governed State they are its best motive power; for it is moral qualities in the main which rule the world – *Samuel Smiles*

The unity is one of character and its ideal. That character of the completed man, raised above what is poor and low, and governed by noble tempers and pure principles, has in Spenser two conspicuous elements. In the first place, it is based on manliness…It is not merely courage, it is not merely energy, it is not merely strength. It is the quality of soul which frankly accepts the conditions in human life, of labour, of obedience, of effort, of unequal success, which does not quarrel with them or evade them, but takes for granted with unquestioning alacrity that man is called – by his call to high aims and destiny – to a continual struggle with difficulty, with pain, with evil, and makes it the point of honour not to be dismayed or wearied out by them. It is a cheerful and serious willingness for hard work and endurance, as being inevitable and very bearable necessities, together with even a pleasure in encountering trials which put a man on his mettle, an enjoyment of the contest and the risk, even in play. It is the quality which seizes on the paramount idea of duty, as something which leaves a man no choice; which despises and breaks through the inferior considerations and motives – trouble, uncertainty, doubt, curiosity – which hang about and impede duty; which is impatient with the idleness and childishness of a life of mere amusement, or mere looking on, of continued and self-satisfied levity, of vacillation, of clever and ingenious trifling – *R.W. Church*

And not only that, but we also boast in our sufferings, knowing that suffering produces character, and character produces hope, and hope does not disappoint us, because God's love has been poured into our hearts through the Holy Spirit that has been given us – *Romans 5.3-5*

God demands an honesty, a dignity, a purity, a beauty of being altogether different from that demanded by man of his fellow – *George MacDonald*

When a man bows down before a power that can account for him, a power that knows whence he came and whither he is going, then the truth of his being, his real nature begins to show itself. Then is his nature coming into harmony with itself – *George MacDonald*

Do you not know that you are God's temple and that God's Spirit dwells in you? – *1 Corinthians 3.16*

A clergyman has to be more of a man than other men – *George MacDonald*

The true measure of a man is how he treats someone who can do him absolutely no good – *Ann Landers*

Show yourself in all respects a model of good works, and in your teaching show integrity, gravity, and sound speech that cannot be censured, then any opponent will be put to shame having nothing evil to say of us – *Titus 2.7-8*

Perhaps there is no more important component of character than steadfast resolution. The boys and girls who are going to make great men and women, or are going to count in any way after life, must make up their minds not merely to overcome a thousand obstacles, but to win in spite of a thousand repulses and defeats – *Theodore Roosevelt*

Alike for the nation and the individual, the one indispensable requisite is character – *Theodore Roosevelt*

For this very reason, you must make every effort to support your faith with goodness, and goodness with knowledge, and knowledge with self-control, and self-control with endurance, and endurance with godliness, and godliness with mutual affection and mutual affection with love. For if these things are yours and are increasing among you, they keep you from being ineffective and unfruitful in the knowledge of our Lord Jesus Christ – *2 Peter 1.5-8*

The highest reward for a person's toil is not what they get for it, but what they become by it – *John Ruskin*

Let him that would move the world, first move himself – *Socrates*

A good character carries with it the highest power of causing a thing to be believed – *Aristotle*

Characters must be kept bright, as well as clean – *Lord Chesterfield*

To enjoy the things we ought and to hate the things we ought has the greatest bearing on excellence of character – *Aristotle*

I have often thought that the best way to define a man's character would be to seek out the particular mental or moral attitude in which, when it came upon him, he felt himself most deeply and intensely active and live. At such moments there is a voice inside which speaks and says "This is the real me!" *William James*

Education has for its object the formation of character – *Herbert Spencer*

The little world of childhood with its familiar surroundings is a model of the greater world. The more intensively the family has stamped its character upon the child, the more it will tend to feel and see the earlier miniature world again in the bigger world of adult life. Naturally this is not a conscious, intellectual process – *C.G. Jung*

Instil the love of you into all the world, for a good character is what is remembered – *The Teaching for Merikare*

A faithful study of the liberal arts humanizes character and permits it not to be cruel – *Ovid*

Daddy said: "All children must look after their own upbringing." Parents can only give good advice or put them on the right paths, but for the final forming of a person's character lies in their own hands – *Anne Frank*

The man that makes a character makes foes – *Edward Young*

When we see men of worth, we should think of equalling them; when we see men of contrary character, we should turn inwards and examine ourselves – *Confucius*

Not a having and a resting, but a growing and becoming is the character of perfection as culture conceives it – *Matthew Arnold*

The intellect, character and skill possessed by any man are the product of certain original tendencies and the training which they have received – *Thorndike*

Sow a thought, and you reap an act; sow an act, and you reap a habit; sow a habit and you reap a character; sow a character, and you reap a destiny – *Samuel Smiles*

It is not what he has, nor even what he does, which directly expresses the worth of a man, but what he is - *Hénri Frédéric Amiel*

Character is better than ancestry, and personal conduct is more important than the highest parentage – *Thomas Barnado*

He is rich or poor according to what he is, not to what he has – *Henry Ward Beecher*

The characters that are great, must, of necessity, be characters that shall be willing, patient and strong to endure for others – *Henry Ward Beecher*

Character may be manifested in the great moments, but it is made in the small ones – *Phillip Brooks*

The purpose of Christianity is not to avoid difficulty but to produce a character adequate to meet it when it comes. It does not make life easy; rather it tries to make us great enough for life – *James L. Christensen*

Of all the properties which belong to honourable men, not one is so highly prized as that of character – *Henry Clay*

What lies beyond us and what lies before us are tiny matters compared to what lies within us – *Ralph Waldo Emerson*

The force of character is cumulative – *Ralph Waldo Emerson*

Our character is but the stamp on our souls of the free choices of good and evil we have made through life – *John Cunningham Geikie*

Out of our beliefs are born deeds; out of deeds we form habits, out of our habits grow our character, and on our character we build our destiny – *Henry Hancock*

Character is not made on the mountain tops of life; it is made in the valleys – *Kathryn Kublman*

The quality of a person's life is in direct proportion to their commitment to excellence, regardless of their chosen field of endeavour – *Vince Lombardi*

The study of God's word for the purpose of discovering God's will is the secret discipline which has formed the greatest characters – *Henry David Thoreau*

Character is a by-product; it is produced in the great manufacture of daily duty – *Woodrow Wilson*

A character filled with the love of God – *Charles Gore*

To hold our nature in the willing service of another is the divine idea of manhood, of the human character – *Henry Ward Beecher*

The only thing that endures is character – *O.J. Simpson*

Your character is what you really are – *John Wooden*

He was simply a good man; he was strong and gentle; firm but understanding with others; kind and fair. Finally he used his understatement with a keen droll sense of humour – which I particularly enjoyed. He was a complete man – *(said of a Gurkha Officer)*

26 COURAGE

Whilst I was Chaplain Fellow at University College, Oxford, we had several physically handicapped undergraduates. All of them had something in common, namely, a quiet courageous approach to life. This has caused me to think about the nature of their courage.

I found some clues in the words of Cardinal Manning. He wrote in *Pastime Papers* – 'the Italians call it *Corragio*, or greatness of heart; the Spaniards, *Corage*; the French, *Courage*, from whom we have borrowed it. And we understand it to mean manliness, bravery, boldness, fearlessness, springing not from a sense of physical power, or from insensibility to danger or pain, but from the moral habit of self-command, with deliberation, fully weighing present dangers, and clearly foreseeing future consequences, and yet in the path of duty advancing unmoved to its execution.

This fits in roughly with my observations. Very rarely have they complained about their condition. Each has had a certain greatness of heart quietly bubbling away in them. All of them have developed this moral habit of self-command, able to face the future, calmly, deliberately and courageously. Somehow they have found an inner strength which carries them in their various difficulties.

Be strong and courageous; do not be frightened or dismayed, for the
> Lord your God is with you wherever you go – *Joshua 1.9*

...but there is a higher sort of bravery, the bravery of self-control –
> *Thomas Bailey Aldrich*

How few there are who have courage enough to own their Faults, or resolution enough to mend them – *Benjamin Franklin*

The most precious thing about Jesus is the fact that he is not the great discourager, but the great encourager – *William Barclay*

One has to be courageous not to let oneself be carried along by the world's march; one needs faith and will power to go cross current – *Carlo Carretto*

People talk about the courage of condemned men walking to the place of execution: sometimes it needs as much courage to walk with any kind of bearing towards another person's habitual misery – *Graham Greene*

Be strong, and let us be courageous for our people and for the cities of our God – *1 Chronicles 19.13*

Great things are done more through courage than through wisdom – *German proverb*

Where true Fortitude dwells, Loyalty, Bounty, Friendship and Fidelity may be found – *Sir Thomas Browne*

Courage is what it takes to stand up and speak; courage is also what it takes to sit down and listen – *Anon*

The courage we desire and prize is not the courage to die decently, but to live manfully – *Thomas Carlyle*

Oh courage...oh yes! If only one had that...Then life might be liveable, in spite of everything – *Henrik Ibsen*

Courage is the basic virtue for everyone so long as he continues to grow, to move ahead – *Rollo May*

His heart was courageous in the ways of the Lord – *2 Chronicles 17.6*

Courage is sustained not only by prayer, but by calling up anew the vision of the goal – *A.D. Sertillanges OP*

The greatest virtue in life is real courage, that knows how to face facts and live beyond them – *D.H. Lawrence*

It requires moral courage to grieve; it requires religious courage to rejoice – *Søren Kierkegaard*

Courage is not simply *one* of the virtues but the form of every virtue at the testing point, which means the point of highest reality – *C.S. Lewis*

The stout heart is also a warm and kind one. Affection dwells with Danger, all the holier and lovelier for such stern environment – *Thomas Carlyle*

Wait for the Lord; be strong and let your heart take courage – *Psalm 27.14*

Courage is required not only in a person's crucial decision for his own freedom, but in the little hour to hour decisions which place the bricks in the structure of his building of himself into a person who acts with freedom and responsibility –
Rollo May

…be like our Saviour, unwearied, who when He was abused and had often been evil-illtreated among men, proceeded courageously through all treacheries and deceits to die for them – *Thomas Traherne*

Heroism is the brilliant triumph of the soul over the flesh – that is to say, over fear; fear of poverty, of suffering, of calumny, of sickness, of isolation, and of death. There is no serious piety without heroism. Heroism is the dazzling and glorious concentration of courage –
Hénri Frédéric Amiel

We must accept our existence as far as ever it is possible; everything, even the unheard of, must be possible there. That is fundamentally the only courage which is demanded of us: to be brave in the face of the strangest, most singular and most inexplicable things that can befall us – *Rainer Maria Rilke*

Each one helps the other saying to one another, 'Take courage!' – *Isaiah*

41.6

God is no refuge for the coward, cringing soul. He is the goal and the sustainer of those who dare. 'Whosoever doth not bear his cross and come after Me cannot be My disciple.' Come then, let us get our backs beneath it – whatever it is. Our God demands courage! May he observe that courage in us all! – *W.E. Sangster*

The world seems somehow so made as to suit best the adventurous and courageous, the men who like Nelson, wear all their stars, like Napoleon's marshals, their most splendid uniforms, not that they may be less but more conspicuous and incur greater dangers than their fellows – *W. MacNeile Dixon*

Life, willing to surpass itself, is the good life, and the good life is courageous life. It is the life of the 'powerful soul' and the 'triumphant body' whose self-enjoyment is virtue. Such a soul banishes everything cowardly; it says 'bad – that is cowardly' – *Paul Tillich*

Courage is not the absence of fear, but the mastery of fear – *Author unknown*

Courage is the strength or choice to begin a change; determination is the persistence to continue in that change – *Author unknown*

Now, therefore, keep your sorrow to yourself, and bear bravely the troubles that have come upon you – *2 Esdras 10.15*

He who is not courageous enough to take risks will accomplish nothing in life – *Muhammad Ali*

You will never do anything in this world without courage – *James Lane Allen*

Courage is reckoned the great test of all virtues; because, unless a man has that virtue, he has no security for preserving any others – *James Boswell*

Courage is the first of human qualities because it is the quality which guarantees all the others – *Winston Churchill*

Without courage, wisdom bears no fruit – *Baltasar Gracian*

Keep alert, stand firm in your faith, be courageous, be strong. Let all that you do be done in love – *1 Corinthians 16.13-14*

It is courage, courage, courage, that raises the blood of life to crimson splendour.
Live bravely and present a brave front to adversity! – *Horace*

The greatest of courage on earth is to bear defeat without losing heart – *Robert G. Ingersoll*

Courage comprises all things: a man with courage has every blessing – *Plautus*

Courage consists, not in blindly over-looking danger, but in seeing and conquering it! – *Jean Paul Richter*

Courage is doing what you're afraid to do. There can be no courage unless you're scared – *Eddie Richenbacher*

He who has prepared us for this very thing is God, who has given us the Spirit as a guarantee. So we are always confident – *2 Corinthians 5.5-8*

It is curious that physical courage should be so common in the world and moral courage so rare – *Mark Twain*

Courage faces fear and thereby masters it, cowardice represses fear and is thereby mastered by it – *Martin Luther King*

Courage is an inner resolution to go forward in spite of obstacles and frightening situations; cowardice is a submissive surrender to circumstances –
Martin Luther King

Courageous men never lose the zest for living even though their life situation is zestless; cowardly men, overwhelmed by the uncertainties of life, lose the will to live – *Martin Luther King*

Whatever you do, you need courage. Whatever course you decide upon, there is always someone to tell you that you are wrong. There are always difficulties arising that tempt you to believe your critics are right. To map out a course of action and follow it to an end requires some of the courage that a soldier needs. Peace has its victories, but it takes brave men and women to win them – *Ralph Waldo Emerson*

Only live your life in a manner worthy of the gospel of Christ, so that, whether I come to see you or am absent and hear about you, I will know that you are standing firm in one spirit, striving side by side with one mind for the faith of the gospel, and are in no way intimidated by your opponents – *Philippians 1.27-28*

Courage is the best gift of all; courage stands before everything. It is what preserves our liberty, safety, life, and our homes and parents, our country and our children – *Plautus*

All our dreams can come true, if we have the courage to pursue them – *Walt Disney*

Courage breeds creative self-affirmation; cowardice produces destructive self-abnegation – *Martin Luther King*

We must constantly build dikes of courage to hold back the flood of fear – *Martin Luther King*

Perfect courage is to do unwitnessed what we should be capable of doing before all the world – *La Rochefoucauld*

I can do all things through him who strengthens me – *Philippians 4.13*

God grant me the courage not to give up what I think is right, even though I think it is hopeless – *Admiral Chester W. Nimitz*

Courage is not the absence of fear, but the judgement that something else is more important than fear – *Ambrose Redmoon*

They believed courage to be the secret of liberty – *Louis Dembitz Brandeis*

To see what is right, and not to do it, is want of courage – *Confucius*

Courage is a virtue only insofar as it is directed by prudence – *French Proverb*

For God did not give us a spirit of cowardice, but rather a spirit of power and of love and of self-discipline – *2 Timothy 1.7*

Have courage for the great sorrows of life, and patience for the small ones, and when you have laboriously accomplished your daily work, go to sleep in peace. God is awake – *Victor Hugo*

To the brave heart nothing is impossible – *French Proverb*

It is better to live one day as a lion than a hundred years as a sheep – *A Motto*

Courage is far more common than is commonly supposed, and it belongs as much, and more, to the ordinary events of life than to the spectacular. Every man who lives in intimate contact with other people, especially the unprivileged people, is amazed at the quiet bravery of obscure folk. To those who have eyes to see, there is evidence of courage on every hand – *W.E. Sangster*

Strange is the vigour of a brave man's soul. The strength of his spirit and his irresistible power, the greatness of his heart, and the height of his condition, his mighty confidence and contempt of danger, his true security and repose in himself, his liberty to dare and do what he pleaseth, his alacrity in the midst of fears, his invincible temper, are advantages which make him master of fortune. His courage fits him for all attempts, renders him serviceable to God and man, and makes him the bulwark and defence of his king and country – *Thomas Traherne*

As you know, we had courage in our God to declare to you the gospel of God in spite of great opposition – *1 Thessalonians 2.2-3*

Courage conquers all things – *Ovid*

The strongest, most generous, and proudest of all virtues is true courage – *Michel de Montaigne*

By courage and faith – *Latin phrase*

To be ready when the day of sorrow and grief came to meet it with the courage befitting a man – *Sir William Osler*

Care sat on his faded cheek, but under brows of dauntless courage – *John Milton*

You gain strength, courage and confidence by every experience in which you really stop to look fear in the face. You are able to say to yourself, "I lived through this horror. I can take the next things that comes along."...You must do the thing you think you cannot do – *Anna Eleanor Roosevelt*

Freedom is a system based on courage – *Charles Péguy*

Give us grace and strength to forbear and to persevere. Give us courage and gaiety and the quiet mind, spare to us our friends, soften to us our enemies – *Prayer*

Life shrinks or expands in proportion to one's courage – *Anais Nin*

For courage mounteth with occasion – *William Shakespeare*

Stay with me God. The night is dark,

The night is cold; my little spark

Of courage dies. The night is long;

Be with me, God, and make me strong – *A Soldier – His Prayer*

What though the field be lost?

All is not lost; th' unconquerable will

And study of revenge, immortal hate

And courage never to submit or yield – *John Milton*

Had we lived, I should have had a tale to tell of the hardihood, endurance, and courage of my companions which would have stirred the heart of every Englishman. These rough notes and our dead bodies must tell the tale – *Robert Falcon Scott*

One man with courage makes a majority – *Andrew Jackson*

Courage is resistance to fear, mastery of fear – not absence of fear – *Mark Twain*

Morale is the state of mind. It is steadfastness and courage and hope. It is confidence and zeal and loyalty – *George Catlett Marshall*

No coward soul is mine,

No trembler in the world's storm-troubled sphere:

I see Heaven's glories shine,

And faith shines equal, arming me from fear – *Emily Brontë*

My sword I give to him that shall succeed me in my pilgrimage, and my courage and skill to him that can get it – *John Bunyan*

Religion in its humility restores man to his only dignity, the courage to live by grace – *George Santayana*

The Western world has lost its civil courage, both as a whole and separately, in each country, each government, each political party, and of course in the United Nations – *Alexander Solzhenitsyn*

Whoever is happy will make others happy too. He who has courage and faith will never perish in misery – *Anne Frank*

For without belittling the courage with which men have died, we should not forget those acts of courage with which men…have *lived*…A man does what he must – in spite of personal consequences, in spite of obstacles and dangers and pressures – and that is the basis of all human morality – *John F. Kennedy*

Without justice, courage is weak – *Benjamin Franklin*

Fix your eyes on the greatness of Athens as you have it before you day by day, fall in love with her, and when you feel her great, remember that this greatness was won by men with courage, with knowledge of their duty, and with a sense of honour in action – *Thucydides*

Because of deep love, one is courageous – *Lao-tzu*